Enterprise Modeling

Janis Stirna • Anne Persson

Enterprise Modeling

Facilitating the Process and the People

 Springer

Janis Stirna
Department of Computer and
Systems Sciences
Stockholm University
Kista, Sweden

Anne Persson
School of Informatics
University of Skövde
Skövde, Sweden

ISBN 978-3-030-06926-1   ISBN 978-3-319-94857-7   (eBook)
https://doi.org/10.1007/978-3-319-94857-7

This Springer imprint is published by the registered company Springer Nature Switzerland AG
The registered company address is: Gewerbestrasse 11, 6330 Cham, Switzerland

Preface

For a number of years now, methods, techniques, and practices for Enterprise Modeling (EM) have been a very important part of our professional lives. We strongly believe that modeling is a key technique for understanding, capturing, and communicating organizational knowledge, and we also believe that it is crucial for successfully mastering change and innovation processes in enterprises.

We have always taken great interest in the practical aspects of Enterprise Modeling, ever since we both started working on our doctoral theses on this subject more than 20 years ago. Since then, we have collected substantial experience and research-based knowledge on the dos and don'ts of EM in different contexts and on the conditions necessary for EM to reach its full potential. A large portion of our experiences and knowledge is collected in this book.

The idea for this book emerged from our observation that it takes considerable time to become a highly professional EM practitioner and that learning the dos and don'ts of the practice often is a matter of learning by committing costly mistakes yourself and/or being dependent on having a highly experienced mentor available, of which there is a shortage. Books on the topic of EM practice have not been available. We therefore decided to collect our experience and knowledge in this book.

This book would not have become a reality without the support of many people in our personal and professional environments.

First of all, we would like to thank all colleagues and friends who actively contributed to the development of the "For Enterprise Modeling" (4EM) method and its predecessor, Enterprise Knowledge Development (EKD), which include not only a modeling language but a process for Enterprise Modeling as well. Experience from working with those methods is the foundation that this book rests upon. Since the list of people would be very long with the imminent danger that we would forget someone, we just want to mention Prof. Emeritus Janis Bubenko Jr. at the Royal Institute of Technology (Sweden) who has inspired us greatly.

When it comes to the process of modeling, and in particular how to facilitate modeling sessions, we want to acknowledge Christer Nellborn, Hans Willars, and

Björn Nilsson, who are good examples of truly professional EM practitioners. Thanks for sharing your knowledge and ideas with us!

This book complements the book on the 4EM method that we wrote together with our colleagues Prof. Kurt Sandkuhl at the University of Rostock (Germany) and Dr. Matthias Wißotzki at the University of Wismar (Germany). A special thanks goes to you.

Furthermore, we would like to thank our colleagues in Jönköping, Riga, Rostock, Skövde, Stockholm, and Valmiera who teach Enterprise Modeling and who contributed ideas, improvement proposals, and practices in many fruitful discussions and joint modeling sessions. You all know who you are!

Moreover, we would like to thank fellow researchers and practitioners that work in the area of Enterprise Modeling and in recent years have been part of forming an active community under the auspices of the IFIP Working Group 8.1 on Design and Evaluation of Information Systems and more specifically the Working Conference on the Practice of Enterprise Modeling (PoEM). Many ideas presented in this book have been put forward for discussion with our peers at these forums.

Kista, Sweden   Janis Stirna
Skövde, Sweden   Anne Persson
May 2018

Contents

Chapter 1
Introduction

Modeling has become a widespread activity in enterprises. Strategy development, business process mapping, requirements engineering, product development, enterprise architecture management, and information system (IS) design are just a few examples of activities that benefit from a model-based way of working and knowledge representation in the form of models. In practice, more and more people in organizations are involved in modeling activities that address various organizational problems. The models are usually relayed to business and IT development or improvement of the quality of business operations. Such modeling tasks can be addressed from a number of perspectives, such as strategy (goals, challenges, opportunities, capabilities), business operations (processes, actors, resources), information (business concepts, products), information technology (requirements, components), etc. However, to develop effective solutions and to ensure they fit in the organization, all of these perspectives need to be analyzed in an integrated way. For example, business processes should support goals, manage the information objects, and motivate requirements for supporting information systems. This integrated and multi-perspective way of capturing and analyzing enterprise solutions is at the core of Enterprise Modeling (EM). EM offers a practical and flexible set of work procedures, tools, and practices, which can be adapted to the situation at hand and to the purpose in focus. The growing applicability of EM was the reason that we wrote a book on EM with a specific method "For Enterprise Modeling" (4EM) in focus (Sandkuhl et al. 2014). According to that book, Enterprise Modeling is a structured way of working, which captures various aspects of an organization or a problem situation, such as business goals, processes, and actors, in an integrated way. EM contributes to the management of an organization by supporting change management, decision-making, and planning processes both within the different organizational functions and for its IT support.

In practice, modeling activities often involve groups of people, which means the models are created in a participatory way. It is also the case that not all participants are experienced in modeling. To be efficient, such participatory modeling sessions need the support of dedicated persons who know how to organize a modeling project

© Springer International Publishing AG, part of Springer Nature 2018
J. Stirna, A. Persson, *Enterprise Modeling*,
https://doi.org/10.1007/978-3-319-94857-7_1

Fig. 1.1 Differences of stakeholder views and perceptions. © Joakim Örvander (2014). Reprinted with permission

and modeling sessions, how to manage discussions during a modeling session, and what aspects influence the success and efficiency of modeling in practice. Hence, this book is about the process of managing modeling projects and the facilitation of participatory modeling sessions as well as the activities that are related to facilitation.

In the participatory approach to modeling, the stakeholders—under the guidance of a facilitator—create models to solve previously defined problems in modeling sessions. The facilitator ensures that the stakeholders involved can focus completely on solving the problem, without the need to learn the syntax of a modeling language first. The participatory approach also allows the model to consolidate and include various stakeholder views and perspectives on the same modeling problem. For example, Fig. 1.1 shows three people perceiving the same company in three different ways that are influenced by their background and role in the company, for example, as an organizational hierarchy, as cash flow, or as production line. The participatory approach is based on the assumption that all three (and probably many more) viewpoints need to be investigated and aligned in order to develop well-fitting solutions to this enterprise.

Due to the participatory approach, the outcome of a modeling project not only includes the models that are developed and the decisions or changes made in the enterprise but also results in stakeholders having a better and joint understanding of the problem and its solution and often a better understanding of their own enterprise and their roles in it. In contrast, modeling results created by analysts on the basis of knowledge discovered by the more traditional methods of elicitation do not lead to these positive effects. Even if the models themselves are marvelous, additional efforts need to be spent in convincing decision-makers and other stakeholders to accept the solutions they convey and to commit to the implementation efforts the models require. No matter how experienced the analysts are and how thorough the elicitation process has been, models created in the analyst-driven way risk missing important aspects and details of the organization. This might further restrict their usefulness to the organization.

Concerning terminology, "enterprise" is sometimes used for private organizations only. In this book's interpretation of Enterprise Modeling, the term is not limited to any specific kind of organization. EM is equally applicable to public organizations, industrial enterprises of any domain, privately run businesses, as well as nonprofit organizations. Hence, we will use "enterprise" and "organization" as synonyms when a specific form of ownership is unimportant to specify. We will use "company" in cases where it is important to specify that it is a privately owned company.

In terms of how broad the EM effort should be, there might be a misconception that Enterprise Modeling means modeling the *whole* enterprise. This does not always have to be so—EM most often focuses only on certain parts or problem areas of the organization. Identifying what the focus of an EM project should be is part of the EM process.

The term Business Modeling is sometimes used as a synonym to EM. In principle, Business Modeling covers a broader range of approaches originating in operations research, economics, management studies, and information systems. Enterprise Modeling as addressed in this book and in Sandkuhl et al. (2014) has two main characteristics: (1) it focuses on addressing multiple perspectives of an enterprise in an integrated way and (2) it offers a set of practical guidelines for knowledge acquisition, modeling, and analysis.

The stance taken in this book concerning the EM process is that the quality of models and the effect of modeling are enhanced if a participatory approach to stakeholder involvement is adopted. By participatory approach we mean a process that has the following characteristics:

- It has a defined way of working, for example, in the form of methodological steps to set up and carry out modeling sessions and report the modeling project, following explicit principles of stakeholder involvement.
- It has a group of stakeholders responsible for the knowledge that goes into the model.

– It has a modeling facilitator responsible for guiding the discussion among the stakeholders and the modeling method used.

1.1   The Goal of the Book: Practical Advice

This book reflects our research and practical experiences from having participated in EM method and tool development projects for the past 20 years. It is also based on our experiences from applying EM methods in a large number of projects as modelers and developers as well as facilitators and project managers. Throughout the years, we have also collected and reflected on experiences that colleagues we worked with have shared with us.

During our work in the field of EM, we have noticed that there is a lack of books that provide guidance on its practice. The main goal of this book is, hence, to provide practical advice on managing EM projects and on facilitating participatory Enterprise Modeling sessions. A limited summary of the theoretical background to EM is also included, but this book is not intended to be a starting point for studies on the subject of EM. While we have attempted to write this book independently of any specific EM method, many of the examples are based on the 4EM method. Participatory modeling can also be used in conjunction with other methods that are not made for EM, such as those made for Goal-Oriented Requirements Engineering and information system analysis. We argue that the principles of facilitation discussed in this book are also applicable to using those methods and languages in a participatory setting.

This book aims to:

– Present the background to modeling (Chaps. 2 and 4) and the EM process (Chap. 5)
– Provide a general introduction to the organizational challenges addressed by the participatory EM (Chap. 3)
– Present roles and competences needed in an EM project (Chap. 6)
– Present typical stakeholder behaviors in modeling sessions (Chap. 7)
– Discuss how situational contingencies in participatory modeling can be managed (Chap. 8)
– Present the typical modeling tools used for facilitation (Chap. 9)
– Discuss how participatory modeling can be used beyond EM (Chap. 10)
– Discuss issues related to the training of modeling experts (Chap. 11)
– Present the outlook on the application of participatory EM in practice and emerging issues for research (Chap. 12)

1.2 Structure and Content

The rest of this book is structured as follows.

Chapter 2 briefly introduces the concept of Enterprise Modeling, the EM process, as well as discusses the main approaches to stakeholder involvement and knowledge elicitation. The concept of model quality is also discussed.

Chapter 3 discusses the three typical types of objectives for using EM, namely, (1) to develop the business, (2) to improve the quality of the business, and (3) to use EM as a problem-solving tool for projects that only need support for resolving a specific problem. These types of objectives determine how the EM project needs to be customized in terms of what kind of input models and documentation it should consider, which model types need to be developed, what modeling language should be used and on what aspects of the language the project should focus, what way of working should be followed, what modeling tools should be used and how, as well as what the main quality criteria are for the models produced and for the way of working. In addition, situations not suitable for participatory EM are also discussed in this chapter.

Chapter 4 gives an overview of the 4EM method for Enterprise Modeling. The purpose of including 4EM in this book is to illustrate the concepts of EM method with an example method. At the same time, the example can be used to explain the different aspects of EM. Throughout the book, we will refer to the concepts of EM methods and base examples on the use of 4EM. An extensive presentation of 4EM and an extensive example case are available in Sandkuhl et al. (2014).

Chapter 5 describes the process of carrying out an EM project using a participatory approach. It consists of the following steps: define the scope and objectives of the project, plan for project activities and resources, plan for modeling session, prepare modeling session, set up the room for modeling, conduct modeling session, analyze and refine models, and present results to stakeholders.

Chapter 6 describes the roles involved in an EM project and their responsibilities. Particular attention is paid to the role of the EM practitioner. We also discuss the competences and abilities needed for modeling, the competences and characteristics needed for facilitation, as well as the competences needed for managing EM projects. The chapter ends with a discussion about the composition of the modeling group.

Chapter 7 discusses a number of stereotypical stakeholder behaviors that EM practitioners may encounter in an EM project. They can be observed in modeling sessions as well as in the project as a whole. During modeling sessions, the following stereotypes of stakeholder behavior have been observed: the seller, the buyer, the questioner, the observer, the boss, the one who always knows best, the border patrol, the comedian, the missionary, the expert, and the representative. On the EM project level, the following types of behavior can be observed: the engaged owner, the client, the pragmatic questioner, the contractor, the demanding boss, the one who has done it all, and the business-as-usual manager.

Chapter 8 discusses a number of situations that can arise in modeling sessions and in EM projects in general. We describe what the signs of a situation are and how to deal with it, including what not to do. Some more common recommendations to avoid in modeling projects are documented in the form of anti-patterns. Anti-patterns are common attractive but bad practices, and the reasons why they appear attractive are discussed. We also briefly discuss the aspects of cultural differences and stakeholder body language that can be observed during a modeling session and how to interpret it.

Chapter 9 describes tool support in modeling sessions. There are two main types of tools: (1) the "plastic wall," which is more suitable for idea generation types of modeling sessions, and (2) a projector and a computerized tool, which is more suitable for modeling sessions devoted to refinement of the existing model. The purpose of this chapter is to discuss the suitability of these two kinds of tools as well as to discuss the main issues that influence their use in practice. We also discuss the main requirements and usage scenarios for EM tools.

Chapter 10 discusses the use of the participatory approach to modeling with other modeling approaches. We address a set of typical requirements for a modeling approach to be considered if the approach is to be used in a participatory setting. We also discuss the main principles of the ways of working with business modeling methods such as Business Model Canvas, Enterprise Architecture frameworks, as well as Balanced Scorecard development. Participatory modeling is also suitable for various activities in IS development. In this regard, we discuss aspects of facilitation using agile approaches, Unified Modeling Language (UML), Goal-Oriented Requirements Engineering, and Capability Driven Development.

Chapter 11 discusses how to become a professional EM practitioner. This chapter provides recommendations on how to build a suitable competence profile for working professionally with EM, in particular participatory EM.

Chapter 12 discusses the issues that are pertinent to the use of participatory EM in practice, such as the adoption of it in organizations, including building the organizational structure for modeling, and integration of EM with other approaches sharing similar principles of work for which participatory EM can help. The chapter ends with a discussion on emerging issues of participatory EM.

1.3   Reading Recommendations

This book is written for all who want to learn more about EM with specific focus on how to facilitate participatory modeling and how to set up and carry out EM projects. The book does not require any deep knowledge about specific EM methods and tools. Some background knowledge and experience in modeling is, however, necessary. For this reason, readers less acquainted with the world of EM should consider reading Sandkuhl et al. (2014) first.

General knowledge about how modern organizations function and awareness of the organizational structures would also help to understand the aspects of facilitation and EM project organization described in this book.

This book is written with three main target groups in mind:

– Practitioners looking to extend their competence and to get practical advice for becoming better modeling facilitators and EM project managers
– Instructors in the field of Enterprise Modeling
– Students in the areas of information systems, computer science, and business administration

1.3.1   Practitioners

Practitioners will probably start reading from Chap. 5 that presents the EM process and roles involved. They might also use the book in different ways, depending on the situation of use, for example, reading up on subjects of interest to the practitioner. Elicitation approaches, necessary competences, actor behavior, tool usage, and situational contingencies are among the subjects covered in chapters that can be studied independently of the other book chapters—if the background knowledge is sufficient. For practitioners who want to make the transition from experienced modeler to experienced facilitator, Chap. 11 is also recommended.

1.3.2   Instructors

The material in this book is suitable for advanced courses in EM. Students taking a course on facilitation should be fairly knowledgeable in EM or modeling in the area of IS development in general. On which level of education (bachelor, master, or PhD level) the course is given is less important than the preexisting knowledge and experience. Instructors need some experience in carrying out modeling projects before taking on the task of teaching such an advanced course.

Parts of this book can also be used in basic courses on EM and IS analysis and design. In these cases, Chap. 3 discussing the applicability of EM, Chap. 5 presenting the EM process, Chap. 10 about the use of participatory modeling with other modeling methods, and Chap. 9 about tool use could be of value.

In the following, a proposed overall structure for a course focusing on facilitation is presented. Additional information, lecture slides, and other teaching material are available on the book's companion website.

The lectures could be organized as follows:

1. Introductory lecture about EM and typical application cases of participatory EM based on Chaps. 3 and 4.

2. One lecture about knowledge elicitation techniques as presented in Chap. 2, depending on whether it is covered elsewhere in the study program.
3. One lecture about the different EM methods, the perspectives they cover, how to approach them, and what notations to use. This part should be based on Chap. 4 and other sources, for example, Chaps. 8 and 14 in Sandkuhl et al. (2014).
4. One lecture about the EM process and roles involved based on Chaps. 5 and 6.
5. One lecture about the tools used to support modeling based on Chap. 9.
6. One lecture about the actor types and how to deal with them based on Chap. 7.
7. One or two lectures about situations in modeling and how to deal with them based on Chap. 8.
8. One lecture about how to use the enterprise models for organizational development and how to introduce EM in organizations based on parts of Chap. 12 and Chaps. 9 and 10 in Sandkuhl et al. (2014).

For a course such as this, a key challenge is how to provide practical experience in facilitation to students, even in an educational setting. The lab part should primarily consist of performing group modeling with an EM language for a given purpose on a sample case. The students should be asked to observe each other and to take turns in facilitation. The work should be allowed to take considerable time (e.g., periodically over several weeks) so that all participants in the group have the opportunity to act as facilitators. Instructors should observe the group work and provide constructive comments. This part of the course is also quite challenging for the instructor, since it requires quite a bit of experience from facilitating participatory modeling.

1.3.3   Students

The book can be of value for broadening and extending the know-how in courses on EM, business process management, and IS analysis and design. For self-study, the sequence in the book should be followed. If the book is used as part of a study course, the instructor will advise on how to proceed.

Reference

Sandkuhl, K., Stirna, J., Persson, A., Wißotzki, M.: Enterprise Modeling—tackling business challenges with the 4EM method. In: Dietz, J.L.G., Proper, H.A., Tribolet, J. (eds.) The Enterprise Engineering Series, pp. 1–299. Springer, Heidelberg (2014). ISBN: 978-3-662-43724-7

Chapter 2
Background to Enterprise Modeling and to Related Elicitation Approaches

This chapter will briefly introduce the concept of Enterprise Modeling (EM), the EM process, as well as discuss the main approaches to stakeholder involvement and knowledge elicitation. The concept of model quality is also discussed.

2.1 What Is Enterprise Modeling?

Changes and improvements in enterprises usually have to be based on understanding the existing situation in the enterprise under consideration. This reality is complex and can be analyzed from different perspectives, but not all perspectives and not all aspects of reality are required and relevant for solving the problem or completing the task at hand. Enterprise Modeling can be used to facilitate this process.

A variety of definitions regarding the discipline of Enterprise Modeling can be found in the literature. The understanding of Enterprise Modeling in this book follows the definition given by Bubenko et al. (2001).

> Enterprise Modeling (EM) is the process of creating an integrated enterprise model, which captures the aspects of the enterprise required for the modeling purpose at hand. An enterprise in this context can be a private company, government department, academic institution, other kind of organization, or part thereof.
>
> An enterprise model consists of a number of related sub-models, each focusing on a particular aspect of the enterprise, e.g. processes, business rules, concepts/information, vision/goals, and actors.
>
> An enterprise model describes the current or future state of an enterprise and contains the commonly shared enterprise knowledge of the stakeholders involved in the modeling process.

© Springer International Publishing AG, part of Springer Nature 2018
J. Stirna, A. Persson, *Enterprise Modeling*,
https://doi.org/10.1007/978-3-319-94857-7_2

As described in Chap. 3, the main purposes of EM are to:

– Develop the business, for example, developing business vision and strategies, redesigning business operations, and developing the supporting information systems (IS)
– Ensure the quality of the business, primarily focusing on two issues—sharing the knowledge about the business, its vision, and the way it operates and ensuring the acceptance of business decisions
– Use EM as a problem-solving tool, where EM is only used for supporting the discussion among a group of stakeholders trying to analyze a specific problem at hand

EM is usually carried out according to certain guidelines for work, and the resulting enterprise models are documented using modeling languages. The following sections will introduce these concepts in more detail.

2.2   What Is a Modeling Language?

The results of the modeling process—the developed models—are documented using modeling languages. In EM, visual modeling languages are normally used to represent the model, resulting in diagrams. In these diagrams, geometric shapes (rectangles, circles, etc.) connected by lines or arrows are used as graphical symbols to denote different concepts in the modeling language. Often, details of how these symbols and connections should be labeled are also specified. One example of a graphical language for Enterprise Modeling is 4EM (Sandkuhl et al. 2014). Other commonly used EM languages are DEMO (Dietz 2006), MEMO (Frank 2014), i* (Yu and Mylopoulos 1994), ArchiMate (The Open Group 2016), and Active Knowledge Models (AKM) (Lillehagen and Krogstie 2008).

In a modeling language, the underlying syntax defines how the symbols can be used and interconnected. In addition to syntax, modeling languages also have semantics, although a distinction must be made between formal and informal modeling languages. Formal modeling languages have precisely defined semantics and provide more reasoning capabilities. In informal modeling languages, however, the semantics is only colloquially defined or indirectly provided through an established practical application. The advantage with formal modeling languages is that syntactic and semantic errors can be detected with tool-based automated checks or even prevented during modeling. This allows these models to be transformed into other modeling languages more easily and often without a loss of semantics, which would, for example, allow enterprise models to be used in the software development process. The disadvantage of formal modeling languages is that they may be challenging for business stakeholders to understand, because some training is usually needed.

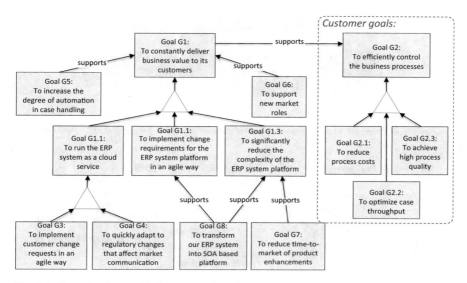

Fig. 2.1 Example of a graphical representation of a model

Figure 2.1 depicts a graphical model, an excerpt of a model describing the goals of an enterprise providing business process outsourcing (BPO) services with a dedicated ERP system. This model also shows a fragment of the customer goals that the BPO service provider aims to support; more about this case is available (Zdravkovic et al. 2014). It is created using the modeling language of the 4EM method (Sandkuhl et al. 2014).

Some EM languages comprise several interrelated model types or sub-models that focus on specific aspects of an enterprise. Examples of such sub-models are process models, goal models, and concept or information models.

Enterprise models for extensive modeling projects or complex processes may consist of a large number of model elements, making them unclear or difficult to display. To allow the complexity of the representation to be reduced, many modeling languages support views and levels.

Most books on EM focus on how to represent enterprise models by using modeling languages. In contrast, this book focuses on the process of modeling and the people involved in the process. With the exception of Chap. 4 presenting an example EM language (4EM), the reader will not find in-depth details about modeling languages in this book. Readers interested in modeling languages should consider the following sources to begin exploring the state of the art in EM: Krogstie (2016), Sandkuhl et al. (2014), Dietz (2006), Lillehagen and Krogstie (2008), and Karagiannis et al. (2016).

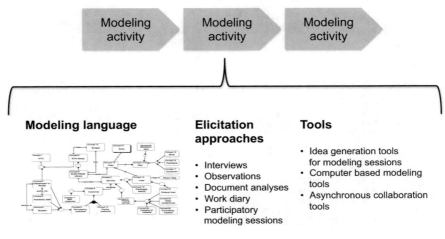

Fig. 2.2 The components of an Enterprise Modeling method

2.3   What Is an Enterprise Modeling Method?

The user of a modeling language needs guidance for how to use it in a practical context, which means that a method is needed. Sometimes in practice, EM languages are referred to as Enterprise Modeling methods. Such views restrict Enterprise Modeling to the graphical representation of models and indicate that having a language is enough to achieve the goals of modeling. In most cases, guidance for questions such as how to organize the modeling activities, how to apply the language to document knowledge elicited in the course of modeling, and how to analyze the modeling results should be explicitly provided. Hence, both a language and a defined process with concrete procedures are needed to support the modeling work.

An *Enterprise Modeling method* describes the approach to Enterprise Modeling by formulating underlying principles as well as detailed and systematic procedures. An Enterprise Modeling method comprises the following components (Fig. 2.2):

1. The Enterprise Modeling process, with a number of defined activities (Chap. 5)
2. The Enterprise Modeling language, with a defined syntax, semantics, and nota-tion, all of which are the building blocks of an enterprise model (an example will be presented in Chap. 4)
3. A set of recommended elicitation approaches (Sect. 2.8)
4. A set of tools (Chap. 9)

2.4   Who Are the Actors Involved in an EM Project?

There are many different actors involved in the modeling process.

All those that have direct or indirect interest in the modeling project or the results are regarded as *stakeholders*. Stakeholders also are those that have no decision-making role in the course of a modeling activity or who do not have relevant information but may still contribute to the project result, for example, with experience in similar projects.

Stakeholders can be divided into two main groups: internal and external stakeholders. External stakeholders include customers, partners, subcontractors, legislators, and shareholders of the enterprise. The employees, project team, the departments concerned, managers, and executives are part of the internal stakeholder group. More about the issue of identifying and managing stakeholder groups is available, for instance, in Cleland (1988) and Freeman (2010).

Stakeholders' relation to a project or its outcome is not always overt. There can also be so-called indirect or hidden stakeholders. They may, for instance, be members of the management hierarchy with some interest in the project outcome and who could be positively or negatively affected by it. The critical factor for the success of Enterprise Modeling and the resulting change initiatives is to involve all relevant stakeholders in the project. Identifying relevant stakeholder groups is a key activity during the preparatory stages of modeling. This is discussed in more detail in Chap. 5.

In modeling activities, two groups of actors can be distinguished, namely, EM practitioners and domain experts:

– *EM practitioners* provide the EM expertise. They have knowledge and experience of the EM method used. They are also tasked with planning the entire modeling project and planning for its modeling activities. Among other things, EM practitioners are responsible for selecting an approach that is suited to the modeling purpose and for ensuring that the resources provided are used in such a way that the project achieves the agreed goals within the allotted time. They are also responsible for ensuring the quality of the methodological process and the quality of the model created. Often, the EM practitioners are engaged from outside the enterprise, for instance, as consultants.
– *Domain experts* have the necessary knowledge of the enterprise in question or domain and application context for the modeling purpose. These subject matter specialists know the organizational structure, business processes, responsibilities, regulations, and problems in the enterprise. This means that any member of staff, from an ordinary worker to executives and enterprise stakeholders, may be a potential domain expert. It also means that domain experts can be found outside the organizational boundaries, within organizations that the enterprise collaborates with. Individuals representing customer groups and other external stakeholders can also act as domain experts. The domain experts group should generally include representatives from different departments and domains, completely covering the enterprise and domain knowledge required for the

modeling purpose. The domain experts are responsible for ensuring that the model content is technically correct and valid for solving the actual problem.

2.5 Why a Participatory Approach to EM and Why It Should Be Moderated or Facilitated?

Approaches to participation in modeling can be categorized according to the degree to which enterprise stakeholders or domain experts participate. Based on Mumford (1983), three levels of participation are identified:

1. *Consultative participation*
   This leaves the main modeling tasks to the EM practitioner, and the enterprise stakeholders are consulted about model content.
2. *Representative participation*
   Here the modeling group consists of EM practitioners as well as stakeholder representatives, but the EM practitioner is still in charge of the content of models.
3. *Consensus participation*
   An EM practitioner, more specifically a facilitator, guides the modeling process, but stakeholders develop the contents of models.

The authors of this book strongly argue for the principle that enterprise stakeholders should participate actively in EM and through a consensus-driven process be responsible for the content of models (c.f. Chap. 6 about responsibilities). This is called the participatory approach to modeling. This principle is implemented in the 4EM method, which the authors have been involved in developing, as a part of the prescribed modeling process. The method developers chose the participatory approach as a result of their practical experience in EM. They recognized that agreements can be reached and problems solved much more effectively when stakeholders, instead of feeling "affected" by EM, become active "participants."

The participatory approach to modeling creates three significant outcomes of a modeling project: (1) the models that are developed, (2) the decisions or changes made in the enterprise, and (3) improved understanding of the problem-solving processes and often even of their own enterprise by the participants. In many cases, the latter two outcomes are overlooked without realizing their significance for the process of implementation of models in real life.

Not every participatory modeling session will produce a high-quality model. However, they almost always add value because the participatory process always produces two results. Firstly, regardless of their state of development, the models that are created can be used as a basis for other activities, whether as a starting point for discussion in further modeling sessions or to capture information that were previously only available in the heads of individual employees. Secondly, the approach changes the problem-solving processes as the participants are guided through a structured and consensus-based process.

1. The participatory approach involves stakeholders in the decision-making and problem-solving process, which increases the participants' acceptance and commitment. This is particularly important if the modeling activities concern changes to organizational units, fields of work, visions and strategies, business processes, or information systems.
2. In the conventional approach to Enterprise Modeling, models are often created by consultants or EM practitioners based on interviews, observations, or workshops, with little active participation by those involved in the enterprise. By contrast, the participatory approach improves model quality as the models are created in cooperation with domain experts and the parties concerned and are constantly reviewed and validated.

EM practitioners also cite a changed attitude to the problem-solving process and enhanced internal knowledge of the organization as the most important reasons for satisfaction with the outcome of a modeling project using the participatory approach. The stakeholders in a modeling project have different and sometimes contradictory success criteria, which must be appropriately investigated during project preparation. Ultimately, the most important gauge of a project's success is that the customer is satisfied with the result, a sign of which is commissioning follow-up projects to tackle further challenges. Moreover, the source of the participating stakeholders' satisfaction and motivation is the fact that they work together in the organization to solve a problem, which can be beneficial for every individual. This motivation is particularly important because improvement and the associated change are a continuous process.

Consequently, a properly conducted modeling project using a participatory approach can provide the following benefits for those involved:

– Better understanding of the relevant parts of the enterprise and how they interrelate
– Problem-solving decisions made by the parties concerned
– A model as a rationale
– Collective discussion of critical issues to find a solution together
– Enhanced organizational learning and communication

It can be tempting to think that if participants in an EM project become active themselves, there is no need for a facilitator or moderator to lead the process of modeling themselves, particularly if they are knowledgeable about modeling. This has been proposed by some researchers (see, e.g., Rittgen 2009), but is not something that we generally recommend. The main argument is that most modeling situations involve an element of negotiation between modeling participants who often represent different stakeholder perspectives. Having a neutral party with the task to manage and balance the negotiation between stakeholder perspectives is, therefore, recommended. This is particularly important if future state models are to be developed. Facilitators can come from the enterprise itself, or they can be external consultants. The important aspect is that the facilitator has no stake in the subject matter.

The participatory approach also comes with some challenges. From both research and experience, we find that a good amount of resources must be put into preparing for modeling sessions. However, the resources initially spent often means that resources can be saved at the end and that the quality of the result often is higher. The problem is only that it sometimes can be difficult to ask for resources before the project starts, more so than asking for resources to deal with emerging problems. Another challenge with this approach is the competence of facilitators. It takes time and experience to become a professional facilitator.

Although there are substantial benefits of adopting a participatory approach, its successful use is restricted by some important organizational characteristics and preconditions, as we will discuss throughout this book.

2.6 How Organizational Culture Matters in Participatory EM

Organizational culture has significant impact on the results and effects of participatory EM. In fact, it seems that failure to properly understand the culture of an organization is perhaps one of the most critical risks in participatory EM. Participatory EM requires that the participants consider themselves authorized to state their opinions and to suggest solutions to the problem at hand. This approach is therefore only suitable in consensus-oriented organizations. In authoritative cultures, it will be extremely difficult to achieve consensus-driven participation in the modeling groups.

Official documents/systems (policy documents, strategy documents, internal instructions, website, etc.) often reveal some of the organizational culture. It can be beneficial for EM practitioners to ask direct questions about how the organization looks upon the concepts of responsibility, cooperation, and participation. This will give an idea of the management philosophy in the organization. Questions could also be asked about how people in the organization will be informed about the project. If strong restrictions are put on the involvement of a circle of people outside the modeling group, this may either indicate an authoritative culture or a hidden agenda. A strong enforcement of the official decision-making structure indicates that the modeling team will not be free to contact people without talking to their superiors first. This may also indicate an authoritative culture.

Attitudes toward participation are often revealed in the way people talk about the problem at hand, other people in the organization, etc. Sometimes this can be seen when observing how people act when talking with each other and with the EM practitioner. Attitudes toward different types of actors (superiors, subordinates, opposite sex, etc.) can be revealing. For example, in a group of people, it can be observed by looking at the faces of people whether or not they agree with what is said or whether they approve of another person or not. Exaggerated agreement with a superior may indicate a need to always express opinions that are in line with those of a superior. This may also indicate an authoritative culture.

In a consensus-oriented culture, which is suitable for participatory modeling, subordinates can question superiors, the dialogue between levels of the organization is open and direct, and reward systems encourage initiatives from all levels of the organization. In an authoritative culture, management is by directives only, the dialogue is indirect, and there are no reward systems for initiatives from different levels of the organization. Note that in an organization, different types of cultures can reside in departments, divisions, subsidiaries, etc. Note also that organizational culture may be amplified by the official decision-making structure. If the organizational culture seems to be authoritative, the participatory approach to EM should not be used. Instead, other approaches such as interviewing and consultative participation could be useful.

If the organizational culture is undecided, maybe modeling can be done in two steps. The first step will function as an initial test of whether or not a participative approach is suitable. If active participation is not achieved in the modeling team, traditional approaches based on interviewing could be used for the remainder of the project. If the culture is mixed, the participatory approach could be used for work in the consensus-oriented part of the organization and some nonparticipatory approach in the more authoritative parts of the organization. However, the two groups should not be mixed.

Hidden agendas will decrease the possibility of achieving the project goals, since different stakeholders will try to steer the project toward their own goals. The project definition states the official goals of the project. It serves as important input to detecting hidden agendas. If the organization has hidden agendas, it may be reluctant to give the necessary authority to stakeholders, which could be "suspected" of jeopardizing that agenda. There can be hidden agendas as a part of a project, and the whole project itself could be a hidden agenda. The latter is the most fatal one.

Interviews with stakeholders before starting the project may reveal hidden agendas, but in that case they need to be carried out by an experienced person with good social skills. Questions about how the project was initiated, how the project is anchored in the organization, and how the result will be used afterward are useful as probes. Hidden agenda may also and will often surface during the project, which calls for open discussions with the customer.

2.7   What Is the Overall Process of an EM Project?

The EM process is discussed in detail in Chap. 5. It follows generic principles of carrying out projects for various purposes. This is because we strongly believe that aligning EM activities with the general project activities improves stakeholder acceptance of the modeling way of working. This section briefly presents the main steps in the process.

2.7.1 Define Scope and Objectives of the Project

There can be a wide variety of reasons for using an EM approach to solve a certain problem in the organization. Regardless of the reason for the project or its trigger, the project goal should be defined at the start of the modeling project. This also involves establishing the expected outcome or what the result should be at the end of the modeling project—"What is the problem that the project intends to solve, and what benefits will it provide?" Since many EM projects start without complete knowledge about the situation in the organization, in the course of the modeling project, the business problem is generally further refined and the goal made more concrete.

Conducting an EM project only makes sense if it meets with approval and support in the enterprise. This requires executives or budget managers and those responsible for the divisions in question to be convinced that the project is beneficial to their areas of responsibility as well as to the organization as a whole. In order to justify the human and monetary resources required for a modeling project, it is often necessary to discuss the expected benefits during project initiation. Preparation for an EM project should not only involve executives but also employees, specialists, and user groups.

2.7.2 Plan for Project Activities and Resources

At this stage, the EM project leader, problem owner, and facilitator plan specific activities to be carried out. This includes the overall number and schedule of modeling sessions, the issues addressed in them, as well as indicating relevant domain experts to be involved in the modeling sessions later. Additional issues to pay attention to at this stage are risk assessment; resource allocation, both for the EM practitioner team and for the domain experts; and establishing the project groups' overall authority, that is, mandate to solve the problem.

Different elicitation techniques can be used for investigating which information should be included in an enterprise model. Selected techniques are presented in Sect. 2.8. In this section, we focus now on the process around facilitated modeling sessions, since that is the main recommended elicitation technique in this book.

2.7.3 Plan for Modeling Session

Each modeling session in the project needs to be carefully planned. It is particularly important that the first session does not fail. Making an overall plan for a modeling session entails setting the goals of the session, selecting the relevant domain experts to participate in the session, and interviewing the participants.

2.7.4   Prepare Modeling Session

A detailed plan for the modeling session is elaborated by analyzing the background material and findings from the interviews. The session should be divided into smaller modeling activities, each with its own focus and driving questions. The modeling facilitator should also assess various risks and scenarios of how the modeling session might develop and plan for alternative actions.

2.7.5   Conduct Modeling Session

The main focus in this phase is to execute the plan of the session. It is important that the participants are made aware of what is going to happen in the session. An essential role of the facilitator is to stimulate and structure the discussion in the session. More on facilitating modeling sessions can be found in Chaps. 7 and 8.

2.7.6   Analyze and Refine Models

Enterprise models created at a modeling session usually need further refinement in terms of presentation and layout, as well as content. The result of the modeling session should also be analyzed with respect to the objectives of the session and the project. This either leads the project team to a conclusion that the expected result is achieved and can be presented to the organization, or the team identifies a set of issues for further modeling and proceeds with planning subsequent project activities and modeling sessions.

2.7.7   Present Results to Stakeholders

The modeling project ends with presenting the results to the problem owner and relevant stakeholders. Larger projects will most likely need several presentations as the project progresses.

A part of this presentation is decision-making on how the results should be implemented or taken up by the organization. It might also be that the stakeholders identify issues that are not resolved and require further development.

2.8   How Can Information to Be Included in Enterprise Models Be Elicited?

Enterprise models represent the situation within the enterprise in question, both in terms of the current state and the future state of affairs. This is only possible if the modeler is able to correctly and fully obtain/elicit relevant knowledge from within the enterprise. Elicitation approaches are essential for this purpose.

One important aspect to be considered in the context of knowledge elicitation is whether or not the models created through EM capture the one and only truth about the problem at hand. We claim that they do not. They can only capture the version of the truth negotiated between the individual stakeholders involved.

Why is this important to keep in mind? Because this will, among other things, prevent the EM practitioner from framing the problem too narrowly or from stopping analysis too soon. Moreover, it helps her or him to realize that more than one person needs to represent a certain stakeholder perspective in the analysis since there can be different opinions about the current and future situation among individuals in a stakeholder group.

Elicitation approaches make it possible to obtain knowledge from different stakeholders about the aspects and parts of an enterprise's situation important for the given modeling purposes. Enterprise employees from various stakeholder groups are often the most important sources of knowledge. The term "stakeholders" generally encapsulates all groups of individuals, both internal and external to the organization, who are involved in its current activities or who affect or will be directly or indirectly affected by future changes.

The approaches covered in this section are interviews, observations, document analysis, and participatory modeling sessions, which are considered to be the main approaches used in practice. The ambition is not to be comprehensive but rather to make an account of the most common approaches.

Table 2.1 summarizes, for the elicitation approaches covered, the appropriate situations where they can be used.

Before starting elicitation activities, the purpose of the activities should be defined, the necessary resources secured, the affected stakeholders informed, and their participation ensured.

All forms of elicitation activities should be carefully prepared. They tie up resources and cost money. Good preparation helps to achieve the goals of this "investment" and to increase the efficiency and effectiveness of Enterprise Modeling.

Before starting any elicitation activity, its purpose and scope should be precisely defined and agreed between those performing the analysis and those in the organization who commissioned it. The aspects and concepts that are important must be derived from the purpose of the activity.

The scope makes it possible to delimit which parts of the enterprise should be included and which should not. The purpose and scope together form the basis for

Table 2.1 Overview of elicitation approaches in Enterprise Modeling

Elicitation approach	Appropriate situation in Enterprise Modeling
Interview	The most important approach when preparing for a participatory modeling session
	Used as an alternative to participatory modeling sessions when the organizational culture or situation does not allow for open discussions in a group setting. Models are then constructed based on the information from interviews
Observation	When more detailed analysis of physically observable current situation is needed and participatory modeling sessions and/or interviews reveal no clear or complete view or result in contradictory information
Document analysis	Preparation of the EM project or as a first step in modeling in order to create a model skeleton
Work diary	Capturing more precise information about durations of tasks, volumes or amounts of resources, or other quantitative information; often used as complement to other elicitation approaches
Participatory model-ing session	Facilitated modeling with a group of stakeholders of current and future situation, if participation is crucial for quality, implementability, and acceptance of models
	Particularly useful: • When an agreement and a joint view of all stakeholders are important • If problems and solutions can only be completely covered and understood if all stakeholders participate in the discussion or development

planning the activities to be carried out, determining the specialists and employees to be involved, and estimating the cost.

In addition, it is important to ensure that the knowledge elicitation activities are approved and supported by enterprise managers—not only the executives that commissioned the overall project but also the managers of the subordinate organizational units from whom enterprise knowledge will be gathered. It is important to ensure that the employees or specialists concerned are allowed time to participate in interviews or sessions, that the necessary information or documents are made available, and that access to the appropriate organizational units and employees is secured.

In addition to managers, the employees involved in or affected by the knowledge elicitation should be involved at an early stage. Comprehensive information about planned activities should be provided to ensure that attitudes toward them are as supportive as possible and to avoid, if at all possible, hostile attitudes. The significance of the overall project to the enterprise, the purpose of the activities, the intended schedule, which activities are planned and who will be involved or affected by them, and how and in what context the collected information is to be used—all of these should be announced before the start of the activities. The key objective here is to ensure that the stakeholders and persons affected have an open attitude toward the activities to be carried out, because this will positively impact the quality and relevance of the knowledge gathered.

The following checklist summarizes the most important points in preparing for knowledge elicitation activities. More detail about preparing for participatory modeling sessions is provided in Chap. 5.

1. Define (as precisely as possible) and agree on the purpose and scope of the investigation between those performing it and those who commissioned it.
2. Obtain approval and support from the relevant managers in the enterprise.

   • Involve all affected organizational units, and don't forget to involve external stakeholders if needed.
   • Agree on sufficient time and resources.
   • Obtain access to existing relevant documentation.

3. Involve those affected within the enterprise at an early stage.

   • Provide information about the purpose of the activities.
   • Announce the schedule and which activities are planned.
   • Communicate who will be involved or affected and why.
   • Provide information regarding how and in what context the collected information will be used.

In the following, the elicitation techniques identified in Table 2.1 are described in some more detail.

2.8.1   Interviews

In EM, interviews are among the most commonly used techniques for gathering information about the enterprise, particular procedures, organizational structures, products, or resources.

Interviews are the most important approach when preparing for a participatory modeling session. More on the role of interviews in that context is found in Sect. 5.4.4. It can also be used as an alternative to participatory modeling sessions when the organizational culture or situation does not allow for open discussions in a group setting. In such cases, the information from interviews is used to construct models, which are then validated with interviewees and other stakeholders.

The various interview formats are summarized in Table 2.2 and explained in more detail in the paragraphs below: face-to-face interviews, telephone interviews, group discussions, written surveys, and computer-based survey processes.

In face-to-face and telephone interviews, the interviewer can provide assistance with unclear questions and answer options. Interviews are relatively quick to conduct, and the interviewer can decide during the interview whether and when to follow up a point in more detail. This is an advantage over written surveys as it allows a closer examination of individual answers to obtain a more comprehensive picture of the interviewee's previous response. An interview that is conducted with support of a guide is called a semi-structured interview. The characteristic feature of

Table 2.2 Interview types, according to Frankfort-Nachmias and Nachmias (2007)

	Interview format			
Medium	Written surveys on paper	Written: computer, e-mail, Internet	Oral; face-to-face	Face-to-face, phone
Definition of questions	Structured interview	Semi-structured interview		Open interview
Definition of answers	Predefined answers (multiple choice)		Free-form answers	
Participants	Single participant		Group	

semi-structured interviews is that the interview is based on a guide containing open questions, which the interviewee can answer freely. The guide merely helps the interviewer not to overlook significant aspects. Structured interviews have a defined set of questions, which the interviewer is supposed to follow rigorously. The advantage of a structured interview is that it provides comparable data. Comparability is achieved by the ability to record information directly during the conversation, which ensures that it is not distorted and can be understood by parties who were not involved in the interview.

A group discussion is a special form of interview where several participants are asked about a subject. It often takes place in the form of a conversation and is led by an interviewer or facilitator. Group discussions make it possible to gather individual opinions, which are expressed more spontaneously and with less control through discussion with the other participants. This allows contrary viewpoints to be identified, which may then need to be examined or investigated in individual interviews. The difference to consultative approaches is that, in group discussions, several individuals are asked about a particular topic, while consultative approaches aim to solve a problem in a purposeful manner.

2.8.2   Observations

Observation makes it possible to collect data and analyze procedures that may be otherwise difficult or impossible to identify. This might concern unconscious, incidental, or routine behavior that is difficult to investigate through other approaches. An important aspect of observation is that the procedures and behavior of interest are studied in the normal operational context, for example, during normal working hours on an ordinary day at the enterprise.

Frankfort-Nachmias and Nachmias (2007) have set out the following points that must apply to every observation:

- The observation must serve a clear purpose (in this case, analysis of an enterprise).
- The start, course, and end must be planned and not left to chance.

– The results of the observation must be systematically recorded according to predetermined criteria.

Observation can be utilized in a variety of forms. A distinction is made between participatory and nonparticipatory observation on the one hand and between structured and unstructured observation in terms of the recording method on the other.

Nonparticipatory observations make use of observers who record and document employees' activities with their knowledge and consent, but do not take part in these activities themselves. In concrete terms, an observer could observe the activities of an entire organizational unit or an operational function, such as the work in a warehouse or the incoming goods department. The observer finds a place from where she or he can see and hear everything but without disturbing the work.

Another option would be to observe a single person in the enterprise as he or she carries out their operational tasks. Here, the observer would shadow the person under observation for a particular period of time in order to record their range of tasks and activities. This could, for instance, be used to document important practices that the observed individual carries out unconsciously. However, the act of observation generally produces the effect that the behavior to be observed is altered by the mere presence of the observer. "If people are aware that they are being observed, they automatically regulate their behavior" (Nerdinger 2008). This fact must be taken into account when evaluating the results of an observation but is not generally an argument against the use of observation to supplement interviews, for example.

In participatory observation, the observer not only observes what is happening but also asks questions about it. This approach makes it possible to capture some of the tacit knowledge and to collect explanations, for example, about why certain things happen in a certain order or a certain manner.

Observation can also take place in a structured or unstructured form. Structured observation is carried out following precise rules with respect to what is recorded about the subject under observation, as well as when, where, and how. For example, if carrying out structured nonparticipatory observation, details of who is observed, for which period of time and during which activities, and how the information is recorded will be predetermined. Unstructured observation is unsuitable for EM because this type of observation is used to formulate hypotheses, which are then verified in a hypothesis-testing process. This is not the purpose of EM. The purpose of EM is to describe an enterprise, in its current or future state, in a model.

2.8.3 Document Analysis

In document analysis, electronic or printed information is viewed and analyzed to obtain relevant findings for the purpose of modeling.

Document analysis provides a valuable contribution to Enterprise Modeling as it offers the opportunity to gain a relatively quick insight into the structures, tasks, processes, and communicative relationships in the investigated enterprise. Available documents that may be potentially relevant to the purpose of modeling are analyzed and relevant enterprise knowledge extracted from them. These documents could include financial reports, business plans, organizational handbooks, standard operation procedures, quality manuals, legislation, organizational charts, service regulations, job descriptions, and flowcharts.

Document analysis is generally a good starting point for an EM project, but it can also provide important reference points for preparing, supplementing, or developing further investigations during the course of an ongoing modeling project.

At the start of the project, potentially relevant documents should be requested from the enterprise by the modeling team. The documents provided are then evaluated, checked for contradictions, and filed for later use in the modeling process. Important findings should be documented separately. Ambiguities, outstanding questions, and contradictions are either resolved with the client in advance or studied during further analysis and information-gathering activities.

During document analysis, it is important to be aware that the information represented therein may be out of date and must therefore be compared by performing at least random checks with other knowledge elicitation approaches.

An example of document analysis with a slightly unusual modeling purpose can be found in a project reported by Persson (1997). Textual requirements specifications were analyzed and the enterprise knowledge contained therein presented in the form of process models, actor models, goal models, concept models, and requirements models. This was done in order to identify missing or contradictory information in the requirements specification. The models revealed numerous unclear aspects of the requirements specification. This indicates that EM also can contribute to reviewing of requirements specifications.

2.8.4 Work Diary

A work diary can be used to collect information about tasks, activities, time, and volumes of work. The involved stakeholders note the requested information themselves. A work diary can be free form, for example, the stakeholders describe their field of work in their own words, without a predetermined structure. It can also be structured, where both the facts to be recorded and a form on which to do so are specified. As the information gathered from free-form diaries takes considerable effort to evaluate, structured work diaries prevail in practice. This requires more preparatory work, but the prestructured information is easier to evaluate, and the information collected is also, in general, more complete.

To ensure that all participants record the necessary information systematically and with comparable content, forms should be prepared and distributed to all the stakeholders involved, along with appropriate instructions for completion. For example, selected stakeholders who perform a particular role in the business process at hand but who work at different departments or related organizations may record all the activities they perform by noting these down at the end of a task/time period along with details of the time and order. This would allow different sites or departments to be compared with the aim of standardization.

Because the information is recorded without any monitoring by an observer, it is necessary to check its plausibility. In addition to tasks, working hours, and volumes, communicative relationships can also be determined. The logging period should be clearly defined, and the method by which the collected information will be evaluated should also be taken into account when creating the forms as well as communicated to the stakeholders involved.

2.8.5   *Participatory Modeling Sessions*

The analysis techniques presented in the preceding sections aim above all to collect information that contributes to an understanding of the current situation in the enterprise or of the future aims. This information is then used to create enterprise models, but these are not actually developed during information gathering. By contrast, participatory modeling is directly geared toward creating models or parts of models. Particular attention is paid to participatory modeling in this book as the technique has proven to be particularly beneficial in EM.

As the employees and domain experts in an enterprise generally have the best knowledge of or ability to judge the current situation and potential avenues for improvements, their active involvement in modeling both the current situation and future improvements is particularly valuable. Participatory modeling aims to make an enterprise's domain experts and employees active participants in model development and to achieve a consensus between the participants regarding all modeling decisions or at least to gain acceptance of the model. Instead of merely acting as sources of information, the participants become active creators, which should result in the participants regarding the developed models as their own development, and not something developed by outsiders.

The participatory approach encourages participants to introduce their "own" modeling contributions, which are negotiated with the group of participants and then incorporated into an overall model that is accepted by the group. In addition to increasing the acceptance of the models among those involved, a further advantage of this approach is that models depicting design decisions about the future state of enterprise affairs are developed by the participants themselves and can therefore be accepted and implemented more quickly.

Modeling sessions are led by a facilitator, whose focus is essentially on achieving the previously defined goal of the modeling session and ensuring that the participants work together in a constructive manner. The role and competences of the facilitator are discussed in more detail in Chap. 6. It should be pointed out, however, that just being able to use a modeling language is not enough to be able to facilitate a modeling session or to manage a modeling project for that matter. It takes a considerable amount of knowledge, on-the-job training, and experience to become an EM professional, particularly when it comes to successfully facilitating modeling sessions and managing larger projects. Novices should never facilitate alone, since the errors made during modeling will negatively influence the outcome of the process where modeling is used.

The participants in a modeling session should generally include representatives from different departments and domains, completely covering the enterprise and domain knowledge required for the modeling purpose. The domain experts are responsible for ensuring that the model content is technically correct and valid for solving the actual problem.

Prior to each modeling session, its goals and topics should be clearly defined and the necessary participants identified, invited, and preinterviewed. The facilitator must prepare the structure of the session, that is, plan the desired order of events so that this can be used as a basis for facilitation of the session.

At the outset of the session, the facilitator introduces the theme and objectives. During the session, it is useful to use a range of resources and tools to enable facilitation and participation. Models are often documented by posting paper cards and by drawing on a large plastic sheet taped to the wall. The plastic sheet is hereafter called the plastic wall. After the session the models are transferred to a computerized tool. More about the tools of modeling can be found in Chap. 9.

The basic idea of the facilitated modeling session is that the session should include a relevant number of loops involving creativity, consolidation, consensus, and critique and new focus; this will be further discussed in the following chapter on the EM process.

The facilitated session may include the following sub-steps or tasks, which are carried out according to the structure planned in advance by the facilitator:

1. *Brainstorming with cards.* The facilitator gives the participants a number of cards. The more cards, the more creative the participants can be. On these cards, the participants simultaneously write down their thoughts and ideas regarding a question asked by the facilitator, using single words or short sentences.

2. *Creating clusters or structures of cards from brainstorming.* The cards resulting from brainstorming are discussed one at a time by the group and divided into particular subtopics or problem areas, also known as "clusters." These clusters are given headings. Individual questions or problems that are mentioned more frequently in the clusters should be marked and weighted. When clustering is complete, the facilitator can decide with the group whether any additions are necessary and if particular aspects or criteria have been disregarded. Other structures can also be created, as prescribed by the chosen EM language. For example, if the task was to identify important activities in a process, the cards can be organized as a process model.

3. *Breaking out into subgroups.* The participants are divided into smaller groups, each of which deals with a specific topic or a part of a cluster/structure already created. The concrete tasks involved in this work depend on the goal and topic of the session. Each subgroup, in a presentation to the whole group, details the

results obtained. This is sometimes called a walk-through. The whole group evaluates the results.

During the sessions, the facilitator should ensure that the participants' attention remains focused on actually solving the problem at hand. Activities such as training in a particular modeling language are therefore not advisable, particularly in the early stages of modeling.

More on how to set up modeling sessions is found in Chap. 5. How to facilitate modeling sessions will be discussed in more detail in Chaps. 7 and 8.

2.9   What Does the Concept of Quality Mean in Enterprise Modeling?

The quality of enterprise models produced in different projects differs depending on the project objectives and the purpose of models. According to Persson (1997), the main overall criteria of successful EM are the following:

1. The quality of the produced models is high.
2. The result is useful and actually used after the modeling activity is completed. The different uses of enterprise models are discussed in Chap. 3.
3. The involved stakeholders are satisfied with the process and the result.

The quality of produced models can be understood to mean that they are correct and consistent with respect to the notation used, or may also concern the model's relevance in solving the given problem. Models that help to solve the specified problem when used as a whole are considered to be of high quality.

High-quality models may:

– Provide a clear business overview
– Support organizational learning
– Help to understand an enterprise's capabilities and processes
– Improve communication between the individual stakeholders about a problem that is to be solved through a modeling project
– Form a rationale for analysis tasks with the help of structured views and descriptions
– Easily extrapolate requirements for process-supporting information systems
– Present a consistent and more comprehensive model by systematically describing business goals, processes, requirements, etc., which is difficult with traditional text-based approaches
– Contribute to continuous improvements in the quality of enterprise processes and structures

From a more formal perspective, a number of model quality criteria can also be applied. In this respect, Larsson and Segerberg (2004) have investigated whether the quality criteria for data models defined by Moody and Shanks (2003) are applicable to enterprise models and proposed several modifications to the original criteria. The resulting quality criteria for EM are as follows:

- Completeness—refers to the degree to which all relevant facts of the problem domain are included in the enterprise model
- Correctness—refers to how well the enterprise model conforms to the rules of the modeling technique
- Flexibility—defined as the ease with which the enterprise model can cope with changes in the modeling domain
- Integration—refers to the degree of consistency between the different sub-models that constitute the enterprise model
- Simplicity—refers to the degree of minimal use of modeling constructs for presenting knowledge in the enterprise model
- Understandability—defined as the ease with which the stakeholders can understand the concepts and structures in the enterprise model
- Usability—defined as the ease with which the enterprise model can be used for its intended purpose

What quality criteria are relevant and how strictly they are to be followed depend on the purpose of modeling or goals of modeling according to Krogstie et al. (2006) and Krogstie (2012). The remainder of this section discusses a number of generic purposes of EM (discussed in Chap. 3) with respect to what quality criteria they require.

If the purpose is to develop vision and strategies, the main quality requirements are understandability, correctness, simplicity, and flexibility, which are the key factors supporting efficient communication among stakeholders.

If the purpose is to design/redesign the business and or information system, the enterprise model presents an organizational and IS design, and hence models should comply with quality requirements in terms of completeness, correctness, flexibility, integration, and usability. Referring to the choice of the modeling language in this case, the understandability for a broad range of stakeholders might be reduced by the need to use a language that allows reaching a higher degree of completeness, correctness, and integration.

If the purpose is to create, maintain, and share knowledge about the business, the main quality requirements are correctness, integration, understandability, and usability. Special emphasis should be put on ensuring that the models are understandable for the target audience without extensive training in a particular modeling approach and language.

In some projects EM is used only as a problem-solving tool, and the models are used only as documentation of the discussion. In such cases, the main quality requirements are correctness, flexibility, and understandability.

2.10   Summary

In this chapter, we have introduced the most important concepts in EM that will be used throughout the book. We defined what EM is and how modeling languages relate to EM methods. An overview of the main actors involved in EM was provided.

The process of EM was also introduced with activities ranging from defining the scope of the modeling project to presenting the results to stakeholders. Arguments for adopting a participatory approach to EM were provided. The main actors in the process were presented, focusing on domain stakeholders and EM practitioners.

Selected elicitation techniques used in EM were discussed. Among them were interviews, observations, document analysis, work diaries, and participatory modeling session.

Finally, an overview of the concept of quality in the context of EM was discussed.

References

Bubenko, J.A., Persson, A., Stirna, J.: User Guide of the Knowledge Management Approach Using Enterprise Knowledge Patterns, Deliverable D3, IST Programme Project Hypermedia and Pattern Based Knowledge Management for Smart Organisations, Project No. IST-2000-28401. Royal Institute of Technology, Sweden (2001)

Cleland, D.: Project stakeholder management. In: Cleland, D.I., King, W.R. (eds.) Project Management Handbook, 2nd edn. Wiley, New York (1988)

Dietz, J.L.G.: Enterprise Ontology—Theory and Methodology. Springer, Heidelberg (2006)

Frank, U.: Multi-perspective Enterprise Modeling: foundational concepts, prospects and future research challenges. Softw. Syst. Model. **13**(3), 941–962 (2014). https://doi.org/10.1007/s10270-012-0273-9

Frankfort-Nachmias, C., Nachmias, D.: Study Guide for Research Methods in the Social Sciences. Macmillan, New York (2007)

Freeman, R.E.: Strategic Management: A Stakeholder Approach. Cambridge University Press, Cambridge (2010)

Karagiannis, D., Mayr, H.C., Mylopoulos, J.: Domain-Specific Conceptual Modeling, Concepts, Methods and Tools. Springer, Heidelberg (2016)

Krogstie, J.: Model-Based Development and Evolution of Information Systems—a Quality Approach, pp. I–XVIII, 1–439. Springer, Heidelberg (2012). ISBN: 978-1-4471-2935-6

Krogstie, J.: Quality in Business Process Modeling. Springer, Heidelberg (2016)

Krogstie, J., Sindre, G., Jørgensen, H.D.: Process models representing knowledge for action: a revised quality framework. EJIS. **15**(1), 91–102 (2006)

Larsson, L., Segerberg, R.: An approach for quality assurance in enterprise modelling. MSc thesis, Department of Computer and Systems Sciences, Stockholm University, No. 04-22 (2004)

Lillehagen, F., Krogstie, J.: Active Knowledge Modeling of Enterprises. Springer, Heidelberg (2008)

Moody, D.L., Shanks, G.: Improving the quality of data models: empirical validation of a quality management framework. Inform. Syst. **28**(6), 619–650 (2003)

Mumford, E.: Designing Participatively. Manchester Business School, Manchester (1983)

Nerdinger, F.: Foundations of Behaviour in Organisations (in German). Verlag W, Kohlhammer, Stuttgart (2008)

Persson, A.: Using the F3 enterprise model for specification of requirements—an initial experience report. In: Proceedings of the CAiSE '97 International Workshop on Evaluation of Modeling Methods in Systems Analysis and Design (EMMSAD), Barcelona, Spain, 16–17 June 1997

Rittgen, P.: Collaborative modeling: roles, activities and team organization. Int. J. Inform. Syst. Model. Des. **1**(3), 1–19 (2009)

Sandkuhl, K., Stirna, J., Persson, A., Wißotzki, M.: Enterprise Modeling: Tackling Business Challenges with the 4EM Method. Springer, Heidelberg (2014)

The Open Group: ArchiMate 3.0 Specification. The Open Group, San Francisco (2016). http://www2.opengroup.org/ogsys/jsp/publications/PublicationDetails.jsp?catalogno=I162

Yu, E.S.K., Mylopoulos, J.: From E-R to "A-R"—modelling strategic actor relationships for business process reengineering. In: Proceedings of the 13th International Conference on the Entity-Relationship Approach, Manchester, England (1994)

Zdravkovic, J., Stirna, J., Kuhr, J., Koç, H.: Requirements engineering for Capability Driven Development. In: Frank, U., et al. (eds.) PoEM 2014, LNBIP, vol. 197, pp. 193–207. Springer, Heidelberg (2014)

Chapter 3
Typical Organizational Problems and How Participatory Enterprise Modeling Helps

Our investigation into the most common purposes for which organizations use EM (Persson and Stirna 2001) shows that there are three main categories of goals (see Fig. 3.1). We first identified goals related to *developing the business*, for example, developing business vision and strategies, redesigning business operations, and developing the supporting information systems (IS). Then goals dealing with *ensuring the quality of the business* were identified, which primarily focus on two issues—sharing the knowledge about the business, its vision, and the way it operates and ensuring the acceptance of business decisions. Finally we identified a third category—*using EM as a problem-solving tool*—where EM is only used for supporting the discussion among a group of stakeholders in their efforts to analyze a specific problem at hand.

In the remainder of this chapter, we will discuss these objectives in terms of the following aspects:

- Input models and documentation—what existing information can be useful to consider.
- Models to be developed—what model types (e.g., business goals, concepts, process, actors, rules, requirements) should be developed to fulfill the purpose of EM.
- EM language requirements—what modeling language should be used and on what aspects of the language should the project focus. In this respect, we are not aiming to recommend any specific language but to provide suggestions about the level of formality and understandability it should provide.
- EM process requirements—what way of working should be used.
- EM tool requirements—what modeling tools should be used, for example, simple or advanced computerized tools or the "plastic wall" for documenting the modeling session.
- Model quality requirements—what are the main quality criteria for the models produced and for the way of working. In this section, we merely point out which quality factors are relevant. A more extended discussion about quality aspects of

© Springer International Publishing AG, part of Springer Nature 2018
J. Stirna, A. Persson, *Enterprise Modeling*,
https://doi.org/10.1007/978-3-319-94857-7_3

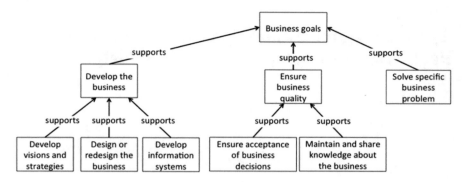

Fig. 3.1 A Goals Model showing the most common purposes of EM, simplified from Persson and Stirna (2001)

enterprise models is available in Sandkuhl et al. (2014) and Krogstie (2012, 2016). A short introduction can also be found in Chap. 2.

The chapter ends with a summary of situations for which participatory EM should not be attempted.

3.1 Business Development

Business development describes all types of purposes associated with developing something new in the organization or substantially improving an existing solution. Business development is frequently done in a change management setting, which requires analyzing the current state in the company, determining the vision for the future, and elaborating pathways for achieving it. Participatory EM is often used in this process with great success because uncovering the facts about the current state and designing solutions that are implementable and have strong impact on the organization often require consolidating the opinions, wishes, and experiences of different stakeholders. The following interview quotation illustrates the typical issues that EM needs to deal with:

> ... questions like strategies, what type of market to participate in, how is the market structured, which are our clients, who are the other interested parties in the organization, how should we structure our work sequencing, how do we structure our products comparing with the clients, and do we sell everything to everyone. EM also aims to describe the reason for the organization, the goals—to relate them to the strategies, to the business idea. EM continues all the way from the strategies through the processes, through the concepts—in order to arrive at a complete picture, or a picture that fits together. [i1 in Stirna (2001)]

Notable specific cases of business development are business process orientation or standardization, new product or service development, and new business model development. The common driving force in these projects is the need to restructure/redesign the business.

Participatory EM is also useful in the early stages of information system development (Bubenko and Kirikova 1999). A common view among business consultants is that the participatory way of modeling is effective for eliciting the business needs and high-level requirements, which are then further refined and implemented into IS designs, as this quotation shows:

> In my experience, the most common modeling I have been doing, has been connected in some way to IT development. There has always been a superior decision of doing something in the IT sphere, which has led to the need to understand the business better and describe it much better, otherwise we can't build the right system. That is very often the situation. On the other hand I have not been very much involved in the rest of the IT development. I have just delivered the results—this is the business, this is how it's working, this is the information that needs to be handled. ... That's one situation. ...Another one is business process definition, where the idea as such has been to describe the business in terms of processes. Then other projects have sort of emerged. E.g. people see that some part of the business should be improved, or this part of the business is not supported by the IT at all. [i2 in Stirna (2001)]

Table 3.1 summarizes the project requirements for business development. Note that in the column "models to be developed," we refer to the common model types of Enterprise Modeling, namely, goals model, concepts model, business process model, actors model, business rules model, and technical components and requirements models. In Chap. 4, we will present the models of the For Enterprise Modeling (4EM) approach (Sandkuhl et al. 2014).

3.1.1 Develop Visions and Strategies

To develop an organization's vision and strategy usually requires setting the goals for the future development as well as elaborating how to reach the goals. In many cases, this work begins with analyzing the current state of affairs, for example, by considering what the current product and service offerings are, what the processes to develop and deliver them are, what organizational units are currently involved in this, as well as what the problems are that influence the current situation and that might be relevant in the future as well.

In the process of developing a vision and related strategies, all kinds of preexisting documentation are valuable as input. It is the responsibility of the modelers to carefully select which documentation can support the modeling process. It is also important to realize that sometimes input to the creative process of defining visions and strategies can come from other organizations as well, for example, in the form of information about technology or market trends, competing products, and new legislation. But considering the innovative nature of this modeling objective, all this information needs to be analyzed together with the stakeholder wishes.

Table 3.1 Summary of EM project requirements for business development

Purpose of EM	Input models and documentation	Models to be developed	EM language requirements	EM process requirements	EM tool requirements	Model quality requirements
Develop visions and strategies	Existing models and other business "blueprints"	Business-oriented models, representing goals, concepts, processes, actors, as well as inter-model links	Notation that domain stakeholders understand	Participatory	Plastic wall, simple documenting tools	Understandability, correctness, simplicity, flexibility
Design/redesign the business	Vision and strategy models and other kinds of business "blueprints"	Business-oriented models, representing goals, concepts, processes, actors, rules, as well as inter-model links	Notation that domain stakeholders understand, established notation	Participatory involving multiple stakeholder groups	Plastic wall, EM tools that make it possible to seamlessly move to requirements analysis and IS design	Completeness, correctness, flexibility, integration, understandability, usability
Develop IS	Business-oriented models	IS-oriented models able to specify IS goals and requirements as well as links with business-oriented models	Enough formality and precision to allow modeling of complex facts	Partly participatory, e.g., to elicit IS goals and high-level requirements and partly analyst driven, e.g., to specify more detailed requirements	Plastic wall, EM tools, or CASE tools depending on the development approach	Completeness, correctness, flexibility, integration, usability

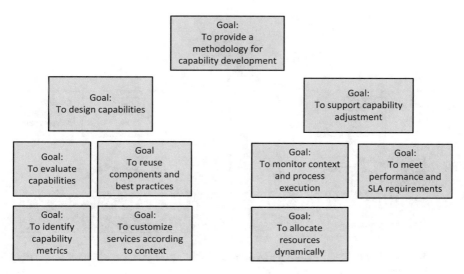

Fig. 3.2 Initial version of a Goals Model showing groupings of goals

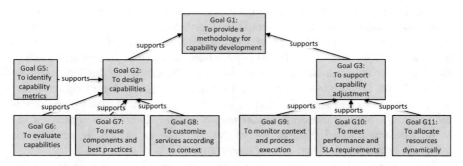

Fig. 3.3 Refined Goals Model with binary relationships of type "supports"

If the modeling project is limited to just developing the strategies, then the modeling language should be chosen such that it ensures understandability and involvement of all stakeholders. Hence, the enterprise model will not need to include the features of a rich modeling notation, and the chosen modeling language can be simplified. For example, in an initial version of the Goals Model, the sub-goals can be arranged in groups (see an example in Fig. 3.2). Later, goal dependencies can be represented by simple binary relationships of the types "supports" (Fig. 3.3) or "hinders," and only in the final stages of the modeling process, AND/OR operationalization relationships could be introduced in the model (Fig. 3.4). This example uses the 4EM notation for goals modeling.

Other model types in an enterprise model might be developed in similar fashion—allowing temporary vagueness at first and refining the model incrementally.

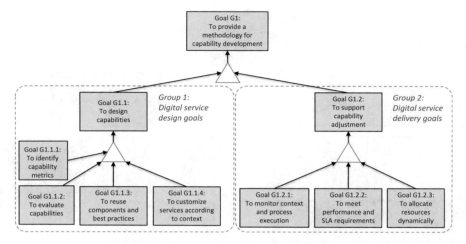

Fig. 3.4 The Goals Model further refined using "AND" goal operationalization relationship (triangle symbol)

The development of visions and strategies is a design process where the views of many organizational stakeholders should be taken into account. A key activity in this process is to elicit as many relevant views as possible and to consolidate them toward a consensus. This ensures that the strategy is feasible and that the different goals of the strategy do not contradict each other. One important aspect of this is to make the arguments for the strategy clear to the stakeholders, which in turn enhances the acceptance of the strategy. For this to be achieved, a participatory approach is indispensable, since it enables the stakeholders not only to listen to arguments and to provide input based on their knowledge but also to essentially become the designers of the future vision of the organization.

Considering that the suggested way of working toward this purpose is a participatory modeling session in need of efficient support for knowledge capture, the preferred modeling tool should be the "plastic wall." After the modeling session, the models can be documented in a simple drawing tool.

The main quality requirements for this EM purpose are understandability, correctness, simplicity, and flexibility, which are the key factors supporting efficient communication among stakeholders.

3.1.2 Design or Redesign the Business

This purpose of EM means that the organization wants to either design a new product or a service, a new work process, or a combination of these. The enterprise models will be used for guiding the implementation of the decisions, that is, they serve as blueprints for new products, services, or work processes.

In designing or redesigning the business, analyzing existing models and documents that define visions and strategies is needed. If no such input exists, then the vision and related strategies should be developed in a separate project or within the current project, because attempting to design the business for the future without them is not recommended.

The typical model types that need to be developed for this purpose concern goals models, concepts models, business process models, actors models, as well as business rules models. A key issue in developing these models is having a holistic view and defining the links between them. Inter-model links used for this purpose are therefore essential.

The modeling language and notation used should be such that it is easy to understand by the stakeholders without extensive training. At the same time, it should be formal enough to represent the knowledge clearly and unambiguously in order to be useful in the process of implementing the models in real life. There are a number of modeling languages that can be useful for this purpose, for example, 4EM (Sandkuhl et al. 2014), ArchiMate (The Open Group 2016), and Value Delivery Modeling Language (VDML) (OMG 2013), to name a few. Furthermore, in choosing which language to use, the modeling languages that have been used in the past and, hence, are known within the organization should be preferred, if they fit the purpose of modeling.

The main goal of this kind of project is to arrive at a feasible and effective solution for implementing the organization's vision in practice. An important quality aspect of an EM that depicts a new design is dependent upon whether or not the design makes sense as a whole and, hence, is possible to implement (Persson 1997). A key aspect of this is consensus among the stakeholders that the new design is the one worth implementing. This requires that the different types of stakeholders be actively involved, which also gives them the opportunity to learn about other parts of the organization represented among the stakeholders. The individual stakeholder's awareness of her or his role in relation to the whole organization is essential for her or his ability to effectively contribute to the overall design. Depending on how big the project is or how large a portion of the organization it influences, a reasonably broad and large stakeholder group may need to be involved. If the group is too large, then several parallel modeling sessions or sub-projects may need to be carried out.

Projects with this objective usually are longer in duration and involve quite diverse activities spanning from idea generation and high-level requirements elicitation to refinement and elaboration of detailed solutions in terms of, for example, business processes and product structures. Some of them require the involvement of larger stakeholder groups, and some can be performed in a more analyst-driven way. Accordingly, the "plastic wall" is well suited for those tasks that require knowledge capture, while computerized modeling tools should be used for model analysis and refinement. In many projects of this kind, the enterprise models serve as input to subsequent implementation activities, such as, new product development projects, new acquisition projects, or new purchase projects. In these cases, the EM tools should be integrated with the IS supporting the business. In some cases, the models represent complete business specifications that can then be deployed by an IT environment, for example, by means of model-driven configuration or even model-based code generation. For example, the MAPPER project proposed an approach and a tool for configuring collaborative work support systems with Active Knowledge Models (AKM) (Lillehagen and Krogstie 2008) supported by the Metis tool. The CaaS project developed an approach of configuring enterprise applications with enterprise models (capability design models) in accordance with run-time context changes (Berzisa et al. 2015).

The enterprise models created in projects with this objective in mind present organizational designs and need to consider quality criteria such as completeness, correctness, flexibility, integration, understandability, and usability.

3.1.3 Develop Information Systems

EM can be efficiently used for the purpose of eliciting and analyzing business requirements to information systems (IS) (Persson 1997; Bubenko and Kirikova 1999). In most projects of this kind, EM is used in the early stages or project inception when the main focus is on business requirements, and hence EM activities can be seen as a "preceding project" that hands over the overall vision in terms of high-level goals, concepts, requirements, etc., to the subsequent implementation project that elaborates these requirements in more detail. In principle, participatory EM shares many common traits with agile development approaches, such as Agile Modeling (Ambler 2002), even if its use in practice in agile projects is unexplored. More about the similarities of EM and Agile Modeling is available in Stirna and Kirikova (2008a, b).

The input documents for EM projects with this purpose are business vision and blueprints in terms of, for example, business process models/descriptions, concepts or information models, and the organization's business rules. If they do not exist or are not described at a sufficient level of detail so as to allow reasoning about what information system support is needed, they need to be created or improved. In addition, the business-oriented models should be extended with links to IS-oriented models, specifying information system goals, problems, and requirements. In this context, it is important to maintain traceability to business-oriented models.

This purpose requires a modeling language that offers means of more precise expression of information in contrast to languages that are primarily used for business development that cater foremost for understandability, often on the expense of formality. The chosen modeling language should preferably have constructs that support the integration of enterprise models with the models used in IS engineering, such as UML models. In such projects, it might even be useful to use the same modeling language for a particular perspective of EM and IS modeling. For example, the concepts modeling language of the 4EM method is fairly similar to UML class diagrams, and hence, a 4EM project focusing on IS development might benefit from replacing the 4EM concepts modeling language with UML class diagrams. Such enterprise concepts models would be easier to refine and evolve to the level of completeness that would be useful for IS development.

The participatory approach is effective for supporting the transition between the business-oriented parts and the more IS-oriented and technical parts of the project. It will also be efficient for eliciting aspects such as IS goals, problems, and high-level requirements because they require stakeholder agreement and consensus. When the high-level goals and requirements are further developed into more detailed IS requirements, a more analyst-driven approach is appropriate, since (1) the more formal models that are used here can be difficult for the organizational stakeholders to comprehend and validate and (2) it might be too resource consuming to involve a group of stakeholders to specify information that is otherwise readily available, for instance, from document analysis or specifications of the current system.

If the goal is to develop an information system, more advanced EM tools should be used. In this case, the repository and versioning functionality will become particularly handy because the models will be used for a longer period of time and they will also be linked to other development artifacts (such as detailed requirements, test cases, architecture specifications) relevant in later IS development stages. In some cases, the team will also reuse the enterprise models.

The main quality requirements for this purpose are completeness, correctness, flexibility, integration, and usability. Referring to the choice of EM language, in this case the requirement for models to be understood by a broad range of stakeholders might take lower priority owing to the need to have a language that better supports model completeness, correctness, and integration.

3.2 Quality Assurance

Many organizations, especially if they are large and distributed, face the challenge of sharing their visions, work procedures, designs, etc., among the different parts of the organization. Many of these aspects can be modeled using enterprise models, and the resulting models can support communication among employees. To this end, we can consider that EM helps to ensure the quality of operations by making organizational knowledge more explicit, thus allowing the stakeholders to better understand the business. For example, in his keynote, Wesenberg (2011) explained how the company Statoil uses models to create a uniform understanding of maintenance procedures among its maintenance crews.

Models also help stakeholders to accept and commit to business decisions, if the models have been created collaboratively and consensus and joint ownership have been established.

Modeling for the purpose of quality assurance contributes to what is commonly known as knowledge management (KM), which concerns creating, maintaining, and disseminating organizational knowledge between stakeholders. While all might not appreciate the concept of KM, we have found that EM can help KM by creating a multifaceted "map" of the business, a common knowledge base for communicating between stakeholders. One KM perspective is keeping employees informed with regard to how the business is carried out.

> ... in those days ... when the company was expanding enormously, they increased by about 100% personnel each year, and it grew very rapidly over the globe. ... So how should we introduce [new people] to the [company E] world and teach [them] how to handle all the things in the [company E] community, etc. It's simply not possible, especially since we don't have good documentation of how we really operate, because everything went on so quickly, that [company E] had to change routines almost every year because of the expansion, etc. So their main motive actually for describing their processes was not to get a lot more efficient, because, maybe rightly, they thought that they were rather efficient, but as a tool to communicate to newly hired personnel, and to show people—this is how we think we are operating, do you have any ideas. [i2 in Stirna (2001)]

Sharing business knowledge is also required when organizations merge or collaborate in carrying out a business process. One aspect of this is terminology as the following citation illustrates.

> I'm thinking about [organization X and organization Y] where they realized that they could use the same data. To be able to do that, they must use the same terms so that they could buy from and sell to each other ... and then it was quite clear that they needed modeling of their business concepts. [i4 in Stirna (2001)]

Stakeholders' commitment to decisions is a critical success factor for achieving high-quality business operations. Differences in opinion about the business must, hence, be resolved, requiring that communication between stakeholders be stimulated. Our investigation (Persson and Stirna 2001) showed that EM, particularly using a participative approach, is effective to obtain such commitment.

> ... if you want people actively involved and if you want them to go along with what is decided, then they have to be allowed to be involved from the beginning and not get decisions forced on them from management. [i5 in Persson (2001)]

> Active participation leads to commitment. So by creating active participation you make it impossible for people to escape commitment. [i5 in Persson (2001)]

Table 3.2 summarizes EM project requirements for the purpose of ensuring the quality of business operations.

3.2.1 Ensure Acceptance for Business Decisions

Modeling with this purpose in mind puts a heavy emphasis on establishing consensus and capturing what the stakeholders decided in their deliberations. The nature of this purpose also implies that reasonably many stakeholders need to be involved. In the process of making decisions, enterprise models serve the purpose of documenting decisions and the arguments for or against them in a graphical form. This is more effective than traditional textual notes, since the notes in the form of an enterprise model are visible throughout the decision-making process and hence are

Table 3.2 Summary of EM project requirements for quality assurance

Purpose of EM	Input models and documentation	Models to be developed	EM language requirements	EM process requirements	EM tool requirements	Model quality requirements
Ensure acceptance for business decisions	Various types of business "blueprints" (e.g., balanced scorecard)	Business-oriented models, e.g., goals, processes, concepts, etc., as well as inter-model links	Notation that domain stakeholders understand	Participatory involving knowledge bearers and users	Plastic wall, simple tools, tools for presentation of models to a wider audience (e.g., web-based tools)	Completeness, correctness, integration, simplicity, understandability, usability
Maintain and share knowledge about the business	Business-oriented models, e.g., goals, processes, concepts, rules, etc., as well as inter-model links	"Cleaned" models that make sense to a wider audience	Simple and intuitive modeling language	Partly participatory, partly analyst driven	EM tools with web interface	Correctness, integration, understandability, usability

jointly owned. Experience has shown that the participatory approach to modeling of decisions fosters a constructive discussion climate.

Various types of business documents, such as vision statements; market analysis; and blueprints, such as Business Model Canvas and balanced scorecards, can be used as input in this process.

Usually business-oriented models, such as those depicting goals, business processes, concepts, and rules, should be developed and linked among themselves with inter-model links. Models are used to capture and document the decisions made by the modeling team. Depending on which kind of decisions or topic they deal with, they can be represented by any model type, but most commonly this is done using goal models or business process models. The responsible parties for implementing each decision can be visualized by links to actors.

Similarly to developing the company vision and strategy, the modeling language should be understandable by all stakeholders in this case. The business decisions should be made clearly identifiable in the models. For this purpose, the modelers might use additional modeling components such as actions. Their main purpose is to visually remind the stakeholders about what the jointly made decisions are and who should do what in order to implement them.

To develop visions and strategies and to design/redesign the business are examples of processes that in essence are decision-making processes, and hence, it is most favorable to adopt a participatory approach.

The "plastic wall" is suitable for capturing the initial model and documenting the decisions as they are made during the modeling session. After the modeling session, the models have to be documented possibly with simple tools, included in a report, and presented to the intended target audience, for example, on the corporate intranet.

The main quality requirements for enterprise models created with this purpose in mind are completeness, correctness, integration, simplicity, understandability, and usability.

3.2.2   Maintain and Share Knowledge About the Business

Modern organizations grow in complexity and size, and as a result, employees find it increasingly difficult to know all aspects of their organizations. Even within their own area of expertise, the complexity and diversity of various knowledge artifacts are such that frequent consultation of manuals and guidebooks is required. Traditionally, such manuals and guidebooks have contained textual descriptions and informal illustrations. In the last decade, with a broader acceptance of modeling, organizations have adopted the approach of expressing part of their business knowledge as models. Hence, the purpose of EM is to support the capture and representation of business knowledge.

All kinds of models that have been used in the organization and are reasonably up to date can be useful to consider. They contain knowledge about how the organization works and how it is intended to work in the future and why. They can be made accessible within the organization after they have been adopted for presentation purposes to their intended audiences. Even if the initial models are too complex, they can serve as the basis on which simpler models or descriptions are created.

In terms of models to be developed, all kinds of models, which convey important messages about how the organization works and why, can be used for this purpose. Models may also be packaged together with information about how they should be used, in which context they are useful, and what the consequences of applying them are. One approach to packaging models is to use organizational patterns and to organize such patterns into a pattern language to support a comprehensive view and to facilitate search and retrieval of models (Rolland et al. 2000).

The modeling language chosen should be relatively commonly used and widely accepted by the intended target audience. It should also to a great extent be intuitive because it is unlikely that all intended users would be trained in the modeling language.

In many ways, the way of working toward this EM purpose is similar to EM for designing or redesigning the business in that different stakeholder types are to be involved and different views are to be consolidated. Additionally, in this case, the knowledge sharing purpose should be taken into account, for instance, by involving both knowledge bearers and users in the modeling sessions.

In terms of tool support, preference should be given to tools with an easy web interface, which include the possibility of annotating the models with text as well as collecting user feedback and comments.

The main quality requirements are correctness, integration, understandability, and usability. Special emphasis should be put on ensuring that the models are understandable for the target audience without extensive training in a particular modeling approach and language.

3.3   Using EM as a Problem-Solving Tool

Even short projects encounter issues and challenges that are unclear, have a multitude of opinions to consider, have changing or unclear requirements, and also have a need to involve a group of stakeholders. Most often, such projects need to resolve a specific problem, decide on the solutions, and then proceed with the implementation of the solution. In such cases, arranging a participatory EM session can be helpful in order to capture, delimit, and analyze the problem situation and to decide on a course of action. In such cases, EM is mostly used as a problem-solving and communication tool. The enterprise models created during this type of modeling only function as the documentation of the discussion and the decisions made. They may not have any further use in terms of specifications for further development or as reusable objects in other projects.

> [in some cases] you can throw [the models] away—they might just have been a sort of drawing for planning your work and afterwards the value of them is already consumed. [i1 in Stirna (2001)]

Table 3.3 summarizes EM project requirements for the purpose to ensure the quality of business operations. The main characteristics of this purpose are that the organization does not intend to use the models for further development work and that the modeling activity has been planned to only be a single iteration. In some cases, this situation changes into one of the other EM purposes discussed in Sects. 3.1 and 3.2. When this happens, it is evidence that the organization sees the benefits of EM or that the problem turns out to be harder to solve than initially expected.

The most important input information is the initial problem statement. In the preparation of modeling, the EM practitioners should also try to identify other relevant documentation that can support the problem-solving process.

Depending on the problem at hand, various types of business-oriented models are developed in this case. However, the models themselves are not the essential output. Sometimes the resulting models are quite incomplete and unrefined, but the ideas and decisions that emerged in the modeling session are much more valuable (Persson 2001).

The modeling language should fit the nature of the problem. For example, if the problem concerns an overall identification and analysis of a problem, the main requirements for the modeling language are understandability and the possibility to use it without extensive training. Modeling with this purpose is used in the context of agile development, in which case a modeling language appropriate for IS design and development should be used, for instance, UML (OMG 2015).

Problem-solving is in most cases a collaborative process, which requires that the creative spirit of the modeling session is supported and that negotiation between stakeholder views is facilitated. We therefore argue that a participatory approach is superior in order to achieve these goals. First of all, it is more or less impossible to support a creative process by analyst-driven interviews of a number of stakeholders. Secondly, negotiation processes tend to be more difficult when arguments are relayed through the analyst instead of stakeholders working out the differences in an interactive setting with the support of a facilitator.

Since the models after the modeling session will only serve as meeting minutes, the "plastic wall" should be used for modeling and simple drawing tools for producing the meeting minutes.

The main quality requirements are correctness, flexibility, and understandability.

3.4   Inappropriate Problems and Situations for Participatory EM

In the previous sections, we have discussed the organizational purposes of using EM with a particular emphasis on the participatory way of working. There are also situations and problems to which participatory EM will either be ineffective or should not be used due to some property of the situation. While much of especially

Table 3.3 Summary of EM project requirements for using EM as a problem-solving tool

Purpose of EM	Input models and documentation	Models to be developed	EM language requirements	EM process requirements	EM tool requirements	Model quality requirements
Use EM to analyze and solve a specific business problem	Initial problem statement and other relevant documentation	Business-oriented models for goals, processes, concepts, rules, etc., and inter-model links	Notation that domain stakeholders understand	Participatory involving multiple stakeholder groups	Plastic wall, simple documenting tools	Correctness, flexibility, understandability

the latter will be discussed at length in later chapters of this book, this section offers a quick summary of when not to use participatory EM.

The Problem Is Trivial   EM requires considerable time to prepare and to carry out, especially considering the involvement of stakeholders. Hence, solving trivial problems that do not require substantial stakeholder input should be solved in an analyst-driven manner. Deciding if the problem is trivial is not always easy; however, it might be that it only appears to be trivial at the outset and many unexpected issues emerge once the investigation begins. This is also one of the reasons why in Chap. 5 we argue that only reasonably experienced practitioners should be the ones defining the project scope and objectives.

The Stakeholders Do Not Possess the Fact Base   The knowledge on the basis of which the problem can be solved can be acquired with other elicitation approaches, such as surveys, observations, and focus groups. Another reason might be that the stakeholders are not knowledgeable about the problem at hand and other methods of elicitation need to be performed. This situation, however, should not be confused with the situation when the stakeholders might not be familiar with the envisioned solution; their views on the organization's requirements are valuable nevertheless.

There Is a Lack of Resources, Authority, and Management Support   EM and especially participatory EM require resources for the EM practitioners (project managers and skillful facilitators) as well as for the stakeholders to participate in the modeling sessions. The project needs to have the authority and management support to address the problem. Without having met all of these requirements, the project will most likely be unable to deliver the expected results, and our recommendation for such cases is not to start the project.

The Situation in the Organization Is Not Favorable for EM   EM requires planned and systematic ways of working. Hence, organizations whose internal cultures are characterized by management by directives, authoritative culture, "firefighting" approaches to daily work, or hidden agendas have difficulties to carry out participatory modeling. In these kinds of situations, open discussions and joint work toward reaching consensus are usually difficult. Therefore, participatory EM will most likely not be able to solve the real problem that the organization faces. A specific case of a situation that is not favorable is that the organization seemingly accepts and wants to do participatory EM but, at the same time, is so used to and is reasonably successful with the analyst-driven way of working that it never manages to model in a participatory way.

   There are specific and strict requirements for the way of working that the project must follow, for example, in terms of using methods or tools that are incompatible with participatory modeling. In such cases, the work procedures of those methods should be followed instead.

3.5 Summary

In this chapter, we discussed the three typical types of objective for using EM:

- To develop the business, which can take the form of developing business vision and strategies, redesigning business operations, as well as developing requirements specifications for information systems.
- To improve the quality of the business. Two main reasons were discussed—sharing the knowledge about the business, its vision, and the way it operates by means of sharing organizational knowledge documented in models and ensuring the acceptance of business decisions.
- To use EM as a problem-solving tool for projects that only need support for resolving a specific problem, deciding on the solution, and then proceeding with the implementation of the solution.

The above types of purposes determine how the EM project needs to be customized in terms of what kind of input models and documentation it should consider, what model types need to be developed, what modeling language should be used and on what aspects of the language should the project focus, what way of working should be followed, what modeling tools should be used and how, as well as what are the main quality criteria for the models produced and for the way of working. In addition, situations not suitable for participatory EM are also discussed in this chapter.

This chapter discussed the basic choices and principles of setting up an EM project. Many of the aspects will be discussed in more detail throughout this book. For example, Chap. 5 presents the EM process in detail, Chaps. 6, 7, and 8 present specific guidelines of organizing EM projects and modeling sessions, while Chap. 9 presents more details about tool support. The purposes of EM also often require integration with other approaches and frameworks, which will be discussed in more detail in Chap. 10.

References

Ambler, S.: Agile Modeling: Effective Practices for Extreme Programming and the Unified Process, 1st edn. Wiley, New York (2002)

Berzisa, S., Bravos, G., González, T.C., Czubayko, U., España, S., Grabis, J., Henkel, M., Jokste, L., Kampars, J., Koç, H., Kuhr, J., Llorca, C., Loucopoulos, P., Pascual, R., Pastor, O., Sandkuhl, K., Simic, H., Stirna, J., Valverde, F., Zdravkovic, J.: Capability Driven Development: an approach to designing digital enterprises. Bus. Inform. Syst. Eng. 57(1), 15–25 (2015)

Bubenko Jr., J.A., Kirikova, M.: Improving the quality of requirements specifications by Enterprise modelling. In: Nilsson, A.G., Tolis, C., Nellborn, C. (eds.) Perspectives on Business Modelling. Springer, Heidelberg (1999)

Krogstie, J.: Model-Based Development and Evolution of Information Systems—a Quality Approach. Springer, Heidelberg (2012)

Krogstie, J.: Quality in Business Process Modeling. Springer, Heidelberg (2016)

Lillehagen, F., Krogstie, J.: Active Knowledge Modeling of Enterprises. Springer, Heidelberg (2008)

Object Management Group (OMG).: Value Delivery MetamodelTM (VDML™) Version 1.0 (2013)

Object Management Group (OMG).: Unified Modeling Language (UML) Version 2.5 (2015)

Persson, A.: Using the F3 enterprise model for specification of requirements—an initial experience report. In: Proceedings of International Workshop on Evaluation of Modeling Methods in Systems Analysis and Design (EMMSAD), Barcelona, Spain, 16–17 June 1997

Persson, A.: Enterprise modelling in practice: situational factors and their influence on adopting a participative approach. Doctoral Thesis, Department of Computer and Systems Sciences, Stockholm University (2001). ISSN 1101–8526

Persson, A., Stirna, J.: Why enterprise modelling?—an explorative study into current practice. In: Proceedings of CAiSE 2001, LNCS, Springer (2001)

Rolland, C., Stirna, J., Prekas, N., Loucopoulos, P., Persson, A., Grosz, G.: Evaluating a pattern approach as an aid for the development of organizational knowledge: an empirical study. In: Proceedings of the 12th Conference on Advanced Information Systems Engineering (CAiSE), LNCS, pp. 176–191. Springer, Heidelberg (2000)

Sandkuhl, K., Stirna, J., Persson, A., Wißotzki, M.: Enterprise Modeling—tackling business challenges with the 4EM method. In: Dietz, J.L.G., Proper, H.A., Tribolet, J. (eds.) The Enterprise Engineering Series, pp. 1–299. Springer, Heidelberg (2014)

Stirna, J.: The influence of intentional and situational factors on EM tool acquisition in organisations. Ph.D. Thesis, Department of Computer and Systems Sciences, Royal Institute of Technology and Stockholm University, Stockholm, Sweden (2001)

Stirna, J., Kirikova, M.: Supporting agile development with participative Enterprise Modeling. In: CAiSE Forum 2008: Ceur-ws.org, vol. 344, pp. 5–8 (2008a)

Stirna, J., Kirikova, M.: How to support agile development projects with Enterprise Modelling. In: Johannesson, P., Söderström, E. (eds.) Information Systems Engineering—From Data Analysis to Process Networks. IGI Publishing (2008b)

The Open Group: ArchiMate 3.0 Specification. The Open Group, San Francisco (2016)

Wesenberg, H.: Enterprise Modeling in an agile world. In: Johannesson, P., Krogstie, J., Opdahl, A.L. (eds.) Proceedings of PoEM 2011, LNBIP, vol. 92. Springer, Heidelberg (2011)

Chapter 4
An Example of an Enterprise Modeling Method: 4EM

This chapter gives an overview of the 4EM method for Enterprise Modeling (Sandkuhl et al. 2014). The purpose of including 4EM in this book is to illustrate the concepts of EM method with an example method. At the same time, the example can be used to explain the different aspects of EM. Throughout the book, we will refer to the concepts of EM methods and base examples on the use of 4EM. An extensive presentation of 4EM and an extensive example case are available in Sandkuhl et al. (2014).

4EM is a representative of the Scandinavian strand of EM methods. It shares many underlying principles of the so-called multi-perspective approaches that recommend the analysis of organizational problems from several perspectives, such as vision (goals, objective), data (concepts, attributes), business processes (processes, tasks, activities), organizational structure (actors, roles, organizational units), etc. Examples of other approaches following the multi-perspective principle are Active Knowledge Modeling (Lillehagen and Krogstie 2008), ArchiMate (The Open Group 2016), and MEMO (Frank 2014).

4EM meets the criteria of being an EM method as it includes a modeling language with graphical representation, a prescribed modeling process, suggested elicitation approaches, and modeling tools. This chapter will present the 4EM language and briefly outline the way of working because the latter will be elaborated in detail in Chap. 5.

4.1 The 4EM Language

The 4EM language consists of six sub-model types, each of them focusing on a specific aspect or perspective of the enterprise—goals, business rules, concepts, business processes, actors and resources, as well as information system (IS) technical components. Table 4.1 shows a summary of the sub-models.

© Springer International Publishing AG, part of Springer Nature 2018
J. Stirna, A. Persson, *Enterprise Modeling*,
https://doi.org/10.1007/978-3-319-94857-7_4

Table 4.1 Summary of sub-models in 4EM (Stirna et al. 2007)

	Goals Model (GM)	Business Rules Model (BRM)	Concepts Model (CM)	Business Process Model (BPM)	Actors and Resources Model (ARM)	Technical Components and Requirements Model (TCRM)
Focus	Vision and strategy	Policies and rules	Business ontology	Business operations	Organizational structure	Information system needs
Issues to model	What does the organization want to achieve or to avoid and why?	What are the business rules, how do they support organization's goals?	What are the things and "phenomena" addressed in other sub-models?	What are the business processes? How do they handle information and material?	Who are responsible for goals and process? How are the actors interrelated?	What are the business requirements to the IS? How are they related to other models?
Components	Goal, problem, external constraint, opportunity	Business rule	Concept, attribute	Process, external process, information set, material set	Actor, role, organizational unit, individual	IS goal, IS problem, IS requirement, IS component

4.1.1   The Goals Model

The Goals Model (GM) focuses on describing the goals of the enterprise. It describes what the enterprise and its employees want to achieve, or to avoid, and when. The Goals Model usually clarifies questions such as:

– Where should the organization be moving and what are the goals of the organization?
– What are the importance, criticality, and priorities of these goals?
– How are goals related to each other?
– Which problems hinder the achievement of goals?

The components of the GM are goal, opportunity, problem (threat and weakness), cause, and constraint. They are linked by binary relationships of the types "supports" and "hinders." Goals are refined by goal operationalization relationships of types AND, OR, and AND/OR.

Figure 4.1 shows a fragment of a GM for a small consulting company. The top goal (G10) is refined into goals G1, G2, G3, and G4 by an AND relationship, which means that in order to achieve G10, all of the sub-goals need to be achieved. Similarly, goal G1 is refined into goals G1.1 and G1.2. Examples of binary relationships in the GM are Weakness 1 hinders goal G2, goal G5 supports goal G3, and Threat 2 hinders Goal 4.

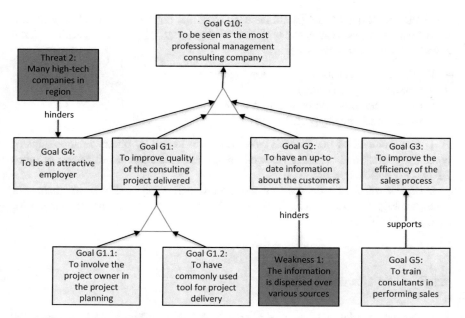

Fig. 4.1 Example fragment of a Goals Model for a consulting company

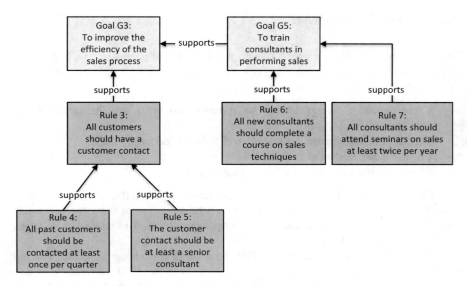

Fig. 4.2 Example fragment of a Business Rules Model for a consulting company

4.1.2   The Business Rules Model

The Business Rules Model (BRM) is used to define and maintain explicitly formulated business rules, consistent with the Goals Model. The Business Rules Model usually clarifies questions such as:

– Which rules affect the organization's goals?
– Are there any policies stated?
– How is a business rule related to a goal?
– How can goals be supported by rules?

The component of the BRM is rule. Rules are linked by binary relationships of types "supports" and "hinders" as well as operationalization relationships of types AND, OR, and AND/OR.

Business rules may be seen as the operationalization or limits of goals. For example, Fig. 4.2 shows how business rules can define more specific means for implementing goals.

4.1.3   The Concepts Model

The Concepts Model (CM) is used to strictly define the "things" and "phenomena" that are mentioned in the other models. Enterprise concepts, attributes, and relationships are represented. Concepts are used to define more strictly expressions in the

Goals Model as well as the content of information sets in the Business Process Model.

The Concepts Model usually clarifies questions such as:

– What concepts are recognized in the enterprise (including their relationships to goals, activities and processes, as well as actors)?
– How are they defined?
– What business rules and constraints monitor these objects and concepts?

The components of the CM are concepts and attributes. The relationship types are binary relationships, generalization/specialization, and aggregation.

Figure 4.3 shows a fragment of a CM for a consulting company. It follows the common notation of concepts modeling with concepts, relationships, and relationship cardinalities. Generalization/specialization is shown by circles; in this example, Concept 5 "offering" is specialized to three concepts—Concept 6 "service," Concept 7 "product," and Concept 8 "customized offering."

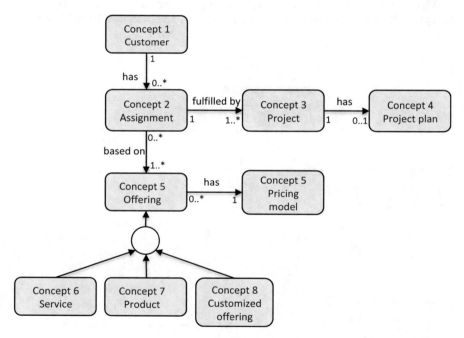

Fig. 4.3 Example fragment of a Concepts Model for a consulting company

4.1.4   The Business Process Model

The Business Process Model (BPM) is used to define enterprise processes, the way they interact and the way they handle information as well as material. A business process is assumed to consume input in terms of information and/or material and produce output in terms of information and/or material. In general, the BRM is similar to what is used in traditional dataflow diagram models.

The BPM usually clarifies questions such as:

– Which business activities and processes are recognized in the organization, or should be there, to manage the organization in agreement with its goals?
– How should the business processes, tasks, etc., be performed (workflows, state transitions, or process models)?
– Which are their information needs?

The components of the BPM are process, external process, information set, and material set.

Figure 4.4 shows a BPM for preparing project after sales at a small consulting company. It shows processes, information sets, and one external process "customer."

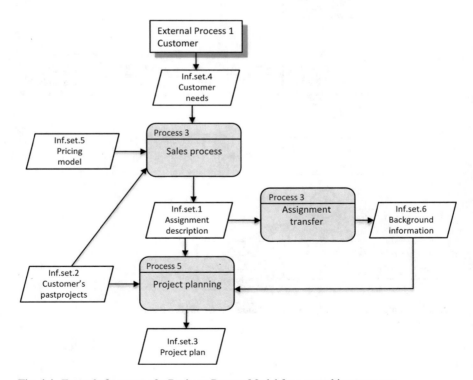

Fig. 4.4 Example fragment of a Business Process Model for a consulting company

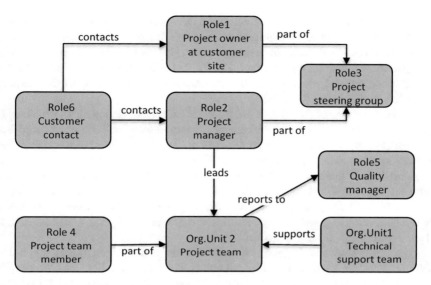

Fig. 4.5 Example fragment of an Actors and Resources Model for a consulting company

4.1.5   The Actors and Resources Model

The Actors and Resources Model (ARM) is used to describe how different actors and resources are related to each other and how they are related to components of the Goals Model and to components of the Business Process Model. For instance, an actor may be responsible for a particular process in the BPM, or the actor may pursue a particular goal in the GM.

The ARM usually clarifies questions such as:

– Who is/should be performing which processes and tasks?
– How is the reporting and responsibility structure between actors defined?

The components of the ARM are role, nonhuman resource, organizational unit, and individual. The relationship types are binary relationships, generalization/specialization, and aggregation.

Figure 4.5 shows a small ARM of roles involved in the sales and project delivery processes at a small consulting company.

4.1.6   The Technical Components and Requirements Model

The Technical Components and Requirements Model (TCRM) becomes relevant when the purpose of EM is to aid in defining requirements for the development of an information system. Attention is focused on the technical system that is needed to support the goals, processes, and actors of the enterprise. Initially, one needs to develop a set of high-level requirements or goals for the information system as a whole. Based on these, we attempt to structure the information system in a number of subsystems or technical components. The TCRM is an initial attempt to define the overall structure and properties of the information system to support the business activities, as defined in the BPM.

The components of the TCRM are information system (IS) goal, IS problem, IS technical component, and IS requirement. IS requirements can be specialized into functional requirements and nonfunctional requirements. Similar to the GM, information system goals and problems are linked by binary relationships of types "supports" and "hinders." IS goals are refined by goal operationalization relationships of types AND, OR, and AND/OR. IS components can have aggregation relationships between them (shown as a small square in Fig. 4.6). Between technical components and IS goals, binary relationships of types "supports," "has goal," and "has requirement" are also possible.

Figure 4.6 shows a fragment of a TCRM for a consultant portal (Technical Component 1) for a small consulting company. It supports the IS Goal 1 "to support information sharing among consultants." The portal consists of several subsystems of which three are shown in this model—time reporting system, project experience

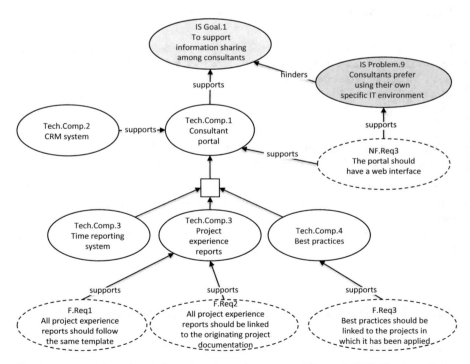

Fig. 4.6 Example fragment of a Technical Components and Requirements Model for an employee portal of a consulting company

reports, and best-practice subsystem. An IS Problem 9 documents that consultants prefer using their own IT environment, which motivates nonfunctional Requirement 3 that states that the portal should have a web interface.

4.1.7 Inter-model Relationships

4EM distinguishes relationships with which the modeling components are related within the sub-model and relationships with components of other sub-models. The latter relationship type is called *inter-model relationship*, sometimes also called inter-model link.

The ability to trace decisions, components, and other aspects throughout the enterprise is dependent on the use and understanding of inter-model relationships. When developing a full enterprise model, these relationships between components of the different sub-models play an essential role. For instance, statements in the GM allow different concepts to be defined more clearly in the CM. A link is then specified between the corresponding GM component and the concepts in the CM. In the same way, goals in the GM motivate particular processes in the BPM. The processes are needed to achieve the goals stated. A link therefore is defined between a goal and the related process. Links between models make the model traceable. They show, for instance, why certain processes and information system requirements have been introduced. Inter-model links are also used as a means to drive the modeling process forward in a modeling session by moving between perspectives. Driving questions like the ones depicted in Fig. 4.8 are then used. They are also a means of making sure that the models make sense. For example, if a process in a BPM does not contribute to fulfilling any business goal in the Goals Model, it is probably not needed. It can also mean that the process is needed but the goal related to the process is missing in the GM.

Table 4.2 summarizes the kinds of relationships that are recommended for use in a 4EM model. Note that the row for the CM does not contain any entries. This means that concepts only have incoming inter-model links. This is done for the purpose of referring components in other sub-model to concepts to clarify terms. Similarly, the ARM does not have any incoming links. This means that the use of ARM components is to specify what goals, rules, process, and requirements they define or are responsible for.

Figure 4.7 shows an example of several fragments of sub-models in a 4EM model and components that are linked between them with inter-model links (dashed arrows).

This model depicts a part of an enterprise model for a consulting company aiming to improve its project delivery (goal G1). This goal is refined using AND decomposition into two sub-goals, namely, G1.1 "to involve the project owner in the project planning" and G1.2 "To have a commonly used tool for project delivery." This figure elaborates only on one of the sub-goals (G1.1) by specifying that it motivates Process 5 "project planning." This process has two information sets as

Table 4.2 Summary of inter-model links in 4EM

To From	GM	BRM	CM	BPM	ARM	TCRM
GM		A goal motivates a rule	A goal refers to a concept	A goal motivates or requires a process		A goal motivates or requires a requirement or component
BRM	A rule affects or influences a goal		A rule refers to a concept	A rule triggers a process		
CM						
BPM	A process supports a goal	A process supports a rule	An information/material set refers to a concept			A process motivates or requires a requirement or component
ARM	An actor defines or is responsible for a goal	An actor defines or is responsible for a rule		An actor performs or is responsible for a process		An actor defines a requirement
TCRM			A TCRM component refers to a concept			

input—"assignment description" and "customer's past project." These information sets are linked to corresponding concepts in the CM by inter-model links of type "refers to" in order to explain information sets in more detail. Of course, in cases like in Fig. 4.7, these kinds of connections might appear to be obvious. However, in real projects when the model complexity is much higher, they need to be documented to increase the overall clarity of the model. Figure 4.8 shows slightly more complex models with more inter-model links and the kind of questions they aim to answer.

4.2   The 4EM Way of Working

The process of 4EM follows the steps described in Chap. 5. The approach to modeling is mainly participatory (Sect. 2.5). Models are developed in sessions involving a group of domain experts and one or two facilitators. In the modeling sessions, models are often documented on large plastic sheets using paper cards (Sect. 9.2). An important part of preparing for the sessions is interviewing the

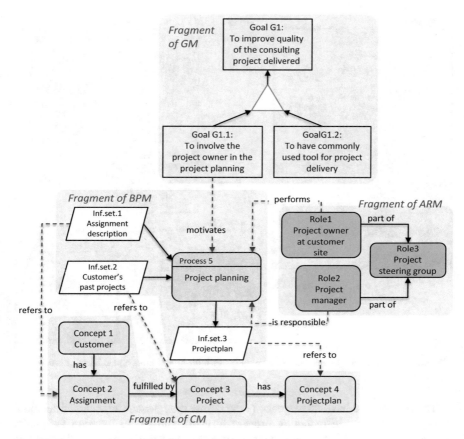

Fig. 4.7 Fragment of an enterprise model with inter-model links

domain experts expected to participate in the session. Document analysis and observation of work practices can also be used.

In a modeling session, the 4EM process populates and refines the sub-model types used in that particular session gradually and in parallel. When working with a model type, driving questions are asked in order to keep this parallel modeling process going. For example, when working with the Business Process Model, we can use the following questions:

– *What does this information set contain?* Go to the Concepts Model to define it and return to the Business Process Model.
– *Who performs this activity?* Go to the Actors and Resources Model to define it and return to the Business Process Model.
– *Why is this activity performed?* Go to the Goals Model to define it and return to the Business Process Model.

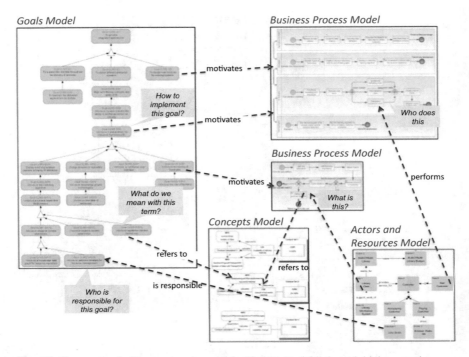

Fig. 4.8 Fragments of a larger enterprise model with inter-model links and driving questions

These questions have three goals: (1) to define the relevant inter-model relationships, (2) to drive the modeling process forward, and (3) to function as quality assurance of the model. It is argued that shifting between model types while focusing on the same domain problem enhances the participants' understanding of the problem domain and the specific problem at hand. Figure 4.8 illustrates working with driving questions and inter-model relationships.

4.3   Summary

In this chapter, we have briefly presented the 4EM method with a particular focus on the modeling language—sub-models, their components, and inter-model relationships. A more extensive presentation of the 4EM language is available in Chap. 8 of Sandkuhl et al. (2014). The 4EM process is participatory and to a large extent similar to that we will describe in the next chapter (Chap. 5). The 4EM language can also be used for creating models in an analyst-driven way.

In this book, 4EM is used as an example EM method that can be used in participatory modeling. Over the years, it has been extensively applied in practice.

The recommendations for participatory modeling have mostly been developed from the cases of using 4EM or its predecessor methods F3 (F3 1994) and EKD (Bubenko et al. 1998, 2001; Loucopoulos et al. 1997).

There are also many other EM approaches that can be used together with the participatory approach to modeling. This means that the contents of the book concerning the EM process (Chap. 5), roles involved (Chap. 6), issues of stakeholder management (Chap. 7), situational contingencies (Chap. 8), and tool use (Chap. 9) to a large extent are independent from the modeling method used.

References

Bubenko Jr., J.A., Brash, D., Stirna, J.: EKD User Guide. Department of Computer and Systems Sciences, Stockholm University and Royal Institute of Technology, Stockholm, Sweden (1998)

Bubenko, J.A., Persson, A., Stirna, J.: User Guide of the Knowledge Management Approach Using Enterprise Knowledge Patterns, Deliverable D3, IST Programme Project Hypermedia and Pattern Based Knowledge Management for Smart Organisations, Project No. IST-2000-28401. Royal Institute of Technology, Sweden (2001)

F3 Consortium: F3 Reference Manual. ESPRIT III Project 6612. SISU, Sweden (1994)

Frank, U.: Multi-perspective Enterprise Modeling: foundational concepts, prospects and future research challenges. Softw. Syst. Model. **13**(3), 941–962 (2014). https://doi.org/10.1007/s10270-012-0273-9

Lillehagen, F., Krogstie, J.: Active Knowledge Modeling of Enterprises. Springer, Heidelberg (2008)

Loucopoulos, P., Kavakli, V., Prekas, N., Rolland, C., Grosz, G., Nurcan, S.: Using the EKD Approach: the Modelling Component. UMIST, Manchester (1997)

Sandkuhl, K., Stirna, J., Persson, A., Wißotzki, M.: Enterprise Modeling—tackling business challenges with the 4EM method. In: Dietz, J.L.G., Proper, H.A., Tribolet, J. (eds.) The Enterprise Engineering Series, pp. 1–299. Springer, Heidelberg (2014)

Stirna, J., Persson, A., Sandkuhl, K.: Participative Enterprise Modeling: experiences and recommendations. In: Krogstie, J., Opdhahl, A., Sindre, G. (eds.) Advanced Information Systems Engineering. CAiSE 2007. Lecture Notes in Computer Science, vol. 4495. Springer, Berlin (2007)

The Open Group: ArchiMate 3.0 Specification. The Open Group, San Francisco (2016)

Chapter 5
The Process of Enterprise Modeling

EM is not merely intended to produce an enterprise model but to serve as the basis for problem-solving, organizational development, and change decisions. The success of EM and its result also depend on how the approach is introduced in an enterprise and how the modeling process is carried out. This chapter will set out guidelines for introducing and using EM in an organization.

5.1 Overview of the EM Process

A modeling project usually involves a number of phases. The subsequent sections of this chapter explain those phases as well as the issues and problems that arise in the process and propose suitable solutions:

1. Define the scope and objectives of the project (Sect. 5.2)
2. Plan for project activities and resources (Sect. 5.3)
3. Plan for modeling session (Sect. 5.4)
4. Prepare modeling session (Sect. 5.5)
5. Set up the room for modeling (Sect. 5.6)
6. Conduct modeling session (Sect. 5.7)
7. Analyze and refine models (Sect. 5.8)
8. Present results to stakeholders (Sect. 5.9)

Figure 5.1 describes the project phases in the form of a process model. It should be considered as a stereotype process, which needs to be adapted to fit each individual project, because in real-life projects, the actual steps and information sets might differ slightly. It is also possible that additional steps are needed, for example, to ensure integration with other development projects or to involve a broader group of stakeholders.

The EM process follows generic principles of carrying out projects for various purposes. This is because we strongly believe that aligning EM activities with the

© Springer International Publishing AG, part of Springer Nature 2018
J. Stirna, A. Persson, *Enterprise Modeling*,
https://doi.org/10.1007/978-3-319-94857-7_5

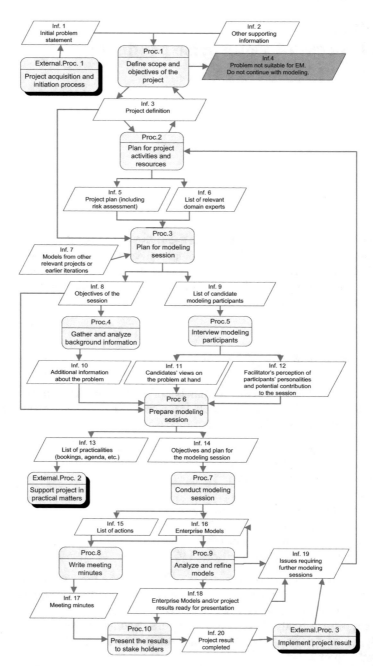

Fig. 5.1 The EM process model showing processes and information sets (Persson and Stirna 2010). © 2010 Springer, Berlin, Heidelberg, reprinted with permission

general project activities improves stakeholder acceptance of the modeling way of working. The actors involved in the process are discussed in more detail in Chap. 6.

Throughout this chapter, references will be made to processes and information sets in this model. In the beginning of each second-level section, an overview of the sub-process in question is provided, before it is discussed in more detail.

It should be noted that the planning and running of an EM project is not a task suitable for novices in the field. For novices, this chapter serves the role of providing insights into the issues and challenges involved. It takes a great deal of practice in the field to master these tasks.

In the following sections, we will describe the steps in the EM process more in detail and also discuss how to supply the EM project with a competent EM practitioner. The EM process described in these sections may appear easy to conduct at the outset. In reality, however, there are many challenges to succeed and pitfalls to avoid, particularly in the project preparation phase (processes 1–6). Much of this knowledge is related to organizational and social issues and hence is not easy to formalize.

5.2   Define the Scope and Objectives of the EM Project

There can be a wide variety of reasons for using an EM approach to solve a certain problem in the organization. Regardless of the reason for the project or its trigger, the project goal should be defined at the start of the modeling project. This also involves establishing the expected outcome, or what the result should be at the end of the EM project. It should also be expected that the business problem is generally further refined and the goal made more concrete during the early stages of the project.

We assume that the EM project is commissioned either as a result of selling consulting services or that another in-house development project has decided to address a specific problem area by a modeling approach. In either case, there usually exist an initial problem statement (information set 1 in Fig. 5.1) and an organizational actor that will benefit from solving the problem—the problem owner.

At this stage, the problem owner and the EM project leader should discuss the problem to find its boundaries, what the likely ways of solving it might be, and what the expected outcomes are. This would form a project definition (information set 3 in Fig. 5.1).

In this process model, we assume that the project manager has chosen participatory modeling sessions as their main preferred elicitation approach after assessing the suitability of the organization to use it (Sect. 2.6). If some doubts arise (e.g., a strong sense of hidden agendas), then the EM project leader should consider other elicitation approaches (Sect. 2.8).

The problem should also be assessed for being suitable for EM. More about assessing the organization and the problem at hand is available in Nilsson et al. (1999), Persson (2001), as well as Stirna et al. (2007). If the organization or the problem is found to be unsuitable for EM, then the problem owner and the project leader should choose other ways of solving it.

Definition of the project goal requires some initial knowledge about the nature of the problem at hand. Some methods, such as "For Enterprise Modeling" (4EM) (Sandkuhl et al. 2014), provide methodological support for this through goal/problem modeling. By analyzing the problems that have been observed and identifying subproblems and the affected or associated processes and organizational units, it is necessary here to determine which parts of the enterprise should be included in a model of the actual situation because they are affected by the problems or the solution and what areas need not be investigated. Although the goal/problem model is the focus here, it should be supplemented by initial versions of the Business Process Model or stakeholder/resource model.

The process of defining the project goal could take the following form:

– Preparing for goal and problem modeling by selecting participants from the enterprise (enterprise employees who know both the problems that have emerged and the processes and organizational units affected), filling the modeling team roles (particularly the role of moderator), agreeing deadlines, and booking rooms. At this stage, the employees selected should be the project commissioner or other relevant stakeholders on the management/problem owner level because the focus of modeling at this stage is to negotiate the project goal with the commissioner.
– Conducting a modeling session to create a goal/problem model, often using conventional tools and plastic sheets. This stage includes identifying relevant business processes (without refining them) and relevant stakeholders or resources.
– Editing the results after the session.
– Holding a workshop with the modeling session participants to present the results and discuss their factual accuracy.
– Deriving and documenting the project goals together with the modeling workshop participants and those responsible for the pre-project planning in the enterprise.

The following example is intended to illustrate how a project goal can be gradually edited and thus refined. In the example, the different sub-models of 4EM are used to illustrate how EM can support also this stage of the project.

Example: Gradual Development and Refinement of a Goals Model
A company wishes to develop a strategy for the long-term development of its human resource capital. This application will initially concentrate on the Goals Model.

• What are the company's long-term goals in general?
• Which goals regarding human resources are recognized and how are these goals related to the company's long-term goals?

(continued)

- Which problems are experienced, which external threats and constraints exist, etc.?

This type of analysis and goal modeling may very well also introduce the need for improved conceptual analysis and modeling of concepts essential for the problem at hand, for example:

- What do we mean by "human resource"?
- How can we measure the current status regarding human resources?
- What do we mean by "competence" and how do we measure competence?
- What kind of competencies may we need in the future regarding the stated goals?

The above questions will help in identifying concepts and creating a Concept Model. The analysis of goals and concepts may also lead to the development of a Business Process Model.

- What qualification measures will be offered to the employees, how can these measures be booked and how are they implemented, and what support for competence development is realized by these processes?
- Which capabilities are required for implementing and performing these processes?
- What kinds of future competences are required to reach the goals defined?
- Should we be interested in developing a "system" for developing and maintaining human resources in the company in the future? New types of positions, roles, and skills may require developing further the Actors and Resources Model.

Regarding the information system support, the overall question to be addressed may be formulated as: "Does our current set of information systems satisfy the need for information support for the long term strategy of the company, and—if not—what has to be changed to arrive at a satisfactory solution?" This question involves, more or less, all sub-models of 4EM. First, the goals of the future situation must be analyzed, as described above. Next, based on this set of goals, the business rules and processes must be examined and redesigned. A new Actors and Resources Model will most probably be developed. The established information systems must be described with their properties in a Technical Components and Requirements Model (TCRM version 1). Afterward, a model of the future set of desired technical components and their requirements (TCRM version 2) must be developed based on documented goals, rules, processes, concepts, and actors for the future business system. A comparison between the properties of the current technical system TCRM version 1 and requirements of the future set of information systems (TCRM version 2) provides here the basis for analyzing needs for changes and further developments. Clearly, in many cases, different alternatives of future information systems may be analyzed.

The above example shows that a relatively unpretentious application case, like the strategy for long-term development of human resource management, requires different perspectives of the enterprise and nearly all 4EM Sub-Models.

An EM project has to start from a clearly defined scope, tasks, and expectations with respect to the results of the project. The tasks and expected results have to be clear to the stakeholders involved in the project. In this context, the following questions can support defining a project's targets completely and concisely:

- What is the goal of the modeling project, which problem has to be solved, and which goals shall be reached?
- What is outside the scope of the project and what is not to be considered within the project?
- Which benefits have to be reached at what point in time for what stakeholder group?
- Who is/are the target group/groups of the project results? Who is the recipient of the final deliverables of the project?
- How does the project support the enterprise strategy and which goals are supported?
- What priority does the project have for the enterprise?
- What is the intended time frame for the project?
- What frame conditions, budget restrictions, and expectations exist with respect to the project?
- Which risks exist and which difficulties are to be expected?
- Which milestones have to be reached and which deliverables have to be produced at what point in time?

When dealing with complex and/or wicked problems (Rittel and Webber 1984), it might be difficult to formulate a clear problem definition. In such cases, the project might organize a modeling session with an objective to find out what the real problem is and how to tackle it. There are two alternative views when it comes to defining the problem at hand. One stresses the importance of obtaining a clear problem definition, assuming that it is possible to acquire such a clear definition. The other assumes that clearly defined problems in most cases are illusions. Instead, they are detected as the project progresses. This has to do with the fact that problems are different in terms of complexity. Problem complexity influences the project planning in terms of necessary activities and resources. Three types of problems can hence be observed:

- *Fairly simple problems.* These problems are possible to clearly define, and they often have a perceivable solution. They do not require the coordination of a large number of different preconditions, activities, actors, and resources.
- *Complex problems.* These problems have a fairly clear definition. They often have a perceivable solution, but they require the coordination of a large number of different preconditions, activities, actors, and resources.

- *Wicked problems.* These problems are ill structured. They have no clear problem definition, and there is no way of measuring that the problem has been solved or testing the solution before it is implemented.

In case of simple and complex problems, planning of the project can proceed. Note, however, that the complex problem will need an experienced project manager and extra resources for coordination activities. If the problem is considered wicked, the project should be carried out in three phases:

1. A pre-study phase where EM, particularly goal modeling, is used to negotiate agreement to the main scope of the project. This is described in the example above.
2. A negotiation phase, where the actual project is negotiated and planned with the relevant stakeholders. Since a wicked problem comprises many unknown factors, the customer must be made aware of them and related risks.
3. A completion phase, where the defined problem is solved as best can be done. Preferably, the project plan should contain a number of evaluation steps, where the results of the project are continuously evaluated and the overall scope is reconsidered before continuing.

5.2.1 Establishing the Project in the Enterprise

Conducting an EM project only makes sense if it receives approval and support from the enterprise. This requires executives or budget managers and those responsible for the divisions in question to be convinced that the project is beneficial to their areas of responsibility as well as to the organization as a whole. To justify the human and monetary resources required for a modeling project, it is often necessary to discuss the expected benefits during project initiation. The following aspects can generally be used when highlighting benefits:

- The project creates value that contributes to the overall success of the enterprise.
- Cost savings through process efficiency and structural improvements.
- Enhanced competitive advantages and corporate agility.
- More efficient IT support for critical business processes.
- Improvements in the documentation and increased transparency of organizational processes.
- Expansion into new markets.

Preparation for an EM project should not only involve executives but also employees, specialists, and user groups. When changes are initiated that affect our status quo, it is human nature to be rather cautious and often distrustful if we cannot assess the potential changes. It is therefore important to establish trust by briefing those concerned according to their initial situation and interests—in other words, motivation points should be produced for the parties involved. These motivation points may take very different forms depending on the individual's role and position.

For instance, executives are motivated more by the project's value contribution to the overall success of the enterprise, but staff members may instead be motivated by work process improvements which they have initiated. The enterprise stakeholders who are relevant to the project should (be made to) feel confident that the modeling project is not a threat to their employment or positions but in fact is intended to support and improve day-to-day work. Concrete examples from previous successful projects within the enterprise or elsewhere should be used as a rationale.

Stakeholder analysis is intended to assist in identifying project participants, their interests, and potential motivation points. To this end, the following questions should be answered:

– Who has an influence on the project?
– Who is affected by it?
– What expectations does the individual/group have of the project?
– What is the attitude toward the project (positive, negative, or neutral)?
– What degree of influence does the individual/group have (low, medium, high, or crucial)?
– Are there any competing projects (in terms of the results, budget, or political power)?

From the project goal, the time frame for implementing changes, and the stakeholder analysis, it is possible to identify the project type or the significance of the project for the enterprise. Firstly, enterprise policy projects and strategic projects can be distinguished. Both are highly interdisciplinary and interdepartmental and hence offer potential for conflicts. Enterprise policy projects are often marked by a specific task (e.g., software rollout), while strategic projects may feature alternative scenarios (reorganization) and a longer duration. It is also possible to identify operational and innovation projects, which, as a rule, are less socially complex (e.g., due to being limited to certain departments or teams) and have shorter implementation timescales. Operational projects have a very limited solution scope and are usually rather short.

At the end of the preparatory phase, the project team should be able to answer the following questions:

– Who instigated the project and why?
– Who is and who must be informed of the project goals/the problem at hand?
– Who is needed to initiate the project and who is affected by the project results?
– Have the answers to these questions been documented in a project description and approved in a project order by the appropriate managers?
– Are there any aspects of the project that cannot be mentioned or documented openly (pointing to hidden agendas)?

5.3   Plan for Project Activities and Resources

At this stage, the EM project leader, problem owner, and facilitator plan specific activities to be carried out. This includes the overall number and schedule of modeling sessions, the issues addressed in them (information set 5 in Fig. 5.1), as well as indicating relevant domain experts to be involved in the modeling sessions later (information set 6 in Fig. 5.1). Additional issues to pay attention to at this stage are risk assessment; resource allocation, both for the EM practitioner team and for the domain experts; and establishing the project group's overall mandate to solve the problem.

5.3.1   Project Activities

The exact activities of a modeling project should be set out in a project plan that identifies the modeling activities to be carried out and defines work packages from them. A work package groups together modeling tasks with related content and defines the deadline by which they should be completed, the necessary effort, and the result to be produced. The content relationships between work packages can be used to establish the order in which they should be handled or whether certain work packages should be completed in parallel. This chronological order is defined in the project plan, which should also define the work package responsibilities. Further general information on project planning techniques and the definition and use of work packages can be found in project management literature.

The project goal determines what modeling activities are required in a project and therefore also which work packages are needed. This means that it is impossible to generalize all projects.

5.3.2   Project Organization

The project organization generally specifies what roles are involved in carrying out the project and what tasks and responsibilities these roles entail. Experience from previously completed EM projects recommends a project structure for EM that contains both roles specific to modeling projects and roles that are generally found in project organization. The roles specific to modeling projects include the facilitator and the modeling group featuring domain experts and EM practitioners. General project organization roles are the project leader, the steering committee, the quality manager, and the reference group.

In a large-scale modeling project, the steering committee is the project's topmost decision-making body, to which the project managers report. The quality manager's role supports the steering committee by reviewing the project results. The project team may include multiple modeling teams. Each team should be led by a facilitator and is also made up of domain and EM practitioners. In addition to the modeling teams, there usually is a method manager, who is responsible for method and tool selection and coordination of individual activities. Reasonably large projects need a documentation manager who is responsible for documenting and versioning the modeling results.

In smaller projects, the steering committee is usually omitted. The manager who commissions the project within the enterprise and the project leader who is in charge of the modeling activities frequently assume these duties. The domain experts involved in the modeling, rather than being specifically assigned to a separate role for the project, perform quality assurance. Tool and documentation management roles are also incorporated into the modeling team. Further information on general project organization roles can be found in the standard literature on this subject. More on the specific roles in an EM project is included in Chap. 6.

Like other types of projects, a modeling project can be unsuccessful without sufficient resources and skills. The individuals involved must be expressly allowed time to participate. Moreover, provisions with regard to modeling tools, modeling kit, rooms, IT, and (if applicable) external domain experts must be organized and made available by the enterprise.

The project managers and participants who are involved in the modeling process must know and understand the goals and expected results of the project. The purpose, goals, and scope of the project must be documented by the time that the project organization and project plan are set, which should also include the allocation of resources (staff, responsibilities, time, money, IT, and other resources). The type of quality assurance with regard to the quality of the results, adherence to milestones, and the validation process must also be defined, generally in a separate quality assurance plan. The outcome of the quality assurance activities should also be documented.

Once the project organization has been established, it should be possible to answer the following questions:

– Who is directing the project and who is part of the project team?
– Have the initiators, commissioner, other authorizers, committees, and reference groups been identified, informed, and involved?
– Have the modeling group participants been identified and involved?
– Are the necessary resources available?
– Has an appropriate reporting system been defined?
– What modeling sessions should be conducted, when, and with what goals?
– What skills and which domain knowledge are required?
– What roles are required for which of these sessions?

The project organization has to be established on the basis of the project goal, which means that all of the roles required for the project are filled. The roles that are generally required in participatory modeling are covered in Chap. 6. The project plan for the modeling project is created, including the schedule and an estimate of the effort involved. Provision of the necessary resources must be agreed with the enterprise. Tools and other necessary aids must be made available or procured.

A typical mistake in planning for resources in an EM project is to underestimate the resources needed for preparing as well as documenting and reporting on modeling sessions. In Persson (2001), we suggest distributing effort as follows:

– Preparing for modeling sessions: ~40% of the total effort
– Carrying out modeling sessions: ~30% of the total effort
– Documenting and reporting the results of the sessions: ~30% of the total effort

This distribution of resources is only given as an indication; depending on the project's aim and duration, they may actually vary by up to 10%. For example, some very short projects might not require extensive documentation, and more complex projects might require even more in-depth preparation.

5.4 Plan for Modeling Session

The first modeling session in a modeling project simply must not fail. This is the time to show to the participants that it is worthwhile to invest time and effort in participating. At this stage, there is no second chance—there is no chance to come back for a second try after a failure. Every outcome that can be perceived as failure by some modeling participants will significantly hamper the future modeling efforts. Preparing for the first session is therefore of utmost importance.

The objective is to plan a specific modeling session, more specifically, to set its overall objective and questions to be addressed (information set 8 in Fig. 5.1). Existing models produced in previous modeling sessions of the project or in earlier projects in the organization and/or other supporting information might also be analyzed. The initial list of relevant domain experts (information set 6 in Fig. 5.1) should be analyzed, and candidates to involve in the modeling session should be selected (information set 9 in Fig. 5.1).

The modeling facilitator usually needs to obtain additional information to learn more about the organization and the background of the problem at hand (process 4: gather and analyze background information). Some of this information can be gathered from documents, such as policy documents. Furthermore, essential enterprise data, such as balanced scorecard data, key performance indicators (KPIs), and business service maps, can be useful. However, the most powerful instrument in planning for the session is interviewing the domain experts that are selected to participate in the modeling sessions.

The candidate modeling participants (information set 9 in Fig. 5.1) are interviewed individually in order to learn more about their views on the problem at hand (information set 11 in Fig. 5.1) and to assess the participant's potential contribution at the modeling session (information set 12 in Fig. 5.1). A benefit for the candidate is that he or she is able to learn about the project and the upcoming modeling session in advance. In some projects, it is beneficial to interview more people than the participants to be involved in the modeling sessions, because this allows the project team to learn more about the organization and, indirectly, to spread the word about the project and the coming change in the organization.

5.4.1   Setting the Goals for the Session

A modeling session is often one instance of a series of modeling sessions, which all have their own goals that are intended to contribute to the overall modeling project goal. It is important that there is a goal for each modeling session. Just gathering a number of people in a room and starting modeling without a clear goal for the session and a plan for the flow of activities within a session will in most cases be disastrous and a waste of effort and resources.

Setting the goal for a modeling session is part of the planning for the overall modeling project. It should be clear what should be produced in the session, which other project results that are input to the session, and how the result of the modeling session is intended to contribute to the overall project.

5.4.2   Selecting the Right Domain Experts to Participate in the Session

Domain experts should be familiar with the problem assigned to the project. Sometimes it may be beneficial to have both the "producer" and the "consumer" side of a particular topic represented to broaden the view. In some stages of the project, it may be necessary to associate specialists in certain areas to the project. These specialists may have the role to suggest organizational or IT solutions to satisfy specific goals stated (e.g., reengineering of some business processes, development of some types of IT solutions).

Who the right domain experts are depends on the goal of the session and models that are to be produced. For example, if a goal model is to be developed, the right domain experts are those who are directly involved in, or have knowledge of, decision-making and goal formulation at the pertinent level of the organization, whether it is operational or strategic. If the goal is to restructure a process, it may not require involvement by formal decision-makers. In all situations, however, it may be necessary to change members of a group as the discussions and models move from one area to another and require people with different knowledge.

5.4.3   Composing the Modeling Group

The composition of the modeling group, the participants in a modeling session, is instrumental to the achievement of the goals for the modeling session. It should therefore be carefully composed based on the goals for the session. It is highly desirable that EM practitioners have a strong influence on the composition of the modeling group. Otherwise the members of the modeling group will not be able to take full responsibility for the results of the modeling session.

The composition of the modeling group should meet a number of criteria:

– The knowledge represented in the group covers the full scope of the problem domain and is able to look at the problem from an overview as well as detailed level.
– The group has adequate domain knowledge.
– The group has the necessary authority to suggest organizational change.
– The group comprises enthusiastic, open-minded, and cooperative people.
– The group consists of people without personal animosity between themselves.

The ideal number of participants is 4–8. If there are less than four people, the discussions tend to become less productive because the number of viewpoints becomes too small. If the number of participants exceeds eight, some individual participants often tend to become less active. It also becomes difficult for the facilitator to manage the group process. Having more than ten people in a modeling group may work if the facilitator is very experienced and the plan for the session allows the facilitator to manage the session in a rather strict way. Alternatively, two modeling facilitators can support each other during the session and take turns as facilitator and observer. In such situations, it is a good idea to plan for frequent short breaks to enable the facilitators to refocus and remedy any problems.

More on how to compose the modeling group in relation to the needed competences is included in Chap. 6.

5.4.4   Interviewing Domain Experts

Before planning for the modeling session, it is strongly recommended to interview the domain experts individually. In most cases, one hour is a reasonable amount of time to spend on the interview, at least to begin with. In preparation for follow-up modeling sessions, it may be necessary to carry out additional shorter interviews, if deemed necessary, for preparing a session properly.

The domain experts need to be prepared for what will happen during the session. This is particularly critical in organizations where the employees are not used to modeling in general and particularly to modeling in a group session. Lindström (1999) recommends that before the modeling session, each individual modeling participant has to:

– Understand the goal of the modeling session
– Agree upon the importance of this goal
– Feel personally capable to contribute to a positive result
– Be comfortable with the rest of the team (including the facilitator)

Note that the purpose of the interviews is *not* to gather information to be included in models but rather to prepare the group process, to select the focus, and to prepare the driving questions for modeling sessions. It is essential that the model group creates the model and develops an ownership of the model. It is not recommended that the EM practitioner prepare models in advance of the modeling session because that tends to decrease the sense of ownership. Both research and practice have also shown that the interpretation of the EM practitioner may not necessarily be the same as that of the group, which tends to cause conflict.

There are several goals with these interviews. They fall into three categories related to the problem at hand, the motivation of domain experts, and the group process.

5.4.4.1   Goals Related to the Problem at Hand

In order to prepare the modeling session in terms of issues to cover, driving questions, etc., the EM practitioner needs to understand the views of the modeling participants regarding the problem, particularly, focusing on goals and possible obstacles to achieve the goals. Their views regarding how other stakeholders might think about the problem at hand are also important. This might reveal potential conflicts of interest and also personal animosities between stakeholders and stakeholder groups. If resolution of potential conflicts of interest or conflict of opinion is essential for solving the problem at hand, driving questions can be posed to the group during the modeling session, in order to make the conflict surface. However, bringing personal conflicts to the surface during a modeling session should be avoided.

5.4.4.2   Goals Related to the Motivation of the Participants in the Group

In order for the goals of the modeling session to be accomplished, the group process should have the highest possible quality so as to utilize to the fullest potential the competencies in the group. Therefore, one goal is to prepare the domain experts with regard to what will happen during the modeling session and why. It is also necessary that they understand in what way their particular competency contributes to the goals of the session and of the project. This clarifies what is expected from them during the session and motivates them to participate actively. To ensure motivation, the attitudes of the domain experts toward the modeling method and the participative approach should also be investigated, if possible.

5.4.4.3   Goals Related to the Group Process

The personalities in a group govern how the facilitator runs the modeling session. The facilitator will, for example, need to neutralize dominant persons and to encourage more introvert persons in order to accomplish full and consensus-driven participation from everyone. The facilitator will also need to ensure that the models produced are the result of consensus between the views represented in the session. Therefore, the facilitator will try to understand as much as possible each individual's personality during the interview. She or he will then be better prepared to facilitate the communication between the members of the modeling group.

Below, we suggest a sample of interview questions assuming a company named COMP, a division of the company named DIV, and a particular function of DIV named F. It is assumed here that the purpose of the project is to analyze F and suggest different possible improvements.

After an initial round of mutual presentations, the facilitator should explain the role of the interview and what will happen in the modeling session. Here it is important to pick up any signs of the domain expert feeling uncomfortable and discuss it up front, for example, starting by saying: "I see that you are a bit uncomfortable with what I say. Can you comment?" In general it is important to make it clear that the information given by the domain expert will only be used to prepare for the session, for example, for formulating driving questions. It is unprofessional to make remarks in the modeling session about who said what in the interviews. The following questions about the problem at hand could be considered, using our example:

- How would you describe the function F, its role, and current activities within division DIV and within company COMP?
- Describe some, in your opinion, important issues within F to be addressed in the next 3–5 years.
- Describe some problems currently experienced by DIV with the function F.
- Give some long-term as well as short-term goals of the function F.
- What makes F a necessary function within DIV?
- What are, in your opinion, the current strengths and weaknesses of function F?
- Which opportunities exist in the area of F?
- Which external constraints would you like to mention regarding F?
- Which external trends may influence the operation of F? How?
- Which management should be particularly concerned with the operation of F?
- Which important decisions, with long-range consequences, will we have to make within a year regarding F? Do you see any problems in carrying out these decisions?
- Which opinions do you think other stakeholders could have about the problems of F?
- What should we not talk about at the modeling session?

The interviews give the project management and the facilitators an improved view of the persons who will participate in the modeling sessions and of their visions, problems, hopes, prejudices, and fears. This gives the facilitator a possibility to plan how to start the modeling session, how to conduct it, and how to handle possible upcoming situations. The interviews may give some hints on organizing the first modeling session depending on situations and opinions revealed in the interviews.

5.5   Prepare Modeling Session

A detailed plan for the modeling session (information set 14 Fig. 5.1) is elaborated by analyzing the background material and findings from the interviews. This plan should include specific objectives of the modeling session, specific questions to be addressed, a preliminary set of enterprise models to be developed (goal models, concepts models, actor models, etc.), a set of driving questions for starting the discussion, and the expected level of model quality.

The session should be divided into smaller modeling activities, each with its own focus and driving questions. Typically a session will move a number of times through four generic phases (Fig. 5.2):

– *Creativity.* The participants are invited to individually write down modeling components, such as activities in a process, concepts, goals, and actors, based on a question, one per paper card. A typical question could be: Which goals does process X need to achieve?
– *Consolidation.* The participants put their cards up on a wall one by one, while the facilitator helps them to consolidate the material into a more coherent view.

Fig. 5.2 The four phases of modeling

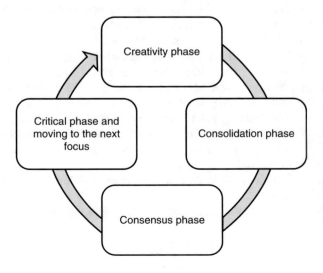

- *Consensus.* The facilitator helps the group to come to consensus about the model.
- *Critique and new focus.* The participants take a step back and analyze the quality of the model, aided by the facilitator. After that, modeling goes on with a new focus. That can entail creating a different type of model or going deeper into the model just having been created.

As described above, domain experts can contribute to creating the model on the plastic wall if deemed suitable. Typically they could group components without consideration for the syntax of the modeling language. Sometimes this improves the sense of ownership of the model. The EM practitioner can then guide the domain experts. In other situations, the EM practitioner adds components to the model after confirmation from the group. Typically this is the preferred approach when syntax of the modeling language is important. Domain experts should not have to learn the syntax. More on the roles and competences of domain experts and EM practitioners is found in Chap. 6. A recommendation is to plan for using both approaches to make the session more interesting to the participants.

More about situations that may occur in modeling sessions is included in Chaps. 7 and 8.

The modeling facilitator should also assess various risks and scenarios of how the modeling session might develop. For example, what are the topics that the participants will not talk willingly about, what are the topics that might lead the discussion astray, what can cause conflicts, and how to act in case of conflict? This should be done in collaboration with the problem owner and project leader. The practicalities of the meeting (information set 13 Fig. 5.1) should also be organized, which include location, agenda, travel plans, etc.

The first modeling session should be organized in a way that promotes concentrated work. This may be achieved by convening in a special room not usually used by the participants or even at other premises, for example, a conference facility. Such a choice of location may provide a more relaxing atmosphere and make interruptions unlikely. Needless to say, mobile phones should be switched off.

Apart from four to eight participants, only a limited number of others should be present:

- One or two facilitators. The number depends on the perceived complexity of the issues to be discussed as well as the number of participants.
- The modeling project leader as an observer who needs an overall knowledge of the modeling work.
- A secretary as an observer with the following tasks:

  • To take care of the practicalities of the plastic sheet, arranging coffee breaks, etc.
  • To document the process of the modeling session.

5.6   Set Up the Room for Modeling

The room must contain at least one large (3 m × 2 m) wall clear of all decoration, to attach a plastic sheet on. There should be precisely enough chairs and tables for the participants. It should be large enough so that nobody could "hide" or make him or her unavailable. There should not be any distractions such as refreshments, telephones, etc.

5.6.1   Equipment

In the room, there should be the following equipment:

– At least one plastic sheet (it can be purchased in most DIY stores and stores selling building materials)

  • The plastic should be relatively thick.
  • Two meters wide, on a roll.

– Pens
– Nonpermanent pens to enable erasure from plastic sheet

  • Medium point
  • At least one for each participant

– Paper

  • Preprinted with components' names if possible.
  • Each component type has a different color to enable easy identification.
  • An A4 page cut into four quarters gives a satisfactory size.
  • A4 papers of different colors.

– Wet rag

  • To wipe off pen drawings from the plastic sheet

– Adhesive putty

  • Two small blobs attached to the back of each piece of paper. Ensure that these stay attached to the plastic sheet when required while allowing them to be easily transferred.

– Scissors
– An overhead projection machine or a beamer connected to a laptop

  • For presenting introduction material and other information necessary to run the session

5.7 Conduct Modeling Session

The modeling session is conducted according to the plans made initially. Here we will not describe details of how a modeling session is conducted. Recommendations of what to do and what not to do are included in Chaps. 7 and 8 and, for example, in Stirna et al. (2007), Sandkuhl and Lillehagen (2008), Jørgensen (2009), Stirna and Persson (2009), and Willars (1999). The tangible outcome of the modeling session is the models produced (information set 16 in Fig. 5.1) and an additional list of actions for implementing the decisions made during the modeling session (information set 15 in Fig. 5.1). Additional intangible outcomes of modeling are participants' improved understanding of the problem area and a firmer commitment to the decisions made (Persson 2001; Lindström 1999).

After the modeling session, it is recommended to write the minutes of the meeting (information set 17 in Fig. 5.1). The minutes should include the models as in the state were produced at the modeling session and action list. At this stage, the models should not be more refined because the main purpose of this activity is to send notes to the participants, which might also serve as a reminder of the actions that they have agreed to be responsible for.

In the following, we provide a set of practical tips to help the modeling team to effectively carry out the session.

5.7.1 Introducing the Session to the Participants

A short introduction is to be given to each of the following:

– All those present
– The agenda of the session
– The topic(s) for discussion
– The ground rules for modeling

The ground rules are necessary since they are not self-evident and are necessary for maximal productivity. They explain the accepted social interactions and means of furthering creativity:

– Everybody participates—no spectators.
– Everybody contributes constructively—differentiate between person and subject matter.
– Everything of importance is written down—talk disappears, the plastic sheet counts.
– Better overexplicit than implied.
– Better half-done here and now than completely brilliant next week.
– Write complete sentences rather than keywords.
– Listen to each other and think individually.
– Build further on each other's thoughts.

- Strive for balance and consensus in the result.
- Search after missing threads of thought.

5.7.2 Stimulating and Structuring Activity in the Modeling Session

The goal of EM is, of course, not only the enterprise model as such. The enterprise model is just a description and representation technique. To obtain an improved understanding, to solve problems, and to develop the enterprise, we should be directed by a critical and analytical study of the enterprise model and its internal relationships. This should be based on good understanding of the principles of EM as they have been presented previously in this book and is the responsibility of the facilitator. Work is often done on more than one model type in one session. Normally, the relationships between sub-models such as in the 4EM method (see Chap. 4) are used as drivers in populating the different sub-models. This may be achieved, to some extent, with the aid of driving questions of the following type:

- Is each goal supported by a process in the Business Process Model? If not, why not?

  - Should we then introduce such a process?
  - Who in the Actors and Resources Model should be responsible for this process?
  - Are they already responsible for a similar process or is there someone else?
  - Should we invest in a new resource to help us run this process?
  - Does this resource need a new or improved information system?

- Can we identify, in the Technical Components and Requirements Model, the requirements for the information system?
- Are there business rules that may put constraints on the requirements?
- Do we have a common enterprise definition of what these constraints and requirements mean, in the Concepts Model?

By searching for relationships and inconsistencies, and discovering gaps, we can increase our knowledge and understanding of the enterprise. The search for knowledge must be made on an individual and group basis in the context of the situation, given the particular intentions of the participants. An EM method such as 4EM (see Chap. 4) will help to work in the right direction, by providing the graphical, structured representation technique in the form of the enterprise model, making the cognitive process of analysis easier. Hence, the lists of driving questions mentioned in previous sections are not complete but only examples that should be further expanded when applicable. Driving questions for each 4EM Sub-Model are presented in Chap. 8 of Sandkuhl et al. (2014).

5.7.3   What to Avoid

There are many pitfalls when one is involved in the communication of ideas between humans, which is what we are dealing with. The following practices should be considered:

- Avoid beginning modeling with long explanations of abstract concepts or focusing on trivial aspects of the problem domain.
- Begin with well-known practical or physical activities, processes, or goals.
- Avoid, if possible, creating unstructured models. This does not mean that the initial model must always be structured. It can be done in such a way that, at first, modeling components are simply grouped together according to some criteria and relationships are introduced later in the modeling session. In fact, the session often involves idea generation and restructuring iterations.
- Conduct additional restructuring and clarification activities as soon as possible after the modeling session; otherwise a lot of information inherent in the unstructured model will be forgotten.
- Avoid having few-worded formulations of modeling components that are not intuitively understood.
- Do not have goals that do not contribute to the overall objectives of the enterprise.
- All goals must be connected so that they contribute to each other. No loose ends should exist.
- Avoid composite statements that have many in and out relationships so that they do not allow for easy understanding and analysis.
- Try to break down statements to the last point at which they are relevant to the issues at hand.
- Avoid detailing attributes before an overall conceptual structure is established.
- Not all attributes are relevant.
- Do not verbalize what is apparent in the model.
- Avoid having concepts that you are unsure why you have them.
- When choosing particular words, confusion and missing concepts may be avoided by creating new words.

More guidelines on what to do and what not to do in a modeling session are included in Chaps. 7 and 8.

5.8   Analyze and Refine Models

Enterprise models created at a modeling session usually need further refinement in terms of presentation and layout, as well as content. The result of the modeling session should also be analyzed with respect to the objectives of the session and the project. This either leads the project team to a conclusion that the expected result is achieved and can be presented to the organization (information set 18 in Fig. 5.1).

Otherwise the team identifies a set of issues for further development and modeling (information set 19 in Fig. 5.1) and proceeds with planning subsequent project activities (process 2 in Fig. 5.1). In many cases, information sets 18 and 19 are reports of the project activities.

After the first modeling session, the EM practitioners document the models using a modeling tool (a software application for model documentation and analysis, see Chap. 9). The first session is often mainly a brainstorming activity. Hence the state of the model is such that:

- It is lacking a clear structure, making it difficult to get an overall picture.
- There are redundant components, for example, there may be two goals stating roughly the same thing.
- There may be missing components.
- Relationships are lacking showing how components are connected to each other.
- The terminology written by domain experts may be ambiguous.

The overall objective of structuring and analyzing the results of the first session is, therefore, to "make sense of the mess." It is to systematically go through all the models, components, and relationships and make them presentable as a basis for further deliberation by the participants in the following session, that is, by clarification, abstraction, structure, simplification, derivation, deduction, and induction.

To achieve progress in terms of structure and clarity of the models, the following strategies can be useful:

- Organize the model to make it more readable. For instance, crossing arrows should be reduced, and grouping of components can be made.
- Introduce relationships. The models are given meaning by drawing relationships so that, if possible, all components in the models are connected to at least one more component. Implicit, undesirable, or overlapping relationships may be discovered and adjusted. Missing components may be discovered. Since the analysts may not have the requisite knowledge, it may be necessary to consult with stakeholders to get a better understanding of the relationships.
- Clarify terminology. Concepts, terms, and abbreviations that are unclear or ambiguous need to be clarified. Domain experts often need to be consulted to explain and define concepts.

After the models produced in the modeling session have been documented, it is time to make sure that they live up to the expectations and correctly capture what has been modeled. More specifically, the models need to be accepted by the modeling group that participated in the session. This can be done in at least two ways that we discuss here: by interviewing stakeholders and by organizing walk-through sessions.

Interviewing stakeholders may seem as a feasible way ahead, since it is easier to schedule an interview with a person than to organize a session with several people, particularly if the people concerned are managers. However, this often causes problems later on. One important purpose of having a walk-through session is, like in participative modeling session, to ensure that different views on the problems are represented in the same room, allowing for quality-enhancing discussions between domain experts.

At the walk-through session, the analysts present work done since the first session and the rationale behind the work on model enhancements. The session should aim to achieve all of the following:

- Review the work from the first session.
- Make corrections and/or additions to the models and descriptions.
- Narrow the field of discussion and specify the domain.
- Expand previous models.
- Suggest further work and future directions.

The resulting models from the first modeling session should be presented to the modeling group precisely in the shape they were created during the modeling session. To present the refined model to the modeling group requires careful planning. The group must be able to trace the results of their efforts, from the original plastic sheet model through the analysis stage to models presented at the next stage, the walk-through session. They must be able to recognize what they have done in the modeling session. A description must acknowledge and give credit to the first session by a verbal description of the results.

At this stage, models produced by computerized tools have replaced models on plastic sheets. Since it is impractical for up to eight people to gather around a normal-sized computer screen, the model should be projected using a projector. As well as the computerized presentation equipment required, all the equipment necessary for modeling as mentioned in Sect. 5.6.1 is also needed. This may entail the use of a larger room or possibly two rooms, one for projection and one for modeling.

A large screen allows all the participants to view the computerized models. In theory, continued modeling directly on the screen together with a tool expert is possible. However, this is not advised as the focus of the group may move from the issues to be discussed to small improvements and/or technical finesses of the modeling tool.

The presentation is a balancing act. The analysts must actually perform an analysis while at the same time not discarding the group work that has been done. When interpretation, change, or deletion is done, it must be explained and justified. This is to ensure that the group will continue to be motivated to contribute. Otherwise, credibility of the analysts and eventually the models is lost.

The results of the first walk-through should be a validation and adjustment of the models being discussed.

Sometimes the modeling project is very small. In fact, for smaller projects, one modeling session is enough. In most cases, more sessions are needed to achieve the modeling project goals. Then the process starts all over with preparations and carries through to validation of models.

5.9   Present the Results to Stakeholders

The modeling project ends with presenting the results to the problem owner and relevant stakeholders. Larger projects will most likely need several presentations as the project progresses.

A part of this presentation is decision-making on how the results should be implemented or taken up by the organization. It might also be that the stakeholders identify issues that are not resolved and require further development (information set 19 in Fig. 5.1).

The EM process we have outlined ends when the problem owner and the involved stakeholders feel that they have a result that can be implemented. In practice the EM project results will most likely serve as input for another development project, including an IT or IS development project.

5.10   Change Management in EM Projects

EM projects, particularly in development situations, typically go through a series of modeling sessions where modeling of the current state of the problem is followed by definition of change requirements. These change requirements are the basis for modeling future state models, which are then used as "blueprints" for the development of, for instance, business processes and/or information systems.

5.10.1   Modeling and Analyzing the Current Situation

As a rule, several models are required to comprehensively model the current situation. Each sub-model is developed in an iterative process, which may include the following steps:

– Modeling starts in a moderated modeling session. Additional sessions may be required for extensive processes or structures.
– The results of the session(s) are documented in the chosen modeling tool.
– The models created with the tool are presented at a workshop with the participants from the initial modeling session(s) and checked for factual accuracy.
– The models are enhanced in workshops of this kind until they reach a state of elaboration that the modeling group and the project manager are comfortable with moving onward to implementation of the model.
– The relationships between the various sub-models are reviewed and expanded if necessary.

5.10.2   Setting Out Change Requirements

Modeling the current situation will have identified the processes, structures, systems, or rules that must be changed in order to remedy the problems that have occurred. There often are several possible ways how changes can be made, and conflicts between enterprise goals often become clear in the goal/problem model. This means that the urgency and priority of the set goals must be decided here, before creating a future state model, and an agreement must be reached as to which of the viable potential changes should be chosen. If it is not possible to decide which potential changes are the most suitable ones based on the goal priorities, multiple versions should be developed during the stage of future state modeling. As the result of this step, which generally takes place in a joint workshop involving a representative of the commissioning party, the project leader is to obtain an agreement as to which versions should be developed in future state modeling.

5.10.3   Creating Future State Models

The future situation that should be brought about to remedy the observed problems is generally defined based on the actual situation. In some cases, this step mostly involves refining the models of the actual situation so that they describe future processes, structures, systems, rules, and concepts. In other cases, new models representing the introduction of completely new processes or structures in the enterprise or radical alterations to processes or structures need to be modeled.

This step produces a description of the enterprise's future situation in the form of a future state model. The future state models can then be used as a "blueprint" for organizational change or as part of the specification of requirements for any necessary software developments.

5.11   Summary

In this chapter, the process of carrying out an EM project using a participatory approach has been described. The process consists of the following steps:

1. *Define the scope and objectives of the project*
   Regardless of the reason for the project or its trigger, the project goal should be defined at the start of the modeling project. This also involves establishing the expected outcome or what the result should be at the end of the modeling project. The defined outcome might also evolve and become more clearly defined as the EM project progresses.

2. *Plan for project activities and resources*

At this stage, the EM project leader, problem owner, and facilitator plan specific activities to be carried out. This includes the overall number and schedule of modeling sessions, the issues addressed in them, as well as indicating relevant domain experts to be involved in the modeling sessions later. Additional issues to pay attention to at this stage are risk assessment; resource allocation, both for the EM practitioner team and for the domain experts; and establishing the project group's overall mandate to solve the problem.

3. *Plan for modeling session*

The first modeling session in a modeling project simply must not fail. This is the time to show to the participants that it is worthwhile to invest time and effort in participating. At this stage, there is no chance to come back for a second try after a failure. Every outcome that can be perceived as failure by some modeling participants will significantly hamper the future modeling efforts. Preparing for the first session is therefore of utmost importance.

4. *Prepare modeling session*

A detailed plan for the modeling session is elaborated by analyzing the background material and findings from the interviews. This plan should include specific objectives of the modeling session, specific questions to be addressed, preliminary set of enterprise models to be developed, a set of driving questions for starting the discussion, and the expected level of model quality. The session should be divided into smaller modeling activities, each with its own focus and driving questions.

5. *Set up the room for modeling*

The room must contain at least one large (3 m x 2 m) wall clear of all decoration, to attach a plastic sheet on. There should be precisely enough chairs and tables for the participants. It should be large enough so that nobody could "hide" or make him or her unavailable. There should not be any distractions such as refreshments, telephones, etc. The modeling material to be used is described in Chap. 9.

6. *Conduct modeling session*

The modeling session is conducted according to the plans made initially. Advice on introducing the session to the participants, stimulating and structuring activity in the modeling session, and what to avoid was given.

7. *Analyze and refine models*

Enterprise models created at a modeling session usually need further refinement in terms of presentation and layout, as well as content. The results of the modeling session should also be analyzed with respect to the objectives of the session and the project. This either leads the project team to a conclusion that the expected result is achieved and can be presented to the organization. Otherwise the team identifies a set of issues for further development and modeling and proceeds with planning subsequent project activities.

8. *Present results to stakeholders*

The modeling project ends with presenting the results to the problem owner and relevant stakeholders. Larger projects will most likely need several presentations as the project progresses. A part of this presentation is decision-making on how the results should be implemented or taken up by the organization. It might also be that the stakeholders identify issues that are not resolved and require further development.

The chapter concluded with a discussion on change management in EM.

References

Jørgensen, H.D.: Enterprise Modeling—what we have learned, and what we have not. In: Proceedings of PoEM 2009, LNBIP, vol. 39. Springer, Heidelberg (2009)

Lindström, C.G.: Lessons learned from applying business modelling: exploring opportunities and avoiding pitfalls. In: Nilsson, A.G., Tolis, C., Nellborn, C. (eds.) Perspectives on Business Modelling. Springer, Berlin (1999)

Nilsson, A.G., Tolis, C., Nellborn, C. (eds.): Perspectives on Business Modelling: Understanding and Changing Organisations. Springer, Heidelberg (1999)

Persson, A.: Enterprise modelling in practice: situational factors and their influence on adopting a participative approach. Ph.D. thesis, Department of Computer and Systems Sciences, Stockholm University (2001)

Persson, A., Stirna, J.: Towards defining a competence profile for the enterprise modeling practitioner. In: The 3rd IFIP WG8.1 Working Conference on the Practice of Enterprise Modelling (PoEM2010), Delft, The Netherlands, November 2010. Springer, Heidelberg (2010)

Rittel, H.W.J., Webber, M.M.: Planning problems are wicked problems. In: Cross, N. (ed.) Developments in Design Methodology. Wiley, New York (1984)

Sandkuhl, K., Lillehagen, F.M.: The early phases of enterprise knowledge modelling: practices and experiences from scaffolding and scoping. In: Proc of PoEM 2008, LNBIP, vol. 15. Springer, Heidelberg (2008)

Sandkuhl, K., Stirna, J., Persson, A., Wißotzki, M.: Enterprise modeling—tackling business challenges with the 4EM method. In: Dietz, J.L.G., Proper, H.A., Tribolet, J. (eds.) The Enterprise Engineering Series, pp. 1–299. Springer, Heidelberg (2014)

Stirna, J., Persson, A.: Anti-patterns as a means of focusing on critical quality aspects in enterprise modeling. In: Proceedings of BMMDS/EMMSAD 2009, LNBIP, vol. 29. Springer, Heidelberg (2009)

Stirna, J., Persson, A., Sandkuhl, K.: Participative enterprise modelling: experiences and recommendations. In: Proceedings of CAiSE'07, LNCS. Springer, Heidelberg (2007)

Willars, H.: Business modeller's checklist: "dos" and "don'ts" in hands-on practice. In: Nilsson, A. G., Tolis, C., Nellborn, C. (eds.) Perspectives on Business Modelling: Understanding and Changing Organisations. Springer, Heidelberg (1999)

Chapter 6
Roles and Competences in an Enterprise Modeling Project

In Chap. 5, we described the EM process and introduced the main roles involved. This chapter describes the roles involved in an EM project and their responsibilities. Particular attention is paid to the role of EM practitioner. We also discuss the competences and abilities needed for modeling, competences and characteristics needed for facilitation, as well as competences needed for managing EM projects. The chapter ends with a discussion about the composition of the modeling group.

6.1 The Main Roles in EM

An overview of the main roles and responsibilities in an EM project is provided in this section. First we discuss the roles related to the customer role in the project followed by the EM practitioner roles as well as the modeling group.

6.1.1 Roles Related to the Customer Role of the Project

The following roles are to be established on the customer side of the project—problem owner, steering committee, project manager, and reference group.

6.1.1.1 Problem Owner

The problem owner is a domain expert who wants to solve some kind of problem in the enterprise as well as has the authority and resources to commission an EM project aiming to solve that problem. The main responsibilities of the problem owner are the following:

© Springer International Publishing AG, part of Springer Nature 2018
J. Stirna, A. Persson, *Enterprise Modeling*,
https://doi.org/10.1007/978-3-319-94857-7_6

- Supporting and "selling" the project within the organization, as well as other internal communication of project goals
- Deciding on the final project plan
- Obtaining official acceptance of milestones and deliverables based on the results of quality control measures
- Deciding about changes in project plans in case of new requirements and delays in project work
- Supporting the acquisition of resources and assigning them to the project
- Deciding about resource allocation

6.1.1.2   Steering Committee

Larger EM projects will need a steering committee, which then takes on the same responsibility as the problem owner. The problem owner, who commissioned the project, is part of and manages this group. The steering committee typically includes domain experts from different areas or departments of the enterprise who are involved in reaching the project's objectives or have an interest in the value the project intends to create. This could be heads of departments, budget-responsible managers, or employee representatives.

6.1.1.3   Project Manager

Project management in large-scale projects often consists of two project managers: the manager from the commissioning enterprise, often called the internal project manager or customer representative, and the manager of the modeling activities, often called the project manager for modeling.

Jointly, these two project managers are responsible for:

- Project planning
- The day-to-day project management (incl. supervision of time plans, resource consumption, and costs)
- Reporting to the steering committee or the problem owner

The *internal project manager* is responsible for and has to coordinate:

- Provision of documents required for the modeling project
- Selection of domain experts required for the modeling and releasing them from their regular duties to allow their participation in modeling activities
- Communication of project goals, expected results, and achievements within the enterprise
- Providing facilities and technical infrastructure for the modeling activities in case they are performed within the enterprise

The *project manager for modeling* is responsible for:

- Planning and organization of all modeling activities following the selected method
- Reaching high-quality modeling results, for example, by organizing workshops for presentation and validation of the models and results
- Assigning EM practitioners to roles and to modeling activities
- Achieving the defined project goals and results

In small- to medium-sized projects, the project manager for modeling may also be fulfilling the role of modeling facilitator. In the following when we refer to the role of project manager, we mean a project manager who also plays the role of modeling facilitator, alone or together with more facilitators. The role of internal project manager will not be discussed further.

6.1.1.4 Reference Group

Large projects often need a reference group, which typically consists of domain experts and experienced employees of the enterprise who are familiar with structures and processes in the enterprise. In smaller projects, the reference group is usually omitted. The reference group is responsible for:

- Supplying domain knowledge, for example, about organization units involved, expertise about the work procedures, and information about the business environment
- Examining and evaluating the results
- Integrating modeling results of different teams into a consistent whole

6.1.2 EM Practitioner Roles

The following roles should be established on the EM practitioner side of the project—facilitator, tool expert, and quality assurance officer.

6.1.2.1 Facilitator

The use of a participatory approach to EM requires the support of a modeling facilitator. The facilitator's task is to direct and guide modeling sessions, which includes the following:

- Prepare modeling sessions.
- Manage sessions in accordance with the method used.
- Manage the modeling process.
- Make sure that all participants are included in the modeling process.

– Make sure that the goals of the modeling activities are reached.
– Support the modeling group in acquiring knowledge and ideas from each other.

6.1.2.2 Tool Expert

In order to use an EM method efficiently, different kinds of modeling tools are needed, and hence, the project should include the role of tool expert. In smaller projects, the project manager or facilitator can play this role. The role of tool expert involves:

– Selecting an appropriate modeling tool for the project
– Documenting the modeling results with the tool, for example, drawing the models on the plastic sheets into a computerized tool
– Preparing models for presentations
– Assisting a modeling facilitator during presentation of models
– Introducing tool in the organization in cases when the organization intends using EM without the support of external method and tool providers

6.1.2.3 Quality Assurance Officer

In small- to medium-sized projects, the project leader plays the role of quality assurance officer, responsible for systematically ensuring the overall quality of the project results. In larger projects, a dedicated expert might need to be assigned for this role. The role of quality assurance officer includes:

– Definition of quality criteria for the different kinds of project results
– Development of a quality plan (which quality result will be evaluated at what point in time according to what criteria?)
– Documentation of the results of quality control activities
– Reporting to project management and steering committee

6.1.3 Modeling Group

A modeling group consists of domain experts who participate in a particular modeling activity. There can be different modeling groups for different modeling activities depending on the purpose of modeling. The tasks of the modeling group are to:

– Actively participate in the modeling sessions
– Contribute with domain knowledge
– Ensure that the models contain relevant and valid domain knowledge
– Assist the facilitators in structuring and describing the models

The composition of the modeling group should meet a number of criteria:

- There are persons from various parts of the enterprise enabling the broadest range of knowledge and views to be available.
- The group has adequate domain knowledge.
- The group has the necessary authority to suggest organizational change.
- The group comprises enthusiastic, open-minded, and cooperative people.

6.2   The Involvement of Main Roles in the EM Process

In essence, there are two types of roles in an EM project: domain experts and EM practitioners. In any EM project, the more specific roles most involved in project activities are:

- Among domain experts: problem owner and participants in modeling groups
- Among EM practitioners: project manager, facilitator, and tool expert

The domain expert group should generally include representatives from different departments and domains, completely covering the enterprise and domain knowledge required for the modeling purpose.

EM practitioners may come from outside as an external consultant or from within the enterprise. The advantage of having an internal EM practitioner is that they will be familiar with the enterprise and the organizational unit under examination. However, an in-house facilitator is not independent of internal authority structures and objectives, which can make an unobtrusive style of workshop facilitation more difficult. A facilitator from an external company might be more impartial to the situation in the enterprise and hence may be able to offer a fresh view as well as bring new ideas and opinions. Of course, an outside facilitator might not always be obtainable, for example, if the content of the modeling project cannot be exposed outside the organization or if the modeling workshop is arranged at short notice, although we would argue against the latter. Regardless of where the facilitators come from, the distribution of responsibilities and tasks should be the same. In the next section, we will discuss the responsibilities of the modeling facilitator in detail.

In Chap. 5, the main steps of the EM process were described, based on Fig. 5.1. Table 6.1 provides an overview of how these roles are involved in the different steps, focusing on whether they participate (P) or are responsible (R).

A key aspect of organizing participatory modeling is the distinction between who is responsible for the knowledge that goes into the model and who for the work procedures and notation used. The domain experts are responsible for ensuring that the model content is correct and valid for solving the actual problem. In essence, the domain experts are responsible for solving the problem. The EM practitioner, particularly the facilitator, is responsible for (1) the modeling process including the practicalities of the sessions such as coffee breaks, (2) the notation used to represent the domain knowledge, and (3) documentation of the minutes of the modeling session. In many cases, the facilitator is also responsible for the preparation of the modeling sessions as well as for model refinement after the session and

Table 6.1 Actor involvement in the EM process steps

EM process step	Domain experts		EM practitioners		
	Problem owner	Participant in modeling group	Project manager	Facilitator	Tool expert
P1 Define scope and objectives of the project	R		P		
P2 Plan for project activities and resources	R		P	P	
P3 Plan for modeling session	P		R	P	
P4 Gather and analyze background information			P	R	
P5 Interview modeling participants		P		R	
P6 Prepare modeling session	P		P	R	
P7 Conduct modeling session		P		R	P
P8 Write meeting minutes			P	R	P
P9 Analyze and refine models	P		P	R	P
P10 Present the results to stakeholders	R	P	P	P	

R responsible, *P* participates

Table 6.2 Responsibilities in modeling

Responsibility areas in modeling	Domain expert responsibility	EM practitioner responsibility
Quality of the modeling process		R
Proper use of the modeling method		R
Model quality		R
Correct and relevant model content	R	

Adapted from Persson (2001)

presentation to the stakeholders. This means that modeling facilitators are not expected to—and in many cases should not—act as domain experts.

An overview of responsibilities is included in Table 6.2. More on the competence of an EM practitioner is included in Sect. 6.3.

6.3   The Competence of EM Practitioners

The competence of EM practitioners is a critical resource in EM application. EM practitioners are responsible for the effective adoption of a chosen method and for the project to reach its goals using the assigned resources.

Fig. 6.1 Core competences of EM in relation to experience

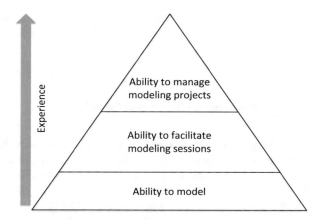

The concept of competence is complex and can be defined in a number of ways. For the purposes of this book, we have chosen to define competence as comprising four main components:

- *Knowledge.* A person's factual knowledge about a specific subject matter, as a result of, for example, education.
- *Ability.* A person's capacity to actually use the knowledge to achieve goals, for example, constructing an enterprise model or facilitating a modeling session.
- *Personal characteristics.* A wide range of personal characteristics are relevant here, such as social skills, intelligence, flexibility, integrity, ability to cooperate, courage, etc. For the EM practitioner, these influence the ability to act as, for example, a facilitator or as negotiator of a modeling project.
- *Willingness to contribute competency.* A person's attitude toward actually contributing her or his knowledge and skills to the achievement of goals other than her or his own.

In the following, the necessary competence of EM practitioners in a modeling project is described, mainly focusing on abilities and personal characteristics.

Persson (2001) reports the core abilities of EM practitioners. Figure 6.1 depicts three types of abilities that are developed with increased experience and which also build on each other.

- *Ability to model*, which means that a person is able to construct an enterprise model which is syntactically correct according to the used EM language and that the model in a reasonable way reflects the domain and problem in question
- *Ability to facilitate modeling sessions*, which means that a person is able to lead a group of domain experts in creating/refining an enterprise model and doing it in such a way that the group's knowledge and abilities work together to create a high-quality model
- *Ability to lead EM projects* toward fulfilling their goals and making the best of the project resources

We claim that in order to target the main challenge of the EM process, which is to produce an EM outcome that is fit for its intended purpose, these are the ones that we need to consider.

6.3.1   Abilities Related to Modeling

The *ability to model* involves making use of the chosen EM language to create and refine enterprise models. The resulting models should reflect the discussion in the modeling session and focus on the problem at hand. Knowing how to use modeling tools for documenting and analyzing the modeling result is also included in this ability. One important, and sometimes neglected, aspect is the ability to create a readable model, because they tend to become large and graphically complex.

6.3.2   Abilities and Personal Characteristics Related to Facilitation

Since we advocate a participatory approach to EM, the *ability to facilitate a modeling session* is essential. Facilitation is a general technique used in group processes for a wide variety of purposes, also within EM (see further Zavala and Hass (2008) and International Association for Facilitators (IAF) http://www.iaf-world.org). This ability is very much based on knowledge about the effects of modeling, the principles of human communication and socialization (especially in groups), as well as the conditions of human learning and problem-solving (cognition). For EM, some of the more important aspects of this competence are to condense and capture important ideas, to pose questions that trigger discussion, to listen, to summarize and generalize, and to drive the discussion toward fulfilling the goals of the EM session.

The following subsections will discuss abilities needed to become a successful modeling facilitator. The degree to which a person has these abilities is dependent on the person's personal characteristics.

6.3.2.1   Ability to Negotiate

Negotiation skills are needed in the early stages of an EM project (processes P1 and P2) as well as during the modeling sessions (process P7). In the preparatory stages, there is usually the need to discuss the different expectations of the problem owner and other parties involved. Often the resources available and required also need to be discussed and in some cases negotiated. For example, it is not uncommon that the problem owner expects the modeling part of the project to be accomplished unreasonably quickly or without the involvement of key domain experts. What is often underestimated is the need for people in key roles in the company to participate in modeling and how much of an in-advance planning this requires. A good negotiator in such cases should be able to present to the decision-makers that the gains from proper project staffing and resource allocation would outweigh the perceived costs and possible productivity losses caused by the domain experts being sidelined from their day-to-day duties.

During the modeling sessions, a good negotiator should be able to identify key differences in opinions related to the modeling domain and to drive the discussion in such a way that a consensus is reached rather than the differences becoming more apparent and a common solution more difficult to find.

6.3.2.2 Ability to Generalize and Make Abstractions

Domain experts very often are talking in terms of concrete examples from their daily work; they talk about specific products, customers, or their production processes. There are two aspects of this competence. First, unless the facilitator comes from the same department as the domain experts, he or she will probably not be able to fully grasp all the details of what is said. In most cases, this is also not needed. What the facilitator should be able to assess is the relevance of the information provided by the domain experts with respect to the modeling objective and the model that is being created. Second, modeling sessions seldom have time to go into a great level of details; hence, even if the domain experts are extremely focused on details, their input might need to be made more abstract. Furthermore, many modeling techniques have built-in mechanisms of generalization and abstraction. For example, generalization and instantiation are techniques of concepts modeling that allow us to create models of concepts or classes, which is far more efficient than creating models of instances. In comparison, creating models of instances usually leads to very large models of restricted usefulness (only for the cases they have originated from) and limited duration (only until the reality they reflect changes). In business process modeling, the technique of process decomposition is used to represent processes that consist of (sub)processes that in turn consist of (sub)processes and so on. While in principle it is possible to model everything in atomic processes that are not possible to divide into more fine-grained processes, such approach is not required in most modeling projects, and it would also be extremely time-consuming to carry out in a modeling session.

The purpose of models also determines what kinds of generalizations and abstractions are appropriate in each case. For example, in an EM setting, focusing on the overall business design specifying attributes or concepts might not be needed, but they might be relevant if the purpose is to specify business requirements for an information system.

In this respect, a skillful modeling facilitator should be able to assess what is the required level of generality and what kinds of abstractions are appropriate to make with respect to the objectives of the modeling session, the purpose of the model, and expectations of the domain experts.

6.3.2.3   Ability to Listen

Modeling sessions often become quite chatty, and hence there is a risk that more people are talking than listening. This should be avoided, because if it happens, then there usually is no control over what is being said and what goes in or not in the model.

Another undesirable situation is that the modeling facilitator takes over and does most of the talking. Instead the facilitator should focus on what the domain experts are saying and direct the attention of the conversation in such a way that all participants have the possibility to express their views and that all relevant views are considered.

6.3.2.4   Ability to Analyze and Synthesize

Models typically evolve iteratively and incrementally, as well as in fragments with respect to the project objective. In many cases, the domain experts tend to tackle the problem by tackling its various subproblems. This is a practicable approach as long as solutions to the subproblems add up to solving the main problem or allow solving the objective of the project. A skillful modeling facilitator therefore should be able to assess the progress of the modeling effort and to make the necessary connections between the different parts that are modeled.

6.3.2.5   Ability to Take a Holistic Perspective

Modeling, especially Enterprise Modeling, involves addressing problems from several perspectives such as business goals, concepts, process, rules, etc. (see Chap. 4). This approach should also be reflected by the way of working. Further- more, this should not be done only from the conceptual perspectives (goals, pro- cesses, etc.) such as the ones included in the modeling method but also perspectives determined by the project problem, for example, development, production, market- ing, sales, human resource management, and customer relations. Similarly, the facilitator should be able to view problems from both technological and business development perspectives. In fact, during one of the early projects in which we applied participatory EM, the users recognized that EM allows strengthening the "business pull" vs. the "technology push," which was achieved by having a holistic view.

6.3.2.6   Ability to Be Creative and Open-Minded

The focus of participatory modeling is to create something new. Even in cases where the task is to model the current state in the organization, there is always a certain need for creativity because participatory modeling is seldom appropriate to capture something well-known and trivial. Hence, the facilitator should be reasonably aware of the state of the art and should be prepared to drive the discussion beyond it. In some cases, especially, when future state of the organization is modeled, or new products or services envisioned, ideas that can be regarded as unconventional or even slightly crazy are suggested. They need to be respected and discussed, because sometimes ideas or solutions that appear unserious or unrealistic can be elaborated into truly innovative and successful solutions. Hence, the task of the facilitator is to support creativity but still stay focused on solving the problem at hand. Different techniques to support creativity can be found in Gray et al. (2010).

6.3.2.7   Ability to Cooperate

Modeling requires collaboration both in terms of generating the idea and of creating the actual model. Hence, the facilitator should be able to cooperate with the assistant facilitator and with the participants of the modeling session.

6.3.2.8   Ability to Be Pedagogical

Modeling sessions typically have cycles or creativity, consolidation, consensus, as well as critique and new focus. These cycles can be longer or shorter, more or less frequent, or about larger or smaller model fragments depending on the situation. During the critique stage, the modeling facilitator often "explains" the model to the participants. She or he tells what the modeling session has achieved up to this point and what would be the next steps. It is at this stage the participants start to realize that the model is the "official" documentation of their discussion and they start paying attention that important parts of the domain knowledge or the discussion they had are correctly included in the model.

Another situation where the facilitator needs to explain the model is process P10 when the model is explained to the stakeholders after it has been refined.

Hence, the modeling facilitator should be able to present the models in such a way that the participants understand it. This should be done without omitting things that are in it and adding things that are not there.

6.3.2.9   Ability to Act with Authority

Modeling facilitator is in charge of the modeling session. This includes what the group discusses, how the model is created, as well as when the coffee breaks take place. It might not be easy to accept for some participants, and it happens that some prefer keeping their organization hierarchy position visible in the session. This is not a good situation, and such people should preferably be identified in the preinterview stage (process P5), but if it happens, the facilitator should be able deal with such participants, for instance, by explaining the procedures of the modeling session in a side discussion.

6.3.2.10   Ability to Act Humbly

Modeling sessions typically involve key domain experts from one or several domains. Their expertise is normally unquestionable and usually exceeds that of the modeling facilitator. This is the intention of participatory modeling and at the core of the principle that the facilitator is there to help. Yet, in some cases, the domain experts point out that the facilitator is not a domain expert implying that he or she should not be listened to. Such participants should have been identified in the preinterview phase, but if they have been missed or such behavior is unexpected, the facilitator should not engage in a demonstration of her or his expertise. Instead, the role and responsibility of the facilitator and the participants should be explained once again. In general, the facilitator should refrain from showing off or jumping into the discussion with his or her expertise and opinions even if she or he is an expert in the subject area, because then the effect of the modeling session is changed—the model created is no longer a result of the joint work of the participants, and instead it becomes "an expert solution" of the often outsider facilitator.

6.3.2.11   Ability to Act Courageously

Modeling sessions are hard work most of the time, but at the same time, great results can be achieved relatively quickly. When it comes to courage, the modeling facilitator should demonstrate the willpower to address hard subjects, deal with people who are hard to deal with, as well as do hard work during the modeling session.

Modeling often touches issues that are known to be sensitive, laid with hidden agendas, and prone to infighting. Such preexisting background will also be present in the modeling project, and even if it should be identified in the preinterview phase, some of it will be brought into the modeling session as well. Very often such issues lie at the core of the problem that needs to be addressed in the modeling sessions, and hence the facilitator should be aware of them and should not shy away from dealing with them.

Modeling projects need to involve people who are the most relevant stakeholders for the problem domain. This often requires dealing with people who for some reason are hard to deal with. This can be due to their human nature or their adverse feelings toward the modeling effort. The modeling facilitator should be aware of such people and predict possible conflict situations. If they are rooted in the human nature, then they are usually solvable and do not pose risks to the modeling session. In such cases, it is often useful to spend additional time for explaining the purpose and roles of the participants of the modeling session. However, if some modeling participants act adversely because they have a hidden agenda, then the modeling facilitator should have a clear plan for dealing with such people. More about dealing with hidden agendas can be found in Chap. 7.

Modeling sessions are also hard work, both mentally, for example, needing to be creative and constantly alert, and physically, for example, standing up for longer periods of time, etc. With time the facilitator and the participants become tired, and this might reflect in the models they create. For example, the participants might feel reluctant to start a new model in the last half hour of the scheduled modeling session. In such cases, the facilitator should show the lead and encourage the rest of the group, for example, by saying that the work can be accomplished in the time remaining or stressing the importance of the work.

6.3.3   Abilities Related to Managing EM Projects

In order for the models to be fit for their intended use, the EM practitioner needs the *ability to select an appropriate EM approach and tailor it in order to fit the situation at hand*. Sometimes that choice is restricted by the requirements of the context of use, as is the case when EM is used in an IS development project that uses a particular method and tool-set. In other cases, the choice of an EM approach is up to the EM practitioner. Based on her or his knowledge about the problem at hand, the requirements on the EM result, the preferences and modeling skill level of the modeling group, and the context in which EM will be used, the EM practitioner will choose an appropriate approach. The professional EM practitioner will have a "toolbox" of potential methods for different purposes that she or he is able to use. Independently of whether the EM practitioner has the choice of approach, the approach often needs to be tailored to fit the situation at hand, and she or he will then need to be able to assess the consequences of any changes made to the approach.

As discussed before, in participatory EM, the *ability to interview involved domain experts* before the EM session is critical. In this situation, the social skills of the EM practitioner are essential, such as ability to listen and ability to read body language. In a discreet way, the EM practitioner needs to ask the domain expert what should be talked about in the modeling session and also try to find out what topics should be avoided and why.

For EM to have effect in its context of use, it needs to be focused toward a particular goal or problem. This pertains both to the overall EM project level and to each EM session. The *ability to define a relevant problem* that is feasible to model based on the information that the EM practitioner can obtain is, therefore, important. This ability is very much related to the ability to interview domain experts. In this ability, the capacities to conceptualize, to generalize, and to assess the relationships between different problems are included. An essential aspect of defining the relevant problems is the ability to spot hidden agendas, which builds both on the practitioner's previous experience and also on her or his social skills and ability to "read between the lines" in a conversation. Unidentified hidden agendas can potentially cause problems later on in the EM project. Assessing the complexity of a problem is also part of defining a problem. Problem complexity has a heavy influence on the planning of the project both in terms of activities and resources. It can be argued that it is impossible to define a clear problem at the outset and that it will change as the project proceeds. This is true, but in order for the project to become operative at least, a "working problem" is needed.

In planning an EM project and an EM session, the *ability to define requirements on the results* is essential in order for project/session goals to be achieved. These requirements relate to the models that are to be produced as well as what is to be achieved by these models. Sometimes the requirements have to do with the process itself. For example, by involving certain stakeholders and having them listen to what other stakeholders have to say in a participatory EM session, certain change decisions can be made less dramatic for the organization. The EM practitioner should also keep in mind that the models produced are the tangible results of modeling, but equally important is the intangible result—participants' changed thinking and understanding of the problem.

The *ability to establish a modeling project* is critical in order to create the most beneficial conditions for the EM project. Favorable conditions will increase the chances of obtaining the desirable effects of EM. Conditions involve resources in terms of time and competence (domain as well as EM practitioner competence) as well as authority for EM project participants to act freely and make decisions within the project definition. This ability is essential in any project.

The result of modeling will be used for a specified purpose. In order for that purpose to be fulfilled, the users of the result need to understand it and its implications. This means that the modeling practitioner will have to present it in oral and/or written form to them. Depending on the target audience, certain aspects of the result will need to be emphasized or toned down. For example, presenting project results to a group of managers the detailed data structure of the supporting IS can be omitted. This requires an ability *to adjust a presentation of project results and issues related to them and to preferences of various stakeholders.*

An EM project is a signal to the organization that change of some kind is imminent. This means that various stakeholders will try to influence the EM practitioner so that their own goals will be those of the EM project. To *navigate between the wishes of various stakeholders while upholding the EM project goal* is, therefore, a critical competence. More about the challenges involved in tackling this problem can be found in Kaarst-Brown (1999).

EM projects typically deliver a solution to a business problem. The solution usually consists of an organizational design proposal (which might include an IT solution) reflected in enterprise models. A partially intangible outcome of the EM project is the supporting set of decisions and commitment to implement the solution. Example issues to consider are as follows: would the solution appear to be inappropriately bureaucratic, democratic, and authoritative; what kind of implementation activities are needed, etc. An ability *to assess the impact of the modeling result and the modeling process in the organization* is therefore needed to drive the modeling effort toward a solution that has a high probability of being implemented within the organization.

In Table 6.3, the core competences are summarized and mapped to the process steps defined in Chap. 5.

6.4   Competence of Domain Experts as Participants in Modeling Groups

In an EM project, the domain experts are in essence responsible for solving the problem at hand, while EM practitioners are responsible for supporting and managing the process that leads up to solving the problem. Having the right domain experts involved in the modeling sessions is, therefore, critical for achieving the goals of the project. Their domain knowledge is the basis on which the results of the project build.

Each modeling session has a goal or several goals that are to be achieved. These goals contribute to fulfilling the project goals. The goals of each modeling session govern the requirements on the competences that should be represented by the participants in the modeling group. It is the task of the facilitator to assess which competences are needed in each modeling session.

The willingness or opportunity of people to contribute their domain knowledge in the sessions is constrained by a number of situational factors such as organizational culture, authority in relation to the problem at hand, time to spend on participation, and method acceptance to mention a few. In the following, we will discuss how some situational factors influence (1) the required competence of individual modeling participants and (2) the composition of the modeling group.

6.4.1   The Competence of Individual Modeling Participants

Participants in a modeling group should, naturally, be well familiar with the problem (s) addressed by the project and session. They also need to be engaged in the

Table 6.3 Matching of EM process steps to core abilities

Ability	Process									
	P1 Define scope and objectives of the project	P2 Plan for project activities and resources	P3 Plan for modeling sessions	P4 Gather and analyze background information	P5 Interview modeling participants	P6 Prepare modeling session	P7 Conduct modeling session	P8 Write meeting minutes	P9 Analyze and refine models	P10 Present the results to stakeholders
To model							X		X	
To facilitate modeling sessions							X			
To interview involved domain experts					X					
To define a problem	X		X						X	
To define requirements on the results	X	X	X							
To establish a modeling project	X									
To adjust presentation of project results						X				X
To navigate between the wishes of stakeholders while upholding a defined project strategy	X	X			X	X	X			X
To assess the impact of the modeling result and the modeling process in the organization	X	X				X			X	X

Persson and Stirna (2010)

problem in order to be willing to contribute in solving it. Each of the participants comes with their own view of the problem based on their role in the organization. Sometimes it may also be beneficial to have both the "producer" and the "consumer" side represented to broaden the view. At some stages of the project, it may also be necessary to associate specialists in certain areas to the project. These specialists may have the role to suggest organizational or IT solutions to satisfy specific goals stated, such as reengineering of some business processes, or development of some types of IT solutions.

In addition to knowledge about the problem addressed, some personal character-istics are desired in an "ideal" modeling participant. One such characteristic is the ability of abstract reasoning and generalization. This is essential in many modeling situations when there is a need to step back and look at the problem at a general level. Also, the social skills, the ability to verbalize and communicate, and creativity contribute greatly to the results of a modeling session. Sometimes participants do not have the desired social skills but have crucial domain knowledge. In those cases, the facilitator needs to actively involve such participants in the discussions. It can often be observed that when such participants are persuaded to be more active, they engage in the discussion as they can see their contribution to the work of the group. However, one of the most important requirements for an individual modeling participant is the motivation to participate and to contribute to solving the problem at hand. This can often make up for the lack of some personal characteristics. More about situations in modeling sessions is found in Chaps. 7 and 8.

6.4.2   Composition of the Modeling Group

The composition of the modeling group is instrumental to the achievement of the goals for the modeling session. An ideal modeling group has the following characteristics:

- The knowledge represented in the group covers the full scope of the problem domain and is able to look at the problem from an overview as well as detailed level.
- The group has adequate domain knowledge.
- The group has the necessary authority to suggest organizational change.
- The group comprises enthusiastic, open-minded, and cooperative people.
- The group consists of people without personal animosity between themselves.

Preferably the group covers the problem domain in terms of scope. It is also important to compose the group so that it includes participants that represent both a detailed view and overview of the problem.

The "direction" of the analysis, if the analysis concerns the current state of affairs or the future state, also defines requirements for the group's composition. People deeply involved in a process can often describe the current state very well. However, when moving toward the future state, a different type of domain experts may be needed. They will, most likely, be visionary and creative people who are able to look at the process from a more holistic perspective, for example, how it relates to other processes and changes outside the organization. In addition, people may not feel that they are authorized to have an opinion about the future state of the enterprise. A clearly stated mandate for the group will help.

When composing the group, it is essential that the domain experts are given sufficient time to participate in the session.

Another aspect to make sure is that the domain experts participate with the intention of actually contributing to solving the problem at hand. For example, having people in the group who are there to just learn or observe will hamper the modeling process. "Everyone contributes!" should be the motto of a modeling session.

The status or rank of certain stakeholders can also restrict the possibilities of composing a group that represents the best available competency. Some people may sometimes falsely be considered highly competent both by themselves and others. To exclude such persons can be difficult but necessary. Sometimes this relates to different "political" views about who should participate or not, stemming from the formal authority of certain stakeholders or conflicts between stakeholders.

It is evidently an ideal situation if all of these requirements are fulfilled. However, reality does often prove to be completely different. Sometimes the organization is mature and understands that only the best people will be able to solve the problem at hand, but sometimes this is not the case. It is then the responsibility of the facilitator or project manager to make clear to the problem owner that restricting the involvement of the key people most likely will negatively influence the quality of the modeling result.

The organization and the facilitator preferably collaborate in choosing the participants in the modeling group. Often it is best that the organization picks out the participants using criteria formulated by the facilitator. Interviewing the potential participants will help the facilitator to make well-argued decisions about the suitability of each person.

For further details about composing the modeling group and the dynamics of a modeling group, c.f. Willars (1999), Nilsson et al. (1999), Astrakan (2001), Bergquist and Eide (1999), and Bubenko et al. (2001).

6.5   Summary

In this chapter, the knowledge, abilities, and personal characteristics of EM practitioners and domain experts have been discussed.

EM practitioners build their abilities over time. Three levels can be observed: (1) the ability to model, (2) the ability to facilitate modeling sessions, and (3) the ability to manage modeling projects. These levels also represent the core abilities of an EM practitioner. Related to these abilities, there are a number of sub-abilities and personal characteristics that are needed in order to be a successful EM practitioner.

For domain experts, the most important competence aspect is their domain knowledge. However, they also need some abilities and personal characteristics in order to be able to contribute properly to the modeling effort. Examples are the ability of abstract reasoning and generalization, the ability to verbalize and communicate, and creativity.

When composing the modeling group, the following aspects need to be considered:

- The knowledge represented in the group covers the full scope of the problem domain and is able to look at the problem from an overview as well as detailed level.
- The group has adequate domain knowledge.
- The group has the necessary authority to suggest organizational change.
- The group comprises enthusiastic, open-minded, and cooperative people.
- The group consists of people without personal animosity between themselves.

References

Astrakan: Högre kurs i modelleringsledning (In Swedish). Course Notes Version 1.1. Astrakan Strategisk Utbildning AB, Stockholm (2001)

Bergquist, S., Eide, H.: Team Games – snabbaste vägen mot högpresterande arbetsprocesser (in Swedish). Frontec AB, Stockholm (1999)

Bubenko, J.A., Persson, A., Stirna, J.: User Guide of the Knowledge Management Approach Using Enterprise Knowledge Patterns, Deliverable D3, IST Programme Project Hypermedia and Pattern Based Knowledge Management for Smart Organisations, project no. IST-2000-28401. Royal Institute of Technology, Sweden (2001)

Gray, D., Brown, S., Macanufo, J.: Gamestorming: A Playbook for Innovators, Rulebreakers, and Changemakers. O'Reilly Media, Sebastopol, CA (2010)

Kaarst-Brown, M.L.: Five symbolic roles of the external consultant—integrating change, power and symbolism. J. Organ. Chang. Manag. **12**(6), 540–561 (1999)

Nilsson, A.G., Tolis, C., Nellborn, C.: Perspectives on Business Modelling: Understanding and Changing Organisations. Springer, Heidelberg (1999)

Persson, A.: Enterprise Modelling in Practice: Situational Factors and Their Influence on Adopting a Participative Approach. Ph.D. Thesis, Department of Computer and Systems Sciences, Stockholm University (2001)

Persson, A., Stirna, J.: Towards defining a competence profile for the enterprise modeling practitioner. In: The 3rd IFIP WG8.1 Working Conference on the Practice of Enterprise Modelling (PoEM2010), Delft, The Netherlands, November 2010. Springer, Heidelberg (2010)

Willars, H.: Business modeller's checklist: "dos" and "dont's" in hands-on practice. In: Nilsson, A. G., Tolis, C., Nellborn, C. (eds.) Perspectives on Business Modelling: Understanding and Changing Organisations. Springer, Heidelberg (1999)

Zavala, A., Hass, B.H.: The Art and Power of Facilitation: Running Powerful Meetings. Management Concepts, Vienna (2008)

Chapter 7
Types of Organizational Stakeholder Behaviors in Participatory Modeling and How to Deal with Them

In participatory EM, we take advantage of the differences in stakeholder views with regard to a particular problem. We use these different opinions in order to construct a multifaceted model of the enterprise. The participatory approach, in fact, claims that having conflicting views with regard to the subject matter is a positive force and that it is useful in the process of arriving at a more complete and better-fitting solution to the problem at hand. This means, however, that we must acknowledge that different stakeholders may have different levels of formal or informal influence in the modeling process.

An EM project is a signal to the organization that change of some kind is imminent. This means that various organizational stakeholders will try to influence the EM practitioners so that their own goals will become those of the EM project. In this chapter, we discuss a number of stereotypical stakeholder behaviors that EM practitioners may encounter in an EM project. They can be observed in modeling sessions as well as in the project as a whole. It is worth noting that the behaviors described here are stereotypical. They are simplified summaries of commonly observed behaviors in EM sessions and projects. Hence, they are different to the stakeholder types commonly seen in areas of stakeholder management and project management (c.f., for instance, Bourne and Walker 2008; Bourne 2011; Cleland 2008; and Freeman 1984).

This chapter is based on our and our colleagues' observations during many years of modeling in practice. Most likely there are more typical behaviors, and some of them may also overlap slightly. Also, the same participant may demonstrate several behaviors in a session. We believe that being able to identify them and to soften their negative impact should be part of a modeling facilitator's skill set. The likelihood of a behavior to appear in a session can be partly assessed in interviews preceding the modeling session, which is yet another argument for the importance of these interviews.

Some of the stereotypical behaviors can also be observed in other types of projects, not just participatory EM, but such a discussion is considered outside the scope of this book.

© Springer International Publishing AG, part of Springer Nature 2018
J. Stirna, A. Persson, *Enterprise Modeling*,
https://doi.org/10.1007/978-3-319-94857-7_7

The stereotypes will be discussed in terms of:

– How to spot them
– What their typical behaviors are
– What their likely impact is (positive and negative) if the situation is unattended
– How to mitigate the negative impacts that they might cause

7.1 Types of Stakeholder Behavior in Modeling Sessions

This section discusses the stereotypical stakeholder behaviors in a participatory EM session. In most cases, they have to be identified and dealt with either during the preparation phase of the modeling session or in the modeling session. Therefore, our recommendation is that the modeling facilitator be aware of them, prepare for the possibility that they emerge in a modeling session, and prepare to deal with them.

The following stereotypes of stakeholder behavior have been observed: the seller, the buyer, the questioner, the observer, the boss, the one who always knows best, the border patrol, the comedian, the missionary, the expert, and the representative.

7.1.1 The Seller

People playing this role typically make other people "buy" their ideas. They keep on explaining them to others and arguing vividly for their relevance. The name of this stereotype is not related to the kind of role or job position one has in the organization.

The seller	
How to spot	Argues vividly for their ideas and tries to make other participants to "buy" them. Is often self-confident, verbally active, knowledgeable, and sometimes insensitive to what is going on in the group. A particular seller is the one who is very convinced about a solution and claims that it is a cure for almost any problem. Often she or he acts as an expert, and other participants are therefore reluctant to disagree
Typical behaviors	Approaches different people, speaks to them directly, and presents his or her proposal from several aspects. Offers "counterproposals" instead of constructive critique to other people's ideas. Aims to get his or her ideas into the model
Likely impact if left unattended	*Positive:* Drives the discussion forward with new ideas that are usually realistic and implementable *Negative:* Tends to dominate the discussion; the ideas might be more incremental improvements than groundbreaking
How to mitigate negative impacts	Balance the discussion, invite other participants to comment, summarize the ideas and contributions of the seller, and move forward once they are documented in the model. Ask questions to clarify which particular problem the proposal of the seller is meant to solve

7.1.2   The Missionary

This is someone who has a specific objective that they think the modeling session should achieve and who acts covertly and overtly toward achieving this objective (his or her mission). The mission can often be quite simple and obvious, such as basing the solution on a specific technology, or more obscure, such as making the parameters of a solution fit certain organizational procedures or personal preferences. In the latter case, the mission might actually involve a hidden agenda, such as competition for resources, influence, and authority, or simply personal dislikes.

The missionary	
How to spot	Keeps repeating the same issue, usually a solution. Can be openly critical to the modeling project as such. Typically hides the negative attitude in face-to-face interviews
Typical behaviors	Speaks a great deal. Is critical of other participants and of the facilitator. Keeps proposing a single solution. Can be destructive, if the mission is to sabotage the modeling project
Likely impact if left unattended	*Positive:* None, because if unaddressed, the solution will most likely turn out focusing on the "mission" which is contrary to the purpose of participatory modeling *Negative:* No real participative effort; the session turns into a battle of arguments between a few participants. One-sided, often dysfunctional solutions. Postponed decisions and real work, which leads to the modeling session having no real effect
How to mitigate the negative impacts	Develop a clear understanding of how each participant is related to the project and the expected result. Clarify issues such as what their stake in the solution is and what else do they do in the organization. Preinterviewing is an opportunity to turn them in a positive direction. Do not take participants on board without preinterviewing

7.1.3   The Buyer

The buyer typically focuses on assessing the ideas of others and seeking to buy into them. The seller and the buyer typically support each other in the sense that the buyer is asking for clarifications and elaborations of the proposal from the seller.

The buyer	
How to spot	Is often engaged in discussions with sellers and prefers listening and sometimes asking questions. Is often impressed by sellers and is a bit too uncritical toward them
Typical behaviors	Listens to other people's ideas and suggestions, particularly the seller's, and is eager to agree with others. Can be perceived as often changing their opinion. Can also ask clarifying questions from time to time. Offers improvements and refinements to improve an idea that

(continued)

The buyer	
	they have bought into. Often offers support in the implementation if she or he has decided to buy into a proposal
Likely impact if left unattended	*Positive:* Supports other participants and makes them feel that they are listened to. Makes unclear and vague ideas and contributions more specific and elaborated. Helps in eliminating ideas that are too wild or out of scope by asking for clarifications *Negative:* May influence the group negatively by seeming uncertain and changing their position a bit too often
How to mitigate negative impacts	Stimulate the buyer's own ideas using creative techniques where each participant is forced to formulate their own ideas. Stimulate other participants to contribute their ideas so that there are more ideas for the buyer to choose from, hence making the buyer take their own stand on the matter

7.1.4   The Questioner

A person who plays this role typically likes to ask a large number of questions. Some of the questions might be useful, but often the questions become self-serving and distracting from the main focus of the modeling session. The approach to burden other participants with a lot of questions might also be a subtle attempt to undermine the effort. Sometimes persons who feel that they have been commanded to be part of the group play this role.

The questioner	
How to spot	Asks a large number of questions to other modeling participants and to the facilitator. Many questions can be quite generic, for example, about the meaning of the modeling effort, and can also be superficial
Typical behaviors	Asks the same or similar questions related to other people's ideas and opinions. Often asks several questions in rapid succession. The questions may be posed in a way that suggests they have genuine interest in the answer but could also be laden with sarcasm, hence questioning the usefulness of the modeling project. Can be difficult to persuade. Can also turn into the border patrol (Sect. 7.1.8)
Likely impact if left unattended	*Positive:* If the questions are asked in a constructive way, this might drive the modeling effort forward *Negative:* If the questions are mostly trivial and repetitive, the modeling session stands the risk of stalling and turning into a useless game of question-answer ping-pong
How to mitigate the negative impacts	Motivate participants in the interview preceding the modeling session. Clarify the issues that are to be discussed in the session and what is to be taken for granted, for example, the purpose of the modeling effort or the modeling method chosen. Explain that sometimes it is valuable to discuss and document ideas that seem difficult or unfeasible at the outset. Point out that participatory modeling should be creative as well as fun. In the session, ask the questioner for his or her own opinions

7.1.5   The Observer

Some people prefer talking and actively engaging in the discussion, while some prefer listening. The observer is someone who does not like talking. The reason for this could simply be human nature or perhaps not knowing other participants in the seminar too well. In most cases, they wait for "their turn" to enter the discussion; hence, the facilitator should make sure they are included in the discussion.

The observer	
How to spot	Does not actively participate in the discussion unless directly approached. Seems otherwise engaged and follows the discussion and the development of the model
Typical behaviors	Prefers to listen. Speaks when approached by a direct question or invitation to contribute. Contributes with valuable ideas but prefers to wait until others have spoken
Likely impact if left unattended	*Positive:* That someone speaks less than others is generally not a problem as long as such persons are given the chance to contribute to the discussion *Negative:* If the facilitators neglect or forget involving such persons, apart from missing their input, this creates a problem that the model might not be seen as jointly owned, and the consensus could be questioned. Over time the observer(s) might turn negative toward the modeling effort
How to mitigate the negative impacts	Suggest that the group take turns in speaking, and make sure that even the observers get equal opportunity to talk. Ask everyone to write down his or her ideas on paper cards (modeling components, see Chap. 4). Ask questions to observers directly Sometimes the behavior stems from skepticism in relation to the modeling effort and not from shyness. If this seems to be the case, explain the purpose and intended effects of the session and why the contributions of the participants are important

7.1.6   The Boss

This stereotype often acts in a dominant manner. According to our experience, they generally have a positive attitude toward the effort and the way of working, but they also have strong opinions about the "right" or the only (their) way the work should be done and what the results entail. If they are used to taking a somewhat authoritative managerial role, it may sometimes be difficult for them to let their guard down in a session involving their subordinate staff.

The boss	
How to spot	Dominates the discussion and usually (but not always) has a managerial role above the rest or some of the other participants
Typical behaviors	Speaks a great deal and usually loudly. Interrupts other participants and the facilitator. Does not engage in consolidating opinions and

(continued)

The boss	
	ideas and, in fact, questions the usefulness of doing so, because his or her opinions should be seen as the only ones valid. Has a tendency to take over the leadership of the group—perhaps unintended. The boss makes summaries and says things like "Can we now agree that. . ."
Likely impact if left unattended	*Positive:* Not many. The boss could be made responsible for implementing some of the decisions, but there is a risk that the session will not result in anything specific enough to implement *Negative:* The model will represent one person's opinions. The other participants will not feel that they have contributed to the model, and hence they will not take responsibility for further actions. This kind of result is a complete opposite of the main purpose and strength of participatory modeling
How to mitigate the negative impacts	Such people should be spotted in the preparation phase. If invited to the modeling session, they should be privately advised about the need to involve everyone. If their dominant behavior becomes unmanageable, the modeling session should be paused for a coffee break, and the facilitator should approach them in private. The facilitator should anticipate such behaviors and build rapport with people who may act in this way. Avoid having managers and their own staff in the same session if possible

7.1.7   The One Who Always Knows Best

This person assumes that they are knowledgeable in almost any subject and not only their own field of expertise. People like these are often intelligent and have a great deal to contribute, provided that they are somewhat restrained in the modeling session. Most likely, these types of people will reveal themselves during the preparatory interview, which allows the facilitator to prepare. They are usually also skeptical about the modeling effort, especially if modeling is new to them, but are generally positive to the purpose of the project. They can be a version of seller and the boss without the management power.

The one who always knows best	
How to spot	This stereotype expresses their opinions loudly and often forcefully. Speaks frequently and gives answers to almost any question. Speaks in a "lecturing" manner
Typical behaviors	Replies to most ideas and suggestions that they have already been done (usually by him or her) sometime in the past. Lectures the rest about the correct, meaning their, way of doing things. Seems to be able to comment on almost any topic in more or less the same fashion
Likely impact if left not dealt with	*Positive:* These people might in fact possess an abundance of knowledge and experience. Some of it might be relevant to the modeling effort and needs to be captured *Negative:* Other participants can feel dominated and shut down their communication in the group. The model does not advance because

(continued)

The one who always knows best	
	there is usually not much to capture from the wordy lectures. Time is wasted
How to mitigate the nega-tive impacts	Ask specific questions that focus on the objective of the session. Say that this is not the time to have long discussions about the past, and stress that all ideas should be documented. Ask the person to summarize and to write down their contribution in terms of modeling components and then introduce them in the model

7.1.8   The Border Patrol

People who play this role have a strong inner wish to do everything as "right" as possible and to make sure that other people do so as well. She or he is, therefore, always looking to find the border between what is permitted and what is not. In most cases, they are knowledgeable about the current state in the organization and in the business sector. But there is also a risk that the knowledge is outdated, and in some cases, the boundaries and rules can be imaginary. Sometimes they use their insistence on following rules as a way of dominating the group and demonstrating their own power. In some cases, it happens that they invent their own rules as a way of restricting the modeling effort.

The border patrol	
How to spot	Often argues against other people's proposals by suggesting compliance to real or imaginary rules. Likes to project authority
Typical behaviors	Injects remarks in the discussion that a particular suggestion is not compliant to a certain rule, policy, or regulation. Should we really. . .? Are we really allowed to. . .? Can it be our place to. . .? May often argue for keeping the status quo or checking the proposals with "higher authorities"
Likely impact if left unattended	*Positive:* Keeps the group within a certain focus area and helps to avoid shifting the discussion toward solutions that would be impossible to implement from a legal or policy point of view. Can be the voice of reason if managed properly *Negative:* Can shut down innovative solutions that challenge the state of the art. Can be perceived as overly critical
How to mitigate the nega-tive impacts	The facilitator should be aware of the basic rule and regulation frameworks that govern the area to which the modeling session relates. Should encourage discussing which rules and policies are relevant and which can be challenged. Seek how to make solutions compliant instead of discarding them at the outset. Consider developing a business rules model, and relate components of other models to it. Support the border patrol to sometimes cross borders

7.1.9   The Comedian

This is somebody who at any time possible cracks jokes or injects comments intended to be funny into the discussion. While modeling should certainly be fun, the facilitator should carefully watch out so that the session does not turn into a casual chat between colleagues. Furthermore, the joking can also be a covert approach to undermine the modeling effort, especially if the jokes are laden with sarcasm or include personal attacks, even if subtle.

The comedian	
How to spot	Someone who frequently cracks jokes and tells funny stories and interjects the discussion
What are the typical behaviors	Adds funny comments to someone else's input, interrupts the discussion, and tells stories about the past. May often shift the discussion toward trivia. Proposes outrageous solutions
What is the likely impact if left not dealt with	*Positive:* Sometimes even ideas that are initially perceived as outrageous or impossible have a rational core and can be elaborated into innovative solutions. Jokes can lighten the mood of the seminar if added to the discussion gracefully and at appropriate moments *Negative:* If the jokes are mostly sarcastic and at someone else's expense, they are most likely meant to disrupt the modeling flow or to shift it toward a certain outcome. In this case, there are few positive outcomes
How to mitigate the negative impacts	The joker should be reminded rather quickly that modeling sessions should focus on modeling the problem at hand and not on simply having a nice chat. It might be that the joker has a hidden agenda in which case he/she should be considered acting more like the missionary

7.1.10   The Expert

This is someone who is an expert in a certain field or problem area. Usually the participants in the modeling session recognize them as experts within the organization. Such people sometimes tend to relate all proposals and solutions through the prism of their own expertise.

The expert	
How to spot	Typically, a recognized expert in a specific subject area.Frequently proposes solutions related to or involving that particular area. Can be an enthusiastic participant as long as they do not feel challenged or threatened
Typical behaviors	Active in discussions. Proposes solutions based on his or her field. Discusses and often criticizes solutions that are not related to his or her area of expertise

(continued)

The expert	
Likely impact if left unattended	*Positive:* Contributes with quite elaborate solutions in a specific area. Can be responsible for implementation if the expertise area is matching
	Negative: One-sided solutions limited to a specific area of expertise
How to mitigate the negative impacts	Explain the purpose of the session, and stress the need to elicit and assess a broad range of solutions. Put them in charge of a certain aspect of the solution if appropriate. They should be reminded to sometimes take a holistic view

7.1.11   The Representative

The representative attends the modeling session instead of someone else, usually a high-ranking manager, and is a direct subordinate of that manager. In these cases, the modeling facilitator is usually not aware that the representative will replace the person who was initially expected. The representative is often unaware of the purpose of the modeling session and might not have the background knowledge about the project. The problem for the facilitator is that this person usually represents someone who is a significant stakeholder in the project and whose input would be highly valuable.

The representative	
How to spot	Wanders in unexpectedly, often late and in the middle of the modeling session. Usually sent in by somebody else with high authority
Typical behaviors	Does not contribute to the discussion. Asks polite questions about the purpose of the project, the session, what modeling is, and why it is any good. Might ask questions that aim to undermine the modeling effort. Periodically leaves the room. Leaves the session early and unannounced
Likely impact if left unattended	*Positive:* None
	Negative: Will most likely pass over incorrect information to the person he/she represented. The modeling facilitator should not accept new and unknown participants, but sometimes it might be difficult to resist. If they are let into the session, the modeling effort needs to halt, and time has to be spent on introducing the project to this person after which there might be too little time to restart
How to mitigate the negative impacts	Do not accept participants without preinterviewing. Plan how you will collect the participants and bring to the location for the modeling session. Arrange the modeling session at a "secret location" or off premises. Start with a lunch together, during which there is a possibility to address the "surprise representative"

7.2 Types of Stakeholder Behavior in Project Management Setting

Managing modeling sessions in terms of organizational stakeholder behaviors is necessary, but it is equally necessary to deal with stakeholders on the EM project level. The following types of behavior can be observed in EM projects: the engaged owner, the client, the pragmatic questioner, the contractor, the demanding boss, the one who has done it all, and the business-as-usual manager. This list is by no means exhaustive, and many more types could be relevant. The ones that we focus on here are important from the point of view of their specific impact to an EM project and how the EM project manager and facilitator should interact with them.

7.2.1 The Engaged Owner

This kind of person often acts as a problem owner in the EM project. This is someone who has a good understanding of the problem area and the expected solution. The exact details of the solution may not be known however; otherwise starting an EM project might not be needed. They are also knowledgeable about the kind of resources that are needed and are prepared to allocate them.

The engaged owner	
How to spot	Is usually identified in the process of project negotiations and preparation. Might be the person who commissions the project
Typical behaviors	Demonstrates good understanding of the overall problem and the business to which it is related. Suggests other stakeholders that could be involved in the project. Is meticulous about defining the problem to be solved by the project
Likely impact if left unattended	*Positive:* The project has a reasonably clear purpose, resources, and management support *Negative:* The scope tends to increase as more and more business challenges are added to the project. This can happen because the engaged owner appreciates the early results of the modeling project and wants to "quickly do more things"
How to mitigate the negative impacts	Frequently discuss the project progress with the engaged owner, and, if needed, define sub-projects or additional projects. Create a plan for how to deal with new challenges as they emerge

7.2.2 The Client

This is someone, usually a top manager, who has a stake in the project, is able to commission the project, but is not prepared to be involved in the project directly. His or her attitude could be characterized as seeking to "purchase" a solution from an external consultant. In this case, the resources might need to be negotiated more carefully, and a particular emphasis should be on securing access to key people and giving them time to participate. Furthermore, finding a problem owner needed for the more day-to-day work in the EM project is also needed.

A more extreme case of the client is what could be called the contractor. The contractor is someone who wants to start an EM project without making the resources of the organization available more than just paying the external consultants their hourly rate. In this case, it needs to be explained that without the involvement of the organizational stakeholders, there is no point in doing participatory EM.

The client	
How to spot	Presents the proposal for solving a problem in reasonably clear terms. Can have a tendency to simplify the problem or the solution. Asks the external consultant or the facilitator to "solve" the problem
Typical behaviors	Wants the overall control of the project but is not prepared to work as the problem owner
Likely impact if left unattended	*Positive:* Does not interfere with running the modeling project *Negative:* May see the result as something up for his or her approval for continued implementation. Might not be favorable to requests for additional resources
How to mitigate the negative impacts	Find a problem owner to involve in the daily work of the project. Report to the client reasonably frequently to ensure his or her support to the solution and to the resource use, particularly to the involvement of stakeholders

7.2.3 The Pragmatic Questioner

Such persons can be versions of the client with considerably more skepticism, but in most cases, they are not the ones that commission the project. Their skepticism manifests itself by them asking seemingly reasonable and professional questions, for example, about how much time this will take, how much it will cost, if it can be done without the involvement of important people because they are always busy, etc. They pretend to act pragmatically, while in fact they try to prove to themselves (and the problem owner) that participatory modeling is not to be used. According to them, it is either ill-suited (see Chap. 2 about appropriate organization's cultures) or it might be or should be applied in a "simplified" or "pragmatic" way. Giving in to such suggestions of cutting corners in terms of resources or stakeholder involvement, even if they appear reasonable at first glance, is not advisable and will most likely lead to failure of the project.

The pragmatic questioner	
How to spot	Usually not the one in charge of commissioning the project and is not the problem owner. Does not stand to lose anything if the project fails but could be in a position of gain, which could be a strong sign of hidden agendas
Typical behaviors	Asks "pragmatic" questions about the resource and stakeholder involvement. Suggests a cap on resources. Proposes trade-offs, for example, in terms of more consultant hours for less stakeholder involvement. Asks for proof that the EM will "deliver" the expected results
Likely impact if left unattended	*Positive:* Can be used to support the implementation of the results, if persuaded to support the EM project. Otherwise, none *Negative:* Can in modeling sessions turn into the questioner, joker, boss, border patrol, or missionary with the mission to restrict or even sabotage the project
How to mitigate the negative impacts	In the project negotiation phase, the questions should be discussed and answered as clearly as possible, without giving in and, for instance, committing to unrealistic deadlines and insufficient resources. If this turns out not to satisfy the questioner, then this indicates that his or her negative attitude is most likely caused by something else, for instance, by hidden agendas

7.2.4   The Grand Manager

These are managers who seek to relate all efforts in the organization to the existing large programs—reengineering, business process standardization, enterprise architecture management, resilience, or digitization. The bigger the better. They seem to be unable to commission a comparably small project that focuses on solving a specific organizational problem. Furthermore, they do not take into account that aligning with the "grand programs" in a large organization may risk the project being slowed down by internal bureaucracy, existing power games, and agendas, while the perceived gains from cliché arguments such as "efficient resource sharing," "pool of people," "having access," "using standard approaches," or "eliminating double work" might not materialize. In fact, suggestions that an EM project is "parachuted" into an existing large project or program have to be carefully assessed for hidden agendas. If that project or program is in trouble already, they might be looking for a "silver bullet" or someone to blame.

A version of this stereotype is "the offended grand manager." This behavior emerges when the grand manager is responsible for a larger organizational program with which the EM project needs to collaborate, but for some reason this manager has not been involved in the process of making the decision to start the EM project. As a result, the manager might feel offended and act in an adverse manner.

The grand manager	
How to spot	Responsible for a major program, project, division, or function in the organization. Is usually not the one directly commissioning the EM project. May have a significant stake in the project, in which case he or she will act more constructively than if the interest is not very significant
Typical behaviors	Asks questions from the point of view of his or her area of responsibility. Suggests approval procedures that stem from those areas of responsibility. Might suggest being in charge of the resources. Asks questions similar to the pragmatic questioner. Suggests that the EM project should be aligned with a particular organizational undertaking and then the grand manager takes ownership of it
Likely impact if left not dealt with	*Positive:* Aligning with a larger project, if done for the right reason, might add additional clout to the EM project *Negative:* Might act counterproductively, for example, by showing off his or her ego. May in modeling sessions turn into the boss, missionary, or border patrol
How to mitigate the negative impacts	Involve the problem owner in the discussions about the project objective. Address the concerns. Try to clearly define relationships and common interests in resources and inputs/outputs between the EM project and the relevant large programs of the organization

7.2.5   The One Who Has Done It All

People playing this role are often very experienced and have done many great things in the past. They may not necessarily have high management positions and, with respect to the EM project, may not have the responsibility to allocate resources. However, they usually have some influence over the decisions about it. Because of their vast experience, they often tell stories about how they have solved the current problems decades ago. The tone and the attitude often suggest skepticism about whether the problem in question is worth solving, the participatory way of working is worth using, and the people currently present are the right ones for the task.

The one who has done it all	
How to spot	This is someone with a great deal of experience. Usually presents himself or herself as someone relevant to the project. Could in some cases be the problem owner
Typical behaviors	Tells stories about past experiences. The stories usually have the flavor of "those were the days" and that the current challenges are less significant than the past ones
Likely impact if left unattended	*Positive:* Knowing past work and the state of the art is beneficial in many projects *Negative:* Projects skepticism on other participants. Can in modeling sessions turn into the one who knows best, the questioner, and sometimes the missionary
How to mitigate the negative impacts	Analyze how the current project is related to past projects. Discuss the innovative aspects and try to define clear goals for the project

7.2.6   The Business-as-Usual Manager

This is someone who is good at what she/he does, and usually the organization is relatively successful. This person does not see the need for doing anything differently and using a different (in this case participatory) way of working. He or she may agree to participate and even be quite enthusiastic in the beginning but will most likely with time suggest working in the old ways. They will try to solve the problem with the old methods and propose a solution that is an increment of the state of the art. In many cases, such approaches are suitable, and if they are, participatory modeling is probably unnecessary to use. However, if this attitude is applied to a problem that cannot be solved in the old-fashioned way, the results will not be satisfactory.

The business-as-usual-manager	
How to spot	Agrees to participate but seeks to work according to the established way of working. Does not see the value of the EM project and the participatory way of working. Injects skeptical and sarcastic comments into the process of planning for the effort
Typical behaviors	Participates in the project activities but tries to suggest working as usual
Likely impact if left unattended	*Positive:* While all EM projects are in some ways improvements of the state of affairs, knowing and documenting the established ways might be a step toward improvements, but EM should also break out new ideas and solutions *Negative:* Can negate the results by delivering an "old-fashioned" solution. If it is sufficient, then no harm is done, other than wasting some resources on the modeling project. But if the solution does not really have the intended effect, the project participants might get too distracted and lose motivation to continue
How to mitigate the negative impacts	Explain early on in the project why the established ways are not feasible for this problem. Define requirements on the solution, and share them with the project team

7.3   Summary

In this chapter, we have discussed a number of stereotypical stakeholder behaviors that EM practitioners may encounter in an EM project. They can be observed in modeling sessions as well as in the project as a whole. During modeling sessions, the following stereotypes of stakeholder behavior have been observed: the seller, the buyer, the questioner, the observer, the boss, the one who always knows best, the border patrol, the comedian, the missionary, the expert, and the representative. On the EM project level, the following types of behavior can be observed: the engaged owner, the client, the pragmatic questioner, the contractor, the demanding boss, the one who has done it all, and the business-as-usual manager.

While this chapter has been based on our and other colleagues' experiences, most likely, there are more behaviors that can be identified. Being able to identify them and soften their negative impact often becomes the distinguishing difference between a successful modeling effort and a failed one.

The presentation of the behaviors in this chapter is generic in principle—we have specified how to spot them, what the typical behaviors are, what is their likely impact, and how to mitigate the negative impacts. There are many ways of dealing with them, and for some of them, it is difficult to describe specific situations and suggest actions. There are, however, other situations in modeling sessions for which more explicit recommendations can be formulated. These will be discussed in Chap. 8 that follows.

References

Bourne, L.: Advising upwards: managing the perceptions and expectations of senior management stakeholders. Manag. Decis. **49**(6), 1001–1023 (2011)

Bourne, L., Walker, D.H.T.: Project relationship management and the Stakeholder Circle. Int. J. Manag. Proj. Bus. **1**, 125 (2008). https://doi.org/10.1108/17538370810846450

Cleland, D.: Project Stakeholder Management. Project Management Handbook. Wiley, Hoboken, NJ (2008). https://doi.org/10.1002/9780470172353.ch13. ISBN 978-0-470-17235-3

Freeman, R.E.: Strategic Management: A Stakeholder Approach. Pitman Publishing, Boston, MA (1984)

Chapter 8
Managing Situations and Related Contingencies in Facilitated Enterprise Modeling Sessions

There are many situations that arise in a modeling session. Many of them require the modeling facilitator to take action. This chapter describes typical situations that we have encountered during our extensive experience in practice. Examples of situations are how to deal with lack of authority given to the modeling project, how to deal with a situation when one participant wants to take over control of the modeling session, and how to proceed if a model is "too polite" and avoids tackling the hard problems in the organization. For each situation, we describe what the likely signs of a situation are and how to deal with it, including what not to do. Some more common recommendations on what to avoid in modeling projects are documented in the form of anti-patterns that represent seemingly attractive but bad practices and argue why they appear attractive. We will also discuss some aspects of stakeholder body language that can be observed during a modeling session and how to interpret such body language.

8.1 Securing the Resources and Authority of the Project

In many cases, especially when EM is used for the first time in an organization, there is a tendency to apply the principles and criteria of other projects to EM projects, for example, assuming that the time and involvement of key stakeholders can be replaced or compensated by involvement of external consultants or junior employees. In some cases, people assume that a complex problem can be solved in a short time or that the modeling project does not need any or much of preparation.

While the EM project manager and facilitator can argue against this, a useful suggestion is to carry out *a 2-hour demonstration* of experience using participatory EM aimed at addressing a specific question, such as defining the objectives of the modeling project or mapping out the landscape of the problems to be addressed in the project. In most cases, management is able to appreciate the results and also to

© Springer International Publishing AG, part of Springer Nature 2018
J. Stirna, A. Persson, *Enterprise Modeling*,
https://doi.org/10.1007/978-3-319-94857-7_8

note how much time and effort is needed. If this does not produce the desired effect, then the best course of action is to proceed with approaches other than EM.

A modeling project, and consequently the modeling teams that comprise it, should be entrusted to make the decisions about how to solve the problem and how to implement the solutions. This requires authority over resources, responsibilities, and work procedures. Without it the group will not be able to elaborate specific solutions, and the discussion about them will quickly become hypothetical requiring continuation at another time and probably with different people. Such a situation greatly diminishes the power of the modeling sessions, and the result will most likely be difficult to implement. Hence, if management is reluctant, give the modeling group the necessary authority to design the change in the organization, and explain that without authority, modeling can be seen merely as a method for brainstorming of ideas.

8.2 Forming the Modeling Team

The process of forming a modeling team is not always easy. In many cases, participants of the modeling team need to be selected from a *large and diverse group of stakeholders*. They will have different backgrounds and are able to contribute to the solution from various perspectives, needed in most cases. They will also have different individual intentions and motivations (stakes in the subject matter of the project). For example, in some cases, potential modeling participants openly admit that they do not feel like contributing to the project because they see it as a competitor in some way. In other cases, this might be less obvious, and potential conflicts should be sensed and identified, for example, by analyzing the different responses in interviews preceding a modeling session. In such cases, the main risk is to form a heterogeneous group without clear and common objectives. To avoid this, the EM process should have good planning, for example, trying to assess how the different participants might act in the modeling sessions. In the preinterviewing stage, a broad group of stakeholders will probably need to be interviewed. It may also be beneficial to organize the modeling project in groups of sessions, each focusing on a specific aspect or part of the problem that the project addresses. More about forming the modeling team can be found in Chap. 6.

8.3 Managing the Modeling Team

In this section, we will present various situations that we have observed during a modeling session along with suggestions of how to manage them.

A participant does not seem motivated to work in the group. This is often demonstrated by not contributing with relevant points to the discussion, engaging in side discussions, or doing other tasks such as reading e-mails or leaving the room to make phone calls. Motivate this participant personally by informing him or her about the consequences (positive) the work will have on his or her work and on the company as a whole. Point out how his or her area of expertise is relevant to the modeling session. This can also be done during interviews in the preparation phase.

A participant has frequent conflicts, regarding modeling, formulation, and interpretation, with another participant. In this case, it might be advisable to discuss the objectives of the modeling task with both participants in private, for example, during a coffee break.

A group member tries to take command of the work. The way this is done should be assessed. If this is suggested and done in a rational manner, then it might be a good solution for part of the work. The facilitator must, in such situations, be prepared to play a different but constructive role in the process. But if this is done in a destructive manner, for instance, to demonstrate one's power or authority, then the modeling effort runs the risk of not resulting in the desired effects. In such cases, the modeling facilitator should be able to assert authority and to explain the roles in the modeling session.

The members of the modeling team are very quiet, appear to be cautious, and utter very few specific statements about the perceived problem area. This situation is often unexpected if compared to how the participants behaved and what views they expressed in the preparation phase. The situation could be an indicator of hidden agendas or that the situation in the company has suddenly changed. The facilitator should consider:

(1) Explaining the role of the facilitator and the objectives of the modeling task
(2) Asking for the participant's views on objectives and then comparing them with the ones given to you by the problem owner
(3) Suggesting taking turns among the participants to express their most important problems/goals/processes or any other aspects relevant to the problem domain
(4) After the modeling session, asking for additional people to be interviewed and potentially included in the following modeling sessions

Participants ask for training in the modeling methods and tools. How much the modeling participants should be trained in modeling methods and tools is a frequent question in modeling projects. Our suggestion is not to "train" the modeling participants in the method knowledge. More specifically, this should not be done for the purpose of the participation in the modeling session. It is the responsibility of the modeling facilitator that the chosen method/notation is correctly used (Chap. 6). Too much attention to the method/notation used will only distract the modeling participants from solving the problem at hand. Our experience is that hands-on practice is the best way of becoming acquainted with a method/notation. If, after the initial experiences with modeling, the participants express an interest in acquiring more in-depth knowledge and understanding of modeling, then training in the chosen method and related tools should be organized as a separate project of transferring the modeling and facilitating competence to the company.

8.4 General Recommendations for EM Sessions

In this section, we will present some tips and suggestions on what to do and what to avoid during modeling sessions. Some of them are applicable to all sub-models of EM, while some are formulated specifically for a specific EM sub-model. The sub-models of the 4EM method (Chap. 4) are used as example models.

The modeling session typically starts with the problem owner or facilitator introducing the objectives of the project and of the current modeling session. Once this is done, the actual modeling should begin. Instead, often a long silent pause follows because it is generally difficult to start the modeling activity. It might be because participants are a bit passive. They do not know where to start or have no experience of how to act. A good way to start modeling is to ask the participants to *each write down the five most important* goals, problems, concept types, etc. Discussing the five components of each participant and introducing them into the model then follow this. Initially, they might simply be grouped according to a theme or similarity. Relationships can be introduced later. The facilitator can initially do this, but other participants should also be encouraged to interact with the model by drawing relationships or rearranging the modeling components.

Concerning the perspectives or sub-models of modeling (see Chap. 4), it is not always best to start with the Goals Model (GM). In some situations, it may be better to start with the Concepts Model (CM), the Business Process Model (BPM), the Actors and Resources Model (ARM), or the Technical Components and Requirements Model (TCRM) and then gradually work toward elicitation of the other models. Working with inter-model links to drive the process forward can be a suitable approach. The facilitator is advised to make a plan in advance about where to start, depending on the goal of the session. The identification of what is the most appropriate model to start with can be done on the basis of analyzing what the modeling participants talk about most or seem most excited about in the preinterview phase. For example, if they talk about the problem and the organization's visions, then the GM could be a good starting point. If they talk mostly about how they work, then the BPM could be used to capture the current work procedures, and if they talk a great deal about their products, materials, or information objects, the most appropriate starting point could be the CM.

Modeling cannot always be performed in a "top-down" fashion by starting from a strategy and then developing operational solutions. It can also happen that the modeling participants feel more at ease discussing the current (or future) operational solutions that are then elaborated "upward," toward a strategic vision. Questions of the type "why?" normally extend the model "upward," since it asks for more generic components, while questions of types "how?" and "what does this mean?" typically extend the model "downward," by specializing a component in sub-components. This principle can be applied when modeling goals, in which case the why and how questions will extend the goal hierarchy toward more strategic or operational goals. It can also be applied to the whole enterprise model—the why questions will trigger looking for goals that motivate business processes and rules, while the how questions will motivate the elaboration of business processes, concepts, and actors needed for solving problems and realizing business goals.

The plastic wall is for creating a working model, not to perfect one. All EM components and relationships must not, and cannot, be clearly and unambiguously defined at the outset. Initial definitions can be vague and elaborated later as long as they are needed. The facilitator expressing explicit permission for (temporary) vagueness may improve creativity.

It might also happen that some objectives, concepts, and activities of the enterprise domain are not clear to the modeling team. In this case, it may be appropriate to seek additional expertise regarding the application domain and to add people who are familiar with the organization's objectives and information needs to the modeling team.

The models created during the initial modeling sessions often seem very superficial and general, and hence, they do not seem to say anything new or essential. As one modeling participant once said to us, this is a general management guidebook of "sell more to make more." In such cases, the facilitator should suggest condensing or making the model more compact, for instance, by asking the participants to individually select the five most central statements in the model and asking them to select a number of statements (e.g., 5) that could be removed, without hurting the model. Once the team sees the individual suggestions (votes), they should discuss them and reach a consensus about what is important and what is to be removed. The important facts in the model should then be the starting points for further in-depth modeling.

Modeling sessions can also involve situations and actions that should be avoided, such as:

- Do not allow the participants to use other discussion tools such as whiteboards, flip boards, paper, notebooks, etc. This only distracts the attention from the model and may also create a false impression that the "real work," in this case meaning the real documentation of the discussion and the decisions, is or will be created somewhere else and not in the model on the wall or in the modeling tool, depending on which modeling technique is used.
- Do not keep working with a model that has an awkward layout and is not good enough for adding new components. In this case, time should be spent on restructuring the model, moving the pieces of paper around. Engage the modeling participants in this, and they will be able to assess the current state of progress. In some cases, a new sheet of plastic can be started and the modeling components transferred to it.
- Do not keep working on one model type until the discussion is completely exhausted and the model seems perfect. Iterate to other sub-models, for example, create a CM to clarify key concepts and information objects and create a BPM to create solutions for goals in terms of work procedures and practices.
- Do not forget about inter-model links. The strength of EM is the multi-perspective view on the modeling problem. The 4EM method (Chap. 4) is an example of a method that addresses this aspect explicitly. Hence, creating links between sub-models allows creating a holistic view of the problem and the

solution. Furthermore, it might be that different stakeholders feel more familiar with certain model types, which could be based on their role or expertise; hence, switching to different model types may enhance their contribution.

Some more attractive but harmful practices are discussed as anti-patterns of modeling in Sect. 8.5.

8.4.1 Goal Modeling

The GM at hand looks and "feels" unstructured, inconsistent, and too complicated. In this case, the participants should set priorities to goals and problems and restructure the model into goal sub-hierarchies. It might also be useful to move some parts of the model to another plastic sheet to avoid the temptation to work with all parts of the model at the same time.

The GM is "too kind, too polite," there are only a few problems listed, and the goals stated are very general and "obvious" and do not lead to constructive actions for further development of the requirements. The actions to consider are as follows: break down goals into more specialized goals, ask why they are needed, make goals measurable, ask what hinders the goals, reduce the existing set of goals, etc. using a number of "driving questions." Another way of dealing with this is to express the goals according to the principle of SMART goals. This means that every goal should be specific (S), measurable (M), accepted (A), realistic (R), and time framed (T). Even if it cannot be applied to all goals, the more strategic goals typically are less specific and hence less measurable. This guideline contributes to increasing the understandability and usability of the model.

A stated GM component is not understood. Even if the group comes from the same organization and aims to use the terminology and vocabulary used in their organization, new solutions often require new terms or concepts or even adjustment of the existing ones. Such concepts or terms should be defined in the CM. They can also be refined by introducing "supports" links to other goals or business rules or by reformulating the GM component.

The GM has a large number of "supports" relationships making it unstructured and difficult to understand and make sense of. Such Goals Models are often the result of "everything being related to everything." This might be a common situation when goals are seen as having a broad relevance and organization-wide influences can be clearly seen. A way to reduce the number of relationships is to introduce goal sub-hierarchies, each of them focusing on a specific area or topic, usually defined by the top goal in that sub-hierarchy. This means that the many "supports" relationships will be transformed to AND, OR, and AND/OR decomposition relationships.

8.4.2   Concepts Modeling

In EM, the Concepts Model is most often used to clarify concepts used in the other models. The main purpose is to increase the overall understandability and clarity of the solution to an enterprise problem. Hence, a certain amount of vagueness and imprecision is acceptable, because Concepts Models are seldom used for information system design in the form they come out of an EM project. The typical aspects that might be too time-consuming to model in an EM project might be attributes and attribute data types, collection classes, and description classes distinguishing the difference between the information and object. While these aspects are important in the process of developing an information system, in an EM setting involving people not experienced with IS design in discussing such details will only lead to the participants feeling confused and disengage them. If such details are needed in the final results of the EM project, then an additional iteration involving stakeholders from the IS design team should be involved at the later stages of the project.

A CM can be seen as complete, if it contains concepts, attributes, and relationship types such that every conceivable information set in the BPM can be formulated in the CM. In practice, this requirement can be seen as somewhat relaxed to only those information sets that are not trivial or easily identifiable. For example, it is understood by default that people have names and last names as attributes or that customers have attributes for representing their contact information. However, such details of what is modeled and what is assumed to be by default need to be discussed and agreed by the modeling team to avoid misunderstandings. This is also influenced by the purpose of the modeling project. For example, if the purpose of the model is to share knowledge about the overall solution, more details can be omitted than if the purpose is to use the enterprise model for IS design.

8.4.3   Business Process Modeling

Business process modeling is done to specify how an organization implements its vision. In modeling sessions, the modeling is usually done according to some agreement or plan about what is important to model in a participatory modeling session because there usually are so many potentially relevant processes that modeling all of them would be too time-consuming.

Often, which processes to model in a modeling session is influenced by the business goals. For example, modeling of new and innovative ways of working and modeling changes in existing processes require reaching consensus. Business processes can also be influenced by business problems. For example, the company might need to model processes that do not function as expected to see where the potential problems can be identified.

The selection of processes to model in a participatory modeling session should be based on those that benefit most from participatory modeling. Common motivators are, for example, the need to elicit knowledge from multiple stakeholders, achieve consensus, and strengthen the implementation of the new process design in the organization. There also are processes that are either fairly clear and stable or relatively straightforward. Modeling these, if needed for the purpose of project documentation, can be done outside the modeling sessions in an analyst-driven manner, or process documentations from other projects, if they are up to date, can be reused.

In the modeling of processes, a key aspect is to clarify their fit within the overall enterprise model representing the whole solution. The most useful tool for this purpose is inter-model links, for example, as specified by the 4EM method. More specifically:

– A process, or its super-process at some decomposition level, should be related to a goal that motivates the existence of this process.
– Business processes are often triggered or governed by business rules. Hence a process that has no identifiable connection to business rules might suggest that the model is incomplete. Likewise, a business rule that is not related to any process at any decomposition level might be difficult to enforce.
– A business process should be connected to at least one actor that performs it at some decomposition level.
– Information and material sets should be defined as concepts. This might not necessarily be a one-to-one relationship (e.g., information set "flight" related to the concept flight). In many cases, the information sets are defined by a set of concepts (e.g., information set "passenger ticket issued" can be defined in terms of several concepts—passenger, ticket, flight, airport, city, ticket class, service class). How much detail should be modeled depends on the purpose of modeling and should be decided during the modeling session.

It often happens that the role/meaning of a larger process is unclear. Relating it to the GM, determining the customer as well as the producer of the process, and analyzing how the customer (internal or external) may get a satisfactory result out of the process usually help to clarify this.

Another common situation is a difficulty to identify information or material sets that processes produce and consume. This might be caused by prior experience with modeling languages that see processes merely as a sequence of activities. The processes do not seem to produce any information or material sets. In such cases, questions about detailed outcomes and relations to concepts and goals should help. We recommend creating an empty information set every time a process is introduced into the model and asking the stakeholders what outcome the process creates.

The complexity of models is also an issue that often requires addressing. Usually it is not a problem per se—a complex reality usually leads to complex models. Unnecessary complexity is however undesired because it makes the model less suitable for the intended purpose. In practice, there usually is no problem to produce very detailed and complex models because business processes in most organizations are fairly complex. This might not be needed in all cases however, especially when one of the purposes of the model is to communicate among stakeholders. For example, models with a large number of processes at one decomposition level are difficult to take in, to understand, and to analyze. In such cases, the decomposition can be restructured, for example, by increasing the decomposition level by clustering processes in larger processes.

8.5   Anti-patterns of Modeling

So far, we have mostly presented best practices of how to prepare, manage, and facilitate successful modeling sessions. In essence, these can be seen as the dos of modeling. We should also give advice with respect to what EM practitioners should *not* do because in relation to some aspects, there are substantially fewer don'ts than the possible dos. By making the don'ts explicit, we can focus on avoiding the most common costly mistakes in EM. For this purpose, we have chosen the format of anti-pattern.

Alexander et al. (1977) define a pattern as describing "a problem which occurs over and over again in our environment and then describes the core of the solution to that problem, in such a way that you can use this solution a million times over, without ever doing it the same way twice." In this regard, patterns represent reusable (good) solutions. Anti-patterns offer a different perspective of reuse—they capture *bad solutions* to common problems. Besides just presenting a bad solution, they also explain why this solution looks attractive in the first place and why it backfires and turns out to be bad when applied. More about anti-patterns is available, for instance, in Brown et al. (1998) and Long (2001).

In this section, we use a template for anti-patterns adopted from Long (2001), shown in Table 8.1.

8.5.1   The Product of Modeling

This section presents anti-patterns that concern the quality of enterprise models created during a participatory EM session.

Table 8.1   The anti-pattern template

The name of the anti-pattern	
Problem	EM-oriented motivation or problem it tries to solve
Anti-solution	What solution was chosen and how it was applied
Actual results and unintended consequences	What happened after the solution was applied
Primary fallacies	What were the likely causes for failure, for example, false assumptions

8.5.1.1   Elaborate Each Model Type Separately and in Detail

Elaborate each model type separately and in detail	
Problem	Your modeling language has a number of model types or sub-models, all of which are to be elaborated to analyze the modeling problem from various perspectives and to create a holistic view
Anti-solution	Each model type, such as process model, concepts model, goal model, is elaborated separately and in detail until its developers feel that the model is complete. In some cases, the different models are assigned to different sub-teams
Actual results and unintended consequences	The different sub-models do not have good integration points, the links between them (inter-model links) are few, and only the most obvious ones are shown. They are created afterward. All models are more or less finished. More refinement based on analyzing the inter-model links has not been done. If all model types are developed in this manner, the modeling result will not be coherent and ultimately cause development efforts based on the models to fail
Primary fallacies	Assuming that (a) we have to complete one model type before we start with the next and/or (b) model types can be created in isolation and integrated later

Note: This anti-pattern is also observed in university teaching of EM and other modeling approaches when student groups divide the work according to modeling artifacts and work on them individually instead of as a group

8.5.1.2   Use UML for EM

Use UML for Enterprise Modeling	
Problem	The EM project needs to choose a modeling language. In most cases, preference should be given to modeling languages that are already known and used within the organization
Anti-solution	Many organizations are well acquainted with UML and use it in information system development projects. Hence, they choose to use UML also for documenting enterprise models. The tools used might also influence this choice
Actual results and unintended consequences	The resulting enterprise models look more like UML models than enterprise models. Non-UML modeling concepts, such as problems and goals, are modeled with the graphical symbols of the UML. EM concepts that are similar to UML concepts are modeled with those that seem most appropriate without recognizing the differences. This raises confusion among the participants of the modeling session and those that need to interpret the models later
Primary fallacies	Assuming that UML should be used for EM. Blindly following the suggestions of those that recommend organizations using only one modeling language and tool
	Confusing other OMG standards for business modeling, such as VDML (OMG 2015), with UML

There are a number of UML extensions and customizations for business modeling and EM. They can be potentially useful if appropriate methodological steps are elaborated and followed.

8.5.1.3 Relate Everything That Seems Related

Relate everything that seems related	
Problem	During the process of model refinement, you discover that there potentially are several undocumented relationships between model components
Anti-solution	Document all possible relationships that you can find between components in the model. Relate components "for good measure" because they "seem somehow related"
Actual results and unintended consequences	The model is muddled and difficult to understand because it contains many relationships and its interconnectedness could be close to a total graph. Such models are sometimes regarded as "spaghetti models." A more serious problem is that the model will become unfocused and not function well as a basis for different types of development
Primary fallacies	Assuming that all possible relationships need to be documented. Our recommendation is to document the relationships that improve understandability and clarity of the model and make the problem that the model addresses clear

8.5.2 Addressing the Modeling Process

This section presents anti-patterns that concern the quality of the EM process addressing situations that risk occurring but need to be identified and mitigated by the modeling facilitator or project manager.

8.5.2.1 Everybody Is a Facilitator

Everybody is a facilitator	
Problem	The modeling group in the modeling session does not have a modeling facilitator available. The causes for this can be (a) the need for a facilitator has not been realized or (b) there is a lack of resources to afford the services of an external facilitator or (c) the facilitator that was planned to participate is unexpectedly unable to attend, for example, due to force majeure
Anti-solution	The group members attempt to do the best they can to "facilitate each other" in various ways according to their knowledge of what facilitation is. In doing this, the group members might engage in a

(continued)

Everybody is a facilitator	
	pseudo competition about who will facilitate more or louder. It is also not uncommon that the highest-ranking manager assumes the role of facilitator
Actual results and unintended consequences	The modeling session might appear creative and inspired at the outset, but in reality it is quite chaotic. It runs the risk of discussing only themes and topics that are very commonly discussed in the organization instead of focusing on the real objectives of the session
The resulting model usually contains a large number of various modeling components dealing with an abundance of issues, most of which are not relevant to the problem at hand. The modeling language that the group ends up using is not according to a real method, and the model may also include informal "drawings" of various kinds
Primary fallacies	The assumptions that participative modeling can be done without a dedicated and skillful facilitator, that anyone can facilitate, and that good facilitation means dominance over other participants and leads to better results
The assumption that facilitators can be trained quickly and on the fly

8.5.2.2   The Facilitator Acts as Domain Expert

The facilitator acts as domain expert	
Problem	The facilitator has previous knowledge about the domain to be modeled. It is difficult to activate the domain experts in the modeling session and to get them to contribute their knowledge to the model. Modeling progresses slowly and time is running out
Anti-solution	Instead of trying to engage the participants, the facilitator tries to make progress by introducing his or her own knowledge in the model. The participants are mostly watching
Actual results and unintended consequences	The domain experts become even more passive, and their motivation to contribute diminishes further. The model ends up by being the facilitator's own solution to the problem at hand, and even if it is a good one, the domain experts will not feel that they are responsible for it and for its implementation. In the worst case, should the model be incorrect in some way or cause problems when implemented, the credibility of the facilitator will be seriously damaged. This could eventually jeopardize the whole EM project
Primary fallacies	Assuming that it is better to get a model that reflects the views of a select few than no model at all. Assuming that the only effect of modeling is the model produced and neglecting the consensus over the implementation of the model

8.5.2.3 Concept Dump

Concept dump	
Problem	Your modeling participants are knowledgeable about the domain and reasonably skillful modelers. They produce an abundance of modeling concepts without much discussion. The facilitator might be reasonably inexperienced
Anti-solution	The facilitator tries to place them all in the model and somehow relate them to each other. This happens without significant discussion and assessment of how the model contributes to the project objectives
Actual results and unintended consequences	The resulting model contains a lot of concepts. It may look really complex and appear advanced. However, many of these concepts will be trivial, and issues addressed will most likely be peripheral to the problem at hand. Hard problems will be unaddressed due to the lack of discussion and reflection during the modeling session
Primary fallacies	The false assumption that all issues brought up and pieces of paper written need to be placed in the model. Following blindly the guideline that stakeholder wishes must be recorded. Replacing quality with quantity—good models need critical discussion and decisions about what goes into the model need to be weighted with respect to the scope of the model

8.5.2.4 Please the Participants

Please the participants	
Problem	The organization and its participants commit to using participative EM, but at the same time, they impose very strict conditions related to schedule, cost, location, and who should participate in the modeling sessions
Anti-solution	To accept the situation as is and to try to make the best possible effort within the frame conditions
Actual results and unintended consequences	The result usually does not meet the expectations because the resources have not been adequately allocated. The people allocated to the project have not been able to present the complete picture when it comes to the issues involved. The resulting models and the decisions are not implementable and are not followed in the organization. At best they are seen as an input to the problem-solving process that followed the EM project. In the worst case, the EM project and the EM practitioners are blamed for the problems that can be associated with the project
Primary fallacies	Assuming that participative EM can be done with very little effort and in any setting. The amount of effort required for preparing and conducting modeling sessions is given in Chap. 5. Assuming that it does not matter who the stakeholders are and, hence, using stakeholder representatives or mediators, rather than stakeholders themselves, for example, involving a secretary or a favorite employee of a manager, rather than the manager himself or herself

8.5.2.5 Hide EM in the Background

Hide EM in the background	
Problem	The participants and the project owner are genuinely interested in solving the problem and generally positive toward participatory modeling, but they do not want to use participatory EM. In such situations, they do not want to upset their existing ways of working by doing something they may not feel 100% sure about
Anti-solution	Cater for this wish by not talking about modeling and EM in particular. The session is run in a traditional manner of discussing issues. The problem owner chairs it, and the facilitator or assistant facilitator creates the model in the background. The participants are invited to look at it, but the model is not presented to them in detail
Actual results and unintended consequences	The discussion might have been quite useful and may have uncovered potentially important ideas, but the model is not used, and it does not represent all that has been decided in the meeting. The model is, therefore, not useful for further work after the meeting
Primary fallacies	Assuming that EM is only about creating the model and the participatory way of working is the same as a normal meeting. Underestimating the impact a facilitator can make on the creative process

8.5.3 Addressing EM Tool Support

This section presents anti-patterns that concern choosing and using tools for supporting various activities of an EM project. More on EM tool usage is discussed in Chap. 9 as well as in Sandkuhl et al. (2014).

8.5.3.1 Models Keep "Alive" by Themselves

Models keep "alive" by themselves	
Problem	The company has created a set of enterprise models that are intended to be used in the future for (1) reference purposes, such as business process standardization, or for (2) reusing them in new organizational solutions
Anti-solution	Store models in the tool repository and/or reports in the hope that people will look at them when they need them
Actual results and unintended consequences	Once the models are created and stored in the repository, they are quickly forgotten. Nobody remembers the details of the models and their purpose, and as a result, the new modeling activities often "reinvent the wheel"
Primary fallacies	Assuming that the models do not need updating or that when updates are needed people will voluntarily do it. Not allocating responsibilities and resources for model updating

(continued)

Models keep "alive" by themselves	
	Assuming that models and reusable model parts can be easily identifiable. Not identifying reusable artifacts, such as patterns, in Enterprise Models. Assuming that people are well acquainted with the contents of the model repository

8.5.3.2   Professionals Use Only Computerized Tools

Professionals use only computerized tools	
Problem	You use a computerized modeling tool in a setting where you need to capture knowledge, which requires collective thinking or consolidating several opinions
Anti-solution	The facilitator uses a computerized modeling tool and a projector. Everyone sits at a round table and tells about what they think should be modeled and what part of the model they would like to be shown on the screen
Actual results and unintended consequences	The process has interruptions because the facilitator has to shift his or her attention between discussing issues with the group and operating the tool. As a result, the model looks visually unappealing; it has many broken links, misspelled words, and awkward placement of modeling concepts. The progress is slow, and not all stakeholders are able to contribute. Several of them quickly become disengaged. The resulting model reflects the knowledge of a select few in the room and most likely needs extensive refinement work including consultations with the stakeholders present
Primary fallacies	Assuming that working with paper stickers on a plastic wall is perceived unprofessional and slow. Wanting to immediately come up with the finished model. Not wanting to spend time on documentation and model refinement

8.5.3.3   Everyone Embraces a New Tool

Everyone embraces a new tool	
Problem	The stakeholders need to review the models produced; you need to communicate with models within the project
Anti-solution	Purchase many licenses of a tool, train all stakeholders in tool usage, and send them models via e-mail. Ask them to enter comments directly in the tool
Actual results and unintended consequences	The communication in the project is hampered. Models are not discussed as the stakeholders spend considerable time discussing how to use the new tool
Primary fallacies	Assuming that the stakeholders have the motivation and sufficient knowledge to use a tool on their own. Failing to focus on well-established tools and packages, such as office software

8.5.3.4   Cloud-Based Tools Replace the Plastic Wall

Cloud-based tools replace the plastic wall	
Problem	The target of the modeling session is to model a specific issue or problem, and it is reasonably clear what needs to be modeled and how, including the model type that should be created
Anti-solution	Instead of modeling on the plastic wall, the participants take out their laptops and create the model with a cloud-based modeling tool
Actual results and unintended consequences	The communication of the group breaks down. Instead of discussing the model and the issue at hand, the group spends most of the time fixing the graphical representation. Since each of them has the possibility to browse their own view of the model, the attention often shifts, and there is no discussion about the resulting model
	The group spends considerable effort on improving the graphical representation of the model. The model does not follow the modeling language that the group should be using because many of the cloud-based tools offer only a limited choice of symbols
Primary fallacies	Assuming that a computerized tool can replace the plastic wall. Currently, cloud-based tools lack functionality for supporting true collaborative modeling the way the plastic wall does

8.6   Unspoken and Intangible Aspects of Modeling Sessions

Facilitating participatory EM sessions is mostly about dealing with people and least with models. Earlier we have argued that it is the participants of the modeling session who are the most valuable resource. Hence, in dealing with them, the EM project manager and facilitator should be aware of a number of aspects such as cultural differences and body language. These are difficult aspects that take years to master. This section does not intend to compress that knowledge to a few pages. We are merely providing a few examples based on our experience meant to show that this is an area that EM practitioners should be aware of and consider learning. The main reason for this is that the stakeholders are not always willing to express all of their thoughts and opinions openly. There might be hidden agendas, personal opinions, organizational taboos, etc. All this is relevant to be aware of in order to develop a solution that has the desired effect. However, the stakeholders will not communicate this up front. Instead, the EM practitioner should be able to listen to what is said and even more carefully sense that which is not said. Being aware of cultural differences and body language helps in achieving this.

8.6.1   Cultural Differences

Nowadays, it is quite common that facilitators get assignments in other countries. Knowing a bit about the local culture and traditions is therefore needed. For the purpose of planning the modeling project, the following issues need to be worked out before starting:

- How to address people? By first names, last names, using titles? In some countries, there are clear norms, but they also get adapted depending on the organization, age of the people, language used for communication, presence of foreigners, presence of outsiders to the organization, etc.
- How to dress? Formally or informally. This might depend on the national culture, on the organization, on the people participating, and on the venue for modeling.
- How to plan for interruptions such as coffee breaks and lunches? How long do they normally take? Are there ways of shortening coffee and lunch breaks that are unnecessarily long? How would the participants perceive this?
- How to plan for modeling participants who arrive late? In some cultures, this is the normal situation.
- How do people behave when disagreements arise? How should the facilitator act in such situations? In some cultures, open conflict is avoided at any cost. In other cultures, people even prefer to act out certain disagreements at first to show their strength and not to appear as pushovers.

Being unaware of the specifics of each culture and organization usually hampers the process of rapport building with the project owner and the stakeholders. For example, in some cases, we have observed that even seemingly minor neglect of the "local customs," geographical or organizational, has led to the stakeholders' perception of the modeling facilitator as an outsider and hence somebody that is not necessarily knowledgeable about their business case. All this might be difficult to ask and investigate in the preparation stage, but some questions, like how do people prefer to be addressed, are acceptable to ask straight up.

8.6.2   Body Language

Body language is part of nonverbal communication in which physical behavior such as facial expressions, body posture, gestures, eye movement, touch, and the use of space is used to express or convey information. Body language may in effect indicate people's attitude toward the situation more accurately than verbal communication.

This section intends to provide only a few examples of body language observations during participatory modeling. The examples aim to show that the modeling facilitator should be aware of the nonverbal clues that the modeling participants display. However, someone who is knowledgeable in body language could skillfully hide between deceptively neutral postures. Our recommendation is to observe body language but, at the same time, not make hasty conclusions if one is not an expert in reading it. Facilitators who aim to develop their skill portfolio further should start by reading books on the topic, such as Hall (1966), Burgoon et al. (1996), Borg (2009), and Houston et al. (2013).

Below are some examples of body language that we have observed and what they indicate:

– Sitting with legs crossed and foot kicking slightly may indicate boredom.
– Arms crossed on the chest is a posture that may indicate defensiveness.
– Standing or walking with hands in pockets and shoulders hunched often indicates dejection.
– Hand to cheek and touching the mouth with a finger or pen are most often signs indicating thinking and evaluating.
– Supporting head with one or two hands may indicate boredom or detachment.
– Touching and slightly rubbing nose can be signs of rejection, doubt, or lying.

Body language also communicates the attitude of a group of people, for example, if several people have the same posture or use the same gestures, their thoughts are most likely aligned (this is called mirroring). Touching the mouth and chin typically indicates that the person is evaluating or thinking. Figure 8.1 shows two situations in a modeling session. The first picture (left) shows two people adding constructs to a model on the plastic wall and two evaluating the model. The second picture, taken a few minutes later, shows that now three participants are assessing the model.

Depending on the body language used, this might indicate consensus or disagreement. A modeling facilitator who is aware of the aspects of body language is able to sense these situations in the modeling session.

The modeling facilitator should also be aware of what body language to use and what to avoid. For example, Fig. 8.2 (left) shows positive body language attempting to express energy and the need to continue the work, while the picture on the right shows a more authoritative posture used to express a directive. The latter should be avoided

Fig. 8.1 An example of body language showing evaluation

Fig. 8.2 An example of body language of a modeling facilitator

because the participants might either interpret it as the facilitator giving orders or trying to solve the problem single-handedly. In either case, this demotivates them.

8.7 Summary

This chapter presented a number of situations that can arise in modeling sessions and in EM projects in general. We have described what the signs of a situation are and how to deal with it, including what not to do. Some more common recommendations to avoid in modeling projects are documented in the form of anti-patterns. We have also briefly discussed the aspects of cultural differences and stakeholder body language that can be observed during a modeling session and how to interpret it. In the next chapter (Chap. 9), we will discuss issues of tool support for EM.

What we have discussed in this chapter and in Chap. 7 represents our recommendations for facilitating EM sessions and carrying out EM projects. They are mostly based on our experiences and discussions with other practitioners in the field. The material in this book is by no means exhaustive, and many more issues and best practices than what can be described in a book such as this need to be discovered and described in depth. As discussed in Chap. 11, this is part of the training for becoming a modeling facilitator.

References

Alexander, C., Ishikawa, S., Silverstein, M., Jacobson, M., Fiksdahl-King, I., Angel, S.: A Pattern Language. Oxford University Press, New York (1977)

Borg, J.: Body Language. Pearson Education Harlow (2009). ISBN 978-0273758792

Brown, W.J., Malveau, R.C., McCormick III, R.C., Mowbray, T.J.: AntiPatterns: Refactoring Software, Architectures, and Projects in Crisis. Wiley, New York (1998). ISBN 0471197130

Burgoon, J.K., Buller, D.B., Woodall, W.G.: Nonverbal Communication: The Unspoken Dialogue. McGraw-Hill, New York (1996). ISBN 978-0070089952

Hall, E.T.: The Hidden Dimension. Anchor Books, New York (1966). ISBN 0-385-08476-5

Houston, P., Floyd, M., Carnicero, S., Tennant, D.: Spy the Lie: Former CIA Officers Teach You How to Detect Deception. St. Martin's Griffin, New York (2013). ISBN 978-1250029621

Long, J.: Software Reuse Antipatterns. Software Engineering Notes, vol. 26, no. 4. ACM SIGSOFT (2001)

OMG: Value Delivery Modeling Language (VDML). Object Management Group. http://www.omg.org/spec/VDML/1.0/ (2015)

Sandkuhl, S., Stirna, J., Persson, A., Wißotzki, M.: Enterprise Modeling – Tack-ling Business Challenges with the 4EM Method. The Enterprise Engineering Series. Springer, Heidelberg (2014)

Chapter 9
Tools for Participatory Enterprise Modeling

This chapter discusses the issue of tool support in modeling sessions. There are two main types of tools: (1) the "plastic wall," which is more suitable for idea generation types of modeling sessions, and (2) a projector and a computerized tool, which is more suitable for modeling sessions devoted to the refinement of an existing model. The purpose of this chapter is to discuss the suitability of these two kinds of tools as well as to discuss the main issues that influence their use in practice.

9.1 The Types of Tools for EM

It is hardly possible to carry out serious modeling projects without tool support because the models need to be documented for further work or at least for the purpose of inclusion in the minutes of the modeling session.

There are two main types of tools, and their use depends on the kind of model that is being developed and the kind of modeling session that takes place. More specifically, the following choice needs to be made in the process of planning a modeling session:

1. The *plastic wall* is more suitable if the modeling session will focus on generating ideas, exploring alternatives, capturing the current state of the organization, and developing new solutions to business problems, all of which involve knowledge elicitation and documentation. The plastic wall is also more suitable for a modeling session that takes place outside the premises and when the modeling group is quite large. After the session, the models on the plastic wall should be documented using a computerized tool.
2. *A projector and a computerized tool* is more suitable if the modeling session will mainly analyze and refine existing enterprise models that have been documented in earlier projects or previous modeling sessions of the same project. The computerized modeling tool is usually used for documenting the results of the modeling sessions.

© Springer International Publishing AG, part of Springer Nature 2018
J. Stirna, A. Persson, *Enterprise Modeling*,
https://doi.org/10.1007/978-3-319-94857-7_9

In the following sections, we will present in detail the use of both types of modeling tools. Computerized tools continuously evolve, which makes mentioning of specific tools difficult. Because the objective of this chapter is not to advocate any specific tool or vendor but to present a number of useful tool categories and core features that are useful in EM projects, specific tools will not be discussed in detail.

9.2 The Plastic Wall

The so-called "plastic wall" approach means that models are documented on large plastic sheets using colored paper cards (Fig. 9.1). The model on the "plastic wall" (e.g., see Fig. 9.2) is then viewed as the official documentation of the modeling session.

A suitable plastic film can typically be purchased in DIY stores. Preferably, the film should be white and nontransparent, taking into account that sometimes walls may not be just one color. The paper cards or stickers need to be firmly attached to the plastic surface. Post-it type of notes come off easily, more so when they have been moved around a few times. This makes them less suitable to use. Small pieces of adhesive putty (top right in Fig. 9.1), found in stores selling office supplies, can be attached to the back of the paper cards to secure them. Lately, a new kind of sticky note that relies on static electricity instead of adhesive has emerged (see, e.g., Stattys[1]), which, if proven useful for modeling sessions, would eliminate the need

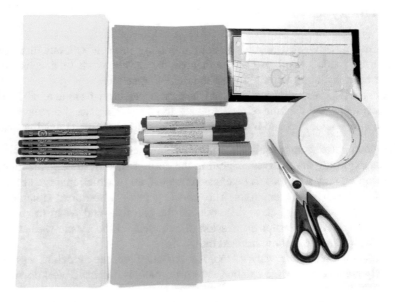

Fig. 9.1 Resources for participatory modeling workshops

---

[1]https://www.stattys.com

Fig. 9.2 Using the "plastic wall"—everyone is involved in modeling

for adhesive putty. Regarding pens, make sure to use nonpermanent felt-tip pens so that writings on the plastic wall can be removed if needed. Taking a picture of models on plastic walls before taking them down is advisable.

From the point of view of conducting a participatory modeling session, the advantages of this approach are the following:

- The plastic wall can be set up in almost any room with a sufficiently large and flat wall. However, we would like to advise that the room for modeling be assessed prior to booking it to avoid the need for cumbersome fixes such as cutting holes in the plastic wall to accommodate wall décor and lighting (see Fig. 9.4 for an example where this had to be done).
- It allows the modeling participants to view and work with the full model instead of the tool operator showing a particular part of the model or doing a specific change. This allows engaging others in a discussion.
- The participants can also improve the model without interfering with what the others are doing, if the situation is appropriate.
- All actions of the modeling facilitators are visible and understandable.

We advise against using a computerized tool in modeling sessions with the primary objective to capture ideas, because if the model is created in the tool, the facilitator or tool operators often need to perform actions that are not related to actual modeling. These actions could be file-saving, changing the font and line sizes, adding more pages to the drawing, etc., all of which slow down the process and distract the participants.

There are a number of misconceptions about the "plastic wall." For example:

- *Plastic wall modeling is a somewhat unserious way of working, and the use of computerized modeling tools should be preferred.* This is in fact an anti-pattern (see Chap. 8). In our experience, using the "plastic wall" makes the modeling session more interactive and inclusive, which outweighs the need to document the model in the computerized tool afterward.
- *There are other idea generation and business planning approaches using large paper or plastic sheets that appear similar to participatory EM, and hence some participatory EM is the same as those.* To avoid this, the facilitators should point out the main differences, such as the modeling notation, the specific way of working (the consensus-driven discussion, focus on concrete actions), and the role of the modeling facilitator (more about preparing and starting a modeling session in Chap. 5).
- *The plastic wall can be replaced by a smart board and a computerized tool.* In our opinion, it cannot because even the best smart boards are still far away from "real-life" resolution and the best multi-touch tables are significantly smaller than a plastic wall, which leads to the same restrictions as using an ordinary projector and a computerized tool.
- *The plastic wall is only a substitute when computerized modeling tools are unavailable.* This is not so. As stated previously, both kinds of tools have their own purposes, and the plastic wall should be used for supporting creativity and knowledge capture even in cases when computerized tools are readily available, as shown in Fig. 9.3.

Computers can still be used for checking existing models and other supporting information, but not for creating the model during the modeling session. Nowadays many tools (for instance, Creately,[2] Lucidchart,[3] Signavio[4]) are available as cloud solutions, running in a browser and offering multiuser and concurrent editing functionality. Many people attempt to use these tools instead of the plastic wall. They sit in the same room but use their own laptops to create a joint model. This way of working usually is not as efficient as the plastic wall because the group often ends up discussing the technical issues of creating the model instead of the actual knowledge that goes into the model. At the moment, the same can be said about emerging technologies such as smart glasses and smart boards—they are currently not suitable for multiuser interaction with the model and knowledge capture the way the plastic wall is.

---

[2]https://creately.com

[3]https://www.lucidchart.com

[4]https://www.signavio.com

Fig. 9.3 The use of plastic wall in a room with available computer equipment

9.3   Computerized Tools

Computerized tools for modeling information system designs emerged in the late 1980s and early 1990s. In those days, their main purpose was to support methods used for tasks such as system analysis, database design, and code design and management. Software packages for automating those tasks became known as CASE (computer-aided software engineering) tools. Some of these tools were adopted to support the early EM methods. At the same time, a class of tools for supporting various modeling methods and offering customization features to support specific modeling methods were developed under the name of meta-tools. Among of the first efforts on meta-tools were RAMATIC (Bergsten et al. 1989), ConceptBase (Jarke et al. 1995), MetaEdit (Marttiin et al. 1996; Kelly 1997), and ADONIS (Jumginger et al. 2000). Tools of this kind were often customized in order to support EM methods. For example, RAMATIC was used and customized to support the 4EM ("For Enterprise Modeling") predecessor F3—"From Fuzzy to Formal" (F3 Consortium 1994; Song 1994). MetaEdit was also used for supporting F3 (Stirna 1995). The resulting tools, albeit successful per se, proved to be rather difficult to use by EM practitioners in their business consulting assignments. This was because the tools of those days lacked in presentation power and required rather powerful computers to run and their licenses were comparatively expensive. As a result, many practitioners chose to document enterprise models in simple drawing tools such as Microsoft Visio and iGrafx FlowCharter. These kinds of tools are still widely used in practice. They offer a rational choice of great presentation power at a low cost. They have proven to be successful because the graphical features are deemed more valuable than the repository support they lack. In our opinion, the simple documenting tools will remain useful for a considerable time because many EM projects are quite small and hence do not gain added value from a tool with a model repository.

Several of the early tools are still widely used and have become more powerful in many aspects of their functionalities, for example, MetaEdit+ (Kelly et al. 2013), ADOxx (Fill and Karagiannis 2013), and Metis that has become Troux Architect and was later acquired by Planview. A new breed of tools for making models executable and hence more organic tools in company management have also emerged, for instance, Active Knowledge Modeling (Lillehagen and Krogstie 2008) and Capability Driven Development environment (Henkel et al. 2017). However, from the point of view of supporting the EM process, the same trade-off of graphical presentation at a low cost and widespread availability vs. more advanced analysis, repository, and model execution functionality at a considerably higher cost and resource commitment has remained.

There also are a number of emerging developments that offer promising technologies and tools that have the potential of being useful for EM but yet lack the maturity or dedicated support from the point of view of participatory EM process. Model annotations (Nolte and Herrmann 2016) and research into collaborative tools and collaborative spaces (Anslow et al. 2016) are among the most relevant developments.

In the area of efforts toward developing tools for supporting participatory modeling, a number of prototype tools have been proposed. Gutschmidt et al. (2017) have developed a tool for the 4EM method that runs on a multi-touch table. It allows each user to work independently on a model fragment and even enter data by means of an on-screen keyboard (see Fig. 9.7). Mangano et al. (2014) have investigated how to support design with interactive whiteboards. While technologies such as interactive boards aim to capture drawings by hand and handwritten text in the computerized format, currently they support only common ways of working without specific considerations for participatory EM. Nevertheless, this area of tool development needs to be continuously monitored because, as these tools will become more mature, they will probably offer more advanced functionality for customized method support. Another area of potentially useful tools is mixed reality tools; see, for instance, Rühmann et al. (2018).

In the following subsections, we will briefly present the most common requirements and usage scenarios for EM tools that should be considered when selecting a tool for participatory EM. We will then discuss some aspects of simple and more advanced EM tools.

9.3.1   Common Requirements for EM Tools

This section summarizes the main requirements for EM tools from the point of view of an EM practitioner. A more extensive discussion on requirements for EM tools is presented in Stirna (2001) and Sandkuhl et al. (2014). Additional requirements for EM tools were also discovered in the requirements elicitation stage of the CaaS project (Bērziša et al. 2014).

In all EM projects, the objective is not just to model. Enterprise models also need to be used for communication and presentation. Hence, they need to be included in other media, for instance, reports, presentations, web pages, and blogs. These are minimum requirements that a simple drawing tool should be able to support. The following requirements are relevant:

- Integrate models in documents produced with commonly used office software for document editing. In many projects, copy/paste functionality has been expressed as the key requirement, and even if this sounds trivial, not all modeling tools support it. There are modeling tools that intend to hold all project documentation in its own repository, and hence including a model in a common document editor might require going through somewhat cumbersome steps of exporting the model to an image format or screen grab, opening the image with an image editing application, copying the desired model or model fragment, and then pasting it in the document. These steps would need to be repeated every time the model is updated.
- Print models in large formats or combine model fragments printed on A4 pages if a larger format is unavailable. This is often needed in the preparation of models for presentations or walk-through modeling sessions.
- Export models to popular graphical formats for presentation on the Internet or the organizational intranet. Some modern tools are able to automate model export to the Internet.
- Create specific graphical symbols for certain modeling components. Simple drawing tools support this functionality, which is an easy way to provide minimal support for a modeling method.

In larger and longer projects, it is hard to use modeling tools only for presentation because considerable effort is also spent on model analysis, refinement, and implementation. Hence the following requirements mandating the use of more advanced tools become relevant:

- Model repository support for storing, maintaining, reusing models or parts of models, ensuring consistency across different models, etc. This is especially important if an organization wants to institutionalize EM and use it continuously.
- Model analysis and quality checking, for example, by creating user-defined views of the model or executing queries over the content of the modeling components, enforcing certain modeling standards.
- Controlled model reuse, for example, by defining reusable model fragments and/or patterns.
- Model integration with external data sources that would allow more advanced model use at information system run-time.
- Model execution and integration with external applications allowing these applications to be configured by models.

- Method customization in order to, for instance, extend an EM method with an additional sub-model or integrate it with another modeling language.
- Collaborative work and multiple user support. Modern tools should be able to support concurrent model editing and management. There should also be support for users who only need to view the models. Recently many tools have been deployed in the cloud, which significantly simplifies meeting this requirement. However, currently many such tools offer very little in terms of custom support for modeling methods, and their graphical presentation capabilities are relatively limited, which will most likely improve as they mature.

In specific projects, many more requirements can be formulated in order to support a specific modeling method or a specific way of working (e.g., numbering the modeling components according to a certain principle, decomposition of modeling components to separate schemas). They should be formulated during the tool acquisition process.

In larger projects that need advanced tools, the list of requirements might become such that no tool might fit or the most fitting tool could turn out to be prohibitively expensive. In such cases, the organization should probably reassess its intentions for tool use and prioritize among requirements. Another solution in such cases is to hire a consultant who can provide tool support for the organization's first projects, during which there will be an opportunity to assess the needed requirements.

9.3.2   Usage Scenarios of EM Tools

The following main EM tool usage scenarios are played out in EM projects.

9.3.2.1   Model Documentation

As discussed previously, the "plastic wall" is suitable for supporting a modeling session that is aimed at capturing the initial version of a model. It allows easy model creation, but once the model has grown and has been discussed for some time, it needs to be documented in a tool. During this process, the model on the plastic wall or its digital images are transferred to the modeling tool (Fig. 9.4). The tool operators usually make the model more readable and understandable, but the main purpose is to document the model as it was created during the modeling session. Too much model improvements at this stage might actually be counterproductive because the stakeholders might not recognize their model as it was at the end of the modeling session.

Fig. 9.4 Result of the "plastic wall" modeling (on the left) and the same model documented in a tool (on the right)

9.3.2.2   Model Refinement Between Modeling Sessions

It might happen that EM practitioners work with the models in between the modeling sessions in order to improve the model quality by, for instance, checking facts with stakeholders, reducing redundancy, improving the syntactic correctness, as well as increasing understandability. Between the modeling sessions, there might also be the need to produce reports or presentation slides. Furthermore, detailed plans for subsequent modeling activities should also be defined. Figures 9.5, 9.6, and 9.7 show the Enterprise Modeling lab of the Chair Business Information Systems at the University of Rostock, Germany. It is equipped with a set of tools, namely, smart board, smart table, whiteboard, and the plastic wall.

9.3.2.3   Model Refinement Session

When a model needs to be refined in a second modeling session, it is more efficacious to introduce changes to it in a computerized tool. In this case, a projector and a computerized tool should support the modeling session. The tool is used to show the model to the participants, and the tool operator makes changes to the model directly in the tool. According to our experience, it is more efficient if this type of modeling session is supported by a modeling facilitator responsible for driving the discussion and a tool expert responsible for operating the tool and introducing the suggested changes in the model. A key activity of the tool operator is to follow the discussion and to present the right part of the model. This requires certain effort, and we recommend that the facilitator and tool operator rehearse their presentation of the model in advance. This can be supported by making models more fit for presentation purposes, for example, by increasing the text size, simplifying the structure, and changing the colors.

 If new models are created during a refinement session, then this should be done on the plastic wall.

Fig. 9.5 A modeling laboratory used for model analysis and refinement. © Institute of Computer Science, University of Rostock. Reprinted with permission from the University of Rostock, IT and Media Center

Fig. 9.6 Smart board used to present a model during a refinement session. © Institute of Computer Science, University of Rostock. Reprinted with permission from the University of Rostock, IT and Media Center

Fig. 9.7 Smart multi-touch table used for jointly working on an enterprise model at the University of Rostock

An emerging type of tools designed to be used together with specific hardware such as smart boards (Fig. 9.6) or multi-touch smart tables (Fig. 9.7) to support modeling sessions can also be used in such modeling sessions. However, in our opinion, they work best with a small number of participants, 3–5, so that all can sit or stand close to the model. Furthermore, smart boards and interactive whiteboards seem to be more suitable for usage in situations where the main emphasis is on presenting the modeling results (e.g., in cases when the project has produced many alternative solutions and the stakeholders are in need to assess them) and occasionally making some annotations or notes.

Among the current drawbacks of these technologies is the relatively limited model size that can be created and shown on the screen at the same time. For example, an example of a Goals Model fragment in Fig. 9.8 occupies half of the screen as can be seen in Fig. 9.7.

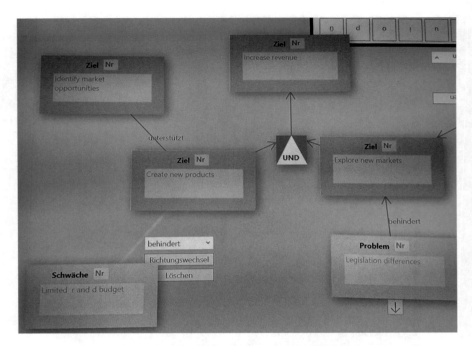

Fig. 9.8 Model fragment created on a multi-touch table by a tool of Gutschmidt et al. (2017)

9.3.2.4   Model Creation Inspired by Reuse

Once the modeling project has advanced beyond the stage of initial model creation or if an organization has adopted a model-based way of working, new models might need to be created on the basis of existing models. In such cases, the projector and EM tool use can be combined with the plastic wall. For example, the plastic wall can be used for the new model, and the computerized tool can be used for browsing existing models and reusable components (Fig. 9.9). In case the new model is only based on the integration of existing model fragments in the tool repository, then this can be done directly in the tool. If a model on the plastic wall is to be combined with a structure of components, such as a sub-hierarchy of goals, in an existing model in the repository, we suggest printing the structure and pasting it on the plastic wall (with a note of which model in the repository it came from). Then the participants can keep on working on the plastic wall and incorporate the structure in their work. In such cases, it is good to have a printer available nearby.

9.3.3   The Process of Tool Acquisition

In practice, the process of tool acquisition is often ad hoc and unplanned, and as a result, tools that are acquired and used do not fit the method used and the way of

Fig. 9.9 A modeling session using a computerized tool and plastic wall

working. This situation needs to be countered by a good understanding of how to use the EM tools and how to introduce them in an organization.

A proposal for EM tool acquisition process is presented in Stirna (2001) and Sandkuhl et al. (2014). It recommends analyzing (1) the organization's intentions (for instance, will the models be kept "alive" over time), (2) situational properties (for instance, the presence of skillful tool operators, availability of resources), and (3) the specific functions that the tool should serve—tool requirements. This should be followed by choosing a tool acquisition strategy (for instance, using simple tools, purchasing a tool, customizing a meta-tool). This allows identifying the candidate tools and then following on with the acquisition of the tools that are decided as the most suitable. More about how to select and introduce EM tools in organizations is available in Stirna (2001).

9.4   Summary

This chapter discussed two main types of tools—the plastic wall and the projector and a computerized tool. The plastic wall is more suitable for participatory modeling with the purpose of capturing and consolidating new ideas and solutions. Computerized tools and models displayed with a projector are more suitable for modeling sessions that aim to discuss and refine existing models and solutions. We have also discussed the main requirements and usage scenarios for EM tools. The objective of this chapter has not been to present the current tools or their features. Moreover, modern tools offer new and exciting features that have the potential of creating novel solutions, but in the quest for new and existing tools, it is important to keep in mind that innovative tool features do not necessarily mean that they will help the organization. In this regard, we would like to point out that the organization's requirements and intentions for use should be the primary guide in the tool acquisition process.

References

Anslow, C., Campos, P.F., Jorge, J.A.: Collaboration Meets Interactive Spaces. Springer, Heidelberg (2016)

Bergsten, P., Bubenko, J., Dahl, R., Gustafsson, M.R., Johansson, L.A.: RAMATIC – A CASE Shell for Implementation of Specific CASE Tools. SISU, Stockholm (1989)

Bērziša, S., Bravos, G., Gonzalez Cardona, T., Czubayko, U., España, S., Grabis, J., Henkel, M., Jokste, L., Kampars, J., Koc, H., Kuhr, J., Llorca, C., Loucopoulos, P., Juanes Pascual, R., Sandkuhl, K., Simic, H., Stirna, J., Zdravkovic, J.: Deliverable 1.4: Requirements Specification for CDD, CaaS – Capability as a Service for Digital Enterprises, FP7 proj. no 611351. http://caas-project.eu/deliverables/ (2014)

F3 Consortium: F3 Reference Manual, ESPRIT III Project 6612. SISU, Sweden (1994)

Fill, H., Karagiannis, D.: On the conceptualisation of modelling methods using the ADOxx meta modelling platform. Enterp. Model. Inf. Syst. Archit. **8**(1), 4–25 (2013)

Gutschmidt, A., Sandkuhl, K., Borchardt, U.: Multi-touch table or plastic wall? Design of a study for the comparison of media in modeling. In: Abramowicz, W., Alt, R., Franczyk, B. (eds.) Business Information Systems Workshops. BIS 2016. LNBIP, vol. 263. Springer, Heidelberg (2017)

Henkel, M., Stratigaki, C., Stirna, J., Loucopoulos, P., Zorgios, Y., Migiakis, A.: Combining tools to design and develop software support for capabilities. Complex Syst. Inform. Model. Quart. **10**, 38–52 (2017). https://doi.org/10.7250/csimq.2017-10.03

Jarke, M., Gallersdörfer, R., Jeusfeld, M.A., Staudt, M., Eherer, S.: ConceptBase – a deductive object base for meta data management. J. Intell. Inf. Syst. **4**(2), 167–192 (1995). https://doi.org/10.1007/BF00961873.

Junginger, S., Kühn, H., Strobl, R., Karagiannis, D.: Ein Geschäftsprozessmanagement-Werkzeug der nächsten Generation – ADONIS: Konzeption und Anwendungen. Wirtschaftsinformatik. **42**(5), 392–401 (2000)

Kelly, S.: Towards a comprehensive MetaCASE and CAME environment: conceptual, architectural, functional and usability advances in MetaEdit+. PhD Thesis, University of Jyväskylä, Finland (1997)

Kelly, S., Lyytinen, K., Rossi, M., Tolvanen, J.: MetaEdit+ at the Age of 20. Seminal Contributions to Information Systems Engineering. Springer (2013)

Lillehagen, F.M., Krogstie, J.: Active Knowledge Modeling of Enterprises. Springer, Heidelberg (2008)

Mangano, N., LaToza, T.D., Petre, M., van der Hoek, A.: Supporting informal design with interactive whiteboards. CHI. **2014**, 331–340 (2014)

Marttiin, P., Harmsen, F., Rossi, M.: A Functional Framework for Evaluating Method Engineering Environments: The Case of Maestro II/Decamerone and MetaEdit+. University of Jyväskylä (1996)

Nolte, A., Herrmann, T.: Facilitating participation of stakeholders during process analysis and design. COOP. **2016**, 225–241 (2016)

Rühmann, L.M., Prilla, M., Brown, G.: Cooperative mixed reality: an analysis tool. In: Proceedings of the 2018 ACM Conference on Supporting Groupwork (GROUP '18), pp. 107–111. ACM, New York, NY (2018). https://doi.org/10.1145/3148330.3154510

Sandkuhl, K., Stirna, J., Persson, A., Wißotzki, M.: Enterprise modeling—tackling business challenges with the 4EM method. In: Dietz, J.L.G., Proper, H.A., Tribolet, J. (eds.) The Enterprise Engineering Series, pp. 1–299. Springer, Heidelberg (2014). ISBN 978-3-662-43724-7

Song, W.: F3 EM Capture Tool. Users Guide. F3 Consortium, SISU, Stockholm (1994)

Stirna, J.: Enterprise modelling tool development. Masters Thesis, Information Technology Institute, Riga Technical University (1995)

Stirna, J.: The influence of intentional and situational factors on enterprise modelling tool acquisition in organisations. PhD Thesis, Department of Computer and Systems Sciences, Royal Institute of Technology, Stockholm, Sweden (2001). ISSN 1101-8526

Chapter 10
Participatory Modeling in Relation to Other Modeling Frameworks and Languages

In this book, we have mostly assumed that facilitation is used in the process of Enterprise Modeling (EM). This chapter will discuss how facilitation can be used to support other types of modeling that in broad terms are similar to EM. We will not present any specific modeling language, method, or framework in detail. Instead, we will discuss what the typical requirements for a modeling approach should be in order for them to be useful in a participatory modeling setting. For example, there is a need for using simpler notation when modeling on the plastic wall. We will also discuss the main principles of the ways of working with business modeling methods as well as Enterprise Architecture (EA) frameworks. Aspects of facilitation using agile approaches, the Unified Modeling Language (UML), Goal-Oriented Requirements Engineering, and Capability Driven Development will also be discussed.

10.1 Requirements on Modeling Methods Related to Facilitation

The process of facilitation poses a number of requirements on the modeling language and the way of working with modeling. This section discusses the most common requirements to be considered in modeling projects. Requirements for modeling tools are discussed in Chap. 9.

10.1.1 Language Requirements

In most cases, using several modeling languages can solve the modeling problem. For the initial phases of modeling, the specifics of the language and notation are usually not that important because the same level of creativity and completeness of

© Springer International Publishing AG, part of Springer Nature 2018
J. Stirna, A. Persson, *Enterprise Modeling*,
https://doi.org/10.1007/978-3-319-94857-7_10

knowledge can be achieved with many languages. Even within the one modeling language, following the same set of model elements, it is possible to introduce modeling "dialects" and sub-notations to cater for the purpose of early knowledge elicitation and capture. Most often this means adding elements of a secondary notation such as comments, groupings of modeling components, as well as including modeling components from other languages. During the planning phase of an EM project, the following main aspects of the modeling language should be considered:

– *Understandability vs. formality* of the modeling language. Johannesson et al. (1997) suggest that the modeling languages that are more understandable by non-experts are less formal and hence the facts are expressed more ambiguously and with less precision. In projects that primarily focus on business aspects and involve business stakeholders with little experience in modeling, understandability is preferred. If, however, development of specific organizational or information system (IS) designs is among the project objectives, formality should be preferred because modeling languages that cater for more formal expression of domain knowledge allow expressing knowledge more precisely. Using more formal languages will also support smoother transition to the subsequent implementation phases of the project.

– *Understandability vs. expressiveness* of the modeling language. All participants of the project (stakeholders, EM practitioners, and developers) should understand the modeling language. Most likely the model will not use all features of the modeling language chosen. For example, in an initial version of the Goals Model, the sub-goals should be arranged in groups rather than linked together with AND/OR operationalization relationships. In the former case, the exact semantics of the chosen language might not be all too important. The Business Process Model might be developed at a high level of detail and initially may omit information sets and specifics of the control flow. However, in cases of not following the modeling languages closely and their notations, the EM practitioners should take care that it does not reach a level of informality where the modeling result is not a model anymore but just a drawing. This can happen if the facilitator is inexperienced or gives excessive freedom to the participants.

– *The appropriateness of the modeling language* for modeling the problem at hand. In most projects, more than one aspect (intentions, procedures, information structure) needs to be analyzed, and hence, approaches that offer multi-perspective views on the problem domain should be preferred. In IS development projects, the specific purpose of creating IS design specifications should guide the language choice, and hence the UML language should be considered as a candidate. For IS development projects, the language chosen should allow integration with other model types used in IS engineering, such as integrating Business Process Models with UML use cases. For modeling business concepts, the project might choose to use class diagrams and gradually refine the Concepts Model into a domain model that can be used in the later stages of the IS development.

– *The acceptance of the modeling language* by the stakeholders and the target audience of models created. This can be influenced by factors such as education and training, organizations' internal standards for methods and tools, as well as IS development technologies used. In the cases when models are used mainly for knowledge sharing in the organization, the modeling language chosen should be relatively commonly used, widely accepted by the intended target audience, and, since organization-wide training in modeling languages is difficult to achieve, intuitive. In this case, models should be expressed by commonly used languages and notations supported by textual descriptions. Potential misunderstandings of the graphical symbols should also be assessed. For example, people might easily perceive ellipses as UML use cases or arrows with large and closed arrowheads as UML generalizations.

In Chap. 9, we present the tools used to support participatory modeling. In general terms, there are two kinds of tools, namely, (1) large plastic sheets and colored pieces of paper representing the different types of modeling components used in modeling sessions with the main focus of eliciting and documenting new knowledge and (2) computerized modeling tools mainly used for model presentation and refinement.

From the point of view of facilitation with the plastic wall, the following aspects of the modeling language should be considered:

– The modeling language needs to be "relaxed." For instance, some aspects of modeling will most likely need to be omitted because they might be seen as too detailed for an idea generation session. For example, in concepts modeling, attributes of classes or concepts are typically left out for further refinement work after the modeling session.
– The modeling language should be able to use the model space efficiently. In this regard, modeling languages that use a location of the modeling component to convey specific knowledge are less preferable because the group will need to rearrange the model if they run out of space on the plastic sheet. Examples of such languages are UML activity diagrams with swim lanes that extend the model horizontally and UML sequence diagrams that extend the model vertically. To deal with this issue, our recommendation would be to model without swim lanes if the number of actors involved is not known in advance and to model UML communication diagrams instead of sequence diagrams because communication diagrams use space more economically and introduction of new objects and messages does not significantly extend the size of the diagram.
– The modeling components should be easily recognizable in a modeling session. This should be realized by either color or shape of the modeling components. It is not necessary that the shape used on the plastic wall is exactly the same as in the specification of the modeling language, but it should not be misleading. Hence, widely known and used symbols, such as UML classes, should not be used for something else.

From the point of view of facilitation with a computerized tool, the following aspects of the modeling language should be considered:

– The tool should be able to document the model from the plastic wall reasonably close to the original in order to avoid the situation that the modeling participants do not recognize their model in the tool. More about this is discussed in Chap. 9.

Hence, the modeling language in the tool should be the same as used by the modeling facilitator.

- The modeling language should be able to include additional components or auxiliary notation for cases where the modeling facilitator has extended the model with additional components.
- The modeling language should consist of modeling components that offer the principle of decomposition of large models into small sub-models or views in order to show the models to the participants at a reasonable zooming scale.

10.1.2   Requirements for the Modeling Process

In practice, this perspective on modeling has largely been overshadowed by the language perspective, even if the outcome of modeling can never be better than the process that was applied to develop the models. Much of this has been presented in Chap. 5. In our opinion, the general principles of organizing a modeling project in organizations and preparing modeling sessions are the same even if modeling is used for other purposes and with other modeling languages, such as those for IS development or EA management. Here are a few aspects that should be taken into account:

- *Implementability.* The model should be created with implementation in mind and make sure that the different goals of the strategy do not contradict each other. One important aspect of this is to make the arguments for the strategy clear to the stakeholders, which in turn enhances acceptance. For this to be achieved, a participatory approach is to be preferred, since it enables the stakeholders to listen to arguments from others and to provide input based on their knowledge about the abilities and shortcomings of the organization. If the EM project leads to commissioning an IT project for implementing support for the business solutions, then this should also be considered, for example, in such a way that specific IT requirements are captured, IS component architecture specified, etc.
- *Iterative and incremental* model development. This principle is at the core of EM, but in the case of IS development projects, the iterations will also include other development activities such as IS design, coding, and testing. Hence, the time to the next modeling effort might be dependent on those activities. It might also be needed to keep track of the models and how they were implemented, which puts additional requirements on the modeling tool and the development process.
- *Guidance for modeling.* Many modeling approaches are mostly focused on specifying the modeling language and leave the way of working up to the interpretation of the modelers themselves. In our opinion, when applied in practice these approaches should be extended with more specific guidelines, such as, driving questions for fact elicitation and quality criteria for models produced, in order to make the participatory modeling session efficient.

10.2 Business Modeling

This section will summarize a number of other types of approaches that are closely related to EM and that in many cases are used together with EM. More specifically, we discuss canvas-based approaches, EA frameworks, as well as other EM and process modeling approaches.

There are a number of approaches similar to the *business model canvas* (Osterwalder and Pigneur 2010). They are mostly presented in the form of a table consisting of a number of cells, each of which is intended to document a specific aspect of the enterprise or business problem/model. For instance, the Business Model Canvas consists of the following building blocks: key partners, key activities, key resources, value propositions, customer relationships, channels, customer segments, cost structures, as well as revenue streams. For each building block, a number of lead questions are recommended in the canvas. They are similar to the driving questions that are suggested, for instance, in the 4EM language (Sandkuhl et al. 2014). Some practitioners have also developed their approaches to business process or product mapping on the principle of canvas. In many cases, these can be used as a starting point for eliciting the overall knowledge about the project, and then more detailed solutions in terms of business processes or information structures can be developed with EM or IS development approaches. In our opinion, the overall process of preparing and facilitating participatory sessions for creating business model canvas is similar to the EM process of Chap. 5.

Enterprise Architecture development and management have become widely used practices in modern organizations. There are a number of suggestions on how to develop Enterprise Architectures, such as TOGAF ADM frameworks (The Open Group) and DoDAF Architecture Development Process (Department of Defense 2009). The EA frameworks are large and consist of many views, each focusing on a specific part or perspective of the Enterprise Architecture. For example, the NAF (UK Ministry of Defence 2013) consists of the following views: All Views, Capability View, Operational View, System View, Service View, Technical View, and Programme View. It is too complex a task to elaborate all views at the same time and grasp them in one modeling session. Even within one view, there are often many issues to cover, which might be too much for one modeling session, and different types of stakeholders need to be involved. For example, the NAF Capability View should address the Capability Taxonomy (view C1) and Capability Dependencies (C3) defining relationships between capabilities; Enterprise Vision (C2) defining goals, measures, enterprise phases, as well as environmental factors; and Standard Activity (C4) defining standard and operational activities for capability. The meta-models of these views are available in the NAF model proposed by the UK Ministry of Defence (2013). It is worth mentioning that they are well elaborated and consist of a significant number of modeling components and relationships, and attempting to work with all of them in one modeling session will not be easy, especially if the modeling participants are inexperienced modelers. To counter this, our recommendation is that for each participatory modeling session, there should be a clear understanding about what parts of the Enterprise Architecture are to be developed.

For example, in the case of capability modeling, the focus could either be based on a topic such as developing capabilities of armored vehicle recovery or on developing detailed solutions in terms of environmental factors, procedures, roles, and resources for a specific capability, such as light armored vehicle recovery on the road.

Concerning *other EM and process modeling approaches*, the EM process and the principles of facilitation discussed in this book are applicable to them as well. Without going into the details of each language, it is worth pointing out that there might be a number of issues to consider, such as how much of the specifics of the modeling method are to be presented to the stakeholders, how to deal with languages and notations that require certain graphical symbols and layouts making them less appropriate for plastic wall modeling, and whether the modeling session should go beyond the "boundaries" of those methods. For example, one issue is should the business process modeling session really be restricted to just processes or also discuss business goals or use cases if appropriate. For most projects, it is advisable not to restrict the creative process and be prepared to extend the modeling effort to other model types.

10.3   Balanced Scorecard Development

The concept of the balanced scorecards (BSCs) (Kaplan and Norton 1996) has been established as an instrument for dealing with major management problems in organizations. The key focus of BSC development is on balancing performance measurements between business strategy and operations. It takes into account various types of measures, such as qualitative and quantitative, and includes various stakeholder perspectives, such as customer or employee perspectives (Kaplan and Norton 1996). In practice, BSC implementation projects often struggle in the process of elicitation and documentation of organizational knowledge because it is difficult to capture. It also requires stakeholder "negotiations" and implies resolution and consolidation of issues. An essential prerequisite when "building a balanced score-card [is to] achieve a consensus on the balanced scorecard that will be used by the organization" (Martinsons et al. 1999, p. 83). Hence, a number of similar issues to what participatory EM deals with need to be addressed. For instance, what are the company goals, what are effective measures to apply, and what are the best resources for the implementation efforts? While this organizational knowledge is needed for achieving a consensus and for an effective BSC implementation (Martinsons et al. 1999), it is often tacit, spread over various organizational entities and people, and associated to diverse beliefs and standpoints. In this regard, little methodological support is available for systematically eliciting knowledge within the BSC process, especially in terms of participatory way of working. To this end, Niehaves and Stirna (2006) have proposed an approach for supporting BSC development with participatory EM taking the EKD approach (Bubenko et al. 2001), a predecessor of the 4EM method, as an example.

Table 10.1 presents BSC implementation steps and outlines how the 4EM method and the participatory approach can support this process.

Table 10.1 4EM support for BSC implementation steps

BSC development phase	Who is involved?	What are the issues?	What are the problems?	How does 4EM address these problems?
(1) Identify and select stakeholders	Top management, BSC project management	How to identify and select the relevant stakeholder groups?	How to identify stakeholder groups that are most relevant to the organization?	EM project preparation, interviews before the EM sessions
(2) Define the vision	Top management, stakeholder representatives, BSC project management, facilitator	How to define a long-term and sustainable vision for the organization?	How to identify and balance distinct concerns? How to create acceptance for the vision?	Participatory EM session—top-level strategic goals. Acceptance and commitment through stakeholder participation
(3) Identify strategic goals in stakeholder perspectives	Management representatives, stakeholder representatives, BSC project management, facilitator	What are the goal landscapes for each stakeholder group?	How to elicit, structure, and document the goals? How to deal with conflicting goals?	Participatory EM session, focus on the landscape of strategic goals for each stakeholder group
(4) Select strategic goals from stakeholder perspective	Top management, BSC project management, facilitator	How to select the strategic goals that should be pursued?	How to identify and manage interrelationships between different goals? How to select the goals according to different stakeholder interests?	Participatory EM session—decision and integration of the different goal landscapes of each stakeholder group. Elaborate operational goals
(5) Define measures	Management representatives, employees involved in the processes, BSC project management, facilitator	What are suitable measures to monitor the goal achievement?	What are the "right" measures to connect goals and actions? How to deal with the diverse perspectives on the measuring systems?	Participatory EM session—develop measurable goals and KPIs. Elicit measurement indicators and KPI calculations
(6) Define actions and resources	Management representatives, employees involved in the processes, BSC project management, facilitator	What is to be done in order to achieve the goals? Who does it and which resources are to be used?	What are the "right" actions and processes? How to deal with the diverse views on the actions to be taken?	Participatory EM sessions—model processes and actors

(continued)

Table 10.1 (continued)

BSC development phase	Who is involved?	What are the issues?	What are the problems?	How does 4EM address these problems?
(7) Performance controlling	Management, controlling, BSC project management	Are the goals achieved? What problems occurred? Where to aim improvements?	Is it the goals, the measures, or the actions that were not suitable? How to solve the problems?	Modeling and analyzing problems and linking them to goals, KPIs, processes, and actions

Adapted from Niehaves and Stirna (2006)

10.4   Information System Analysis and Design

Modeling is widely used in connection to IS analysis and design, for example, for capturing requirements, for domain analysis, and for information system architecture and code design. The participatory approach is most appropriate for Goal-Oriented Requirements Engineering (GORE) and IS analysis and design. This section will therefore discuss issues of facilitation for GORE and IS analysis and design with UML. There are other approaches addressing specific aspects of IS development that can also benefit of participatory modeling. For example, Capability Driven Development, presented later in this chapter, incorporates EM and hence can benefit from the use of a participatory approach.

10.4.1   Agile IS Development Approaches

For more than a decade, the IS development community has been trying out and adopting various agile development approaches, such as eXtreme Programming (XP) (Beck 2004), Scrum (Schwaber and Beedle 2002), and DevOps (Hüttermann 2012). One of the strengths of agile development approaches is their flexibility and ability to deal with change efficiently. They typically do not prescribe which methods, languages, and tools to use. Instead, their main emphasis is on choosing the simplest and most effective approaches that enable software development. The underlying assumption of agile projects is that the customer is fairly certain about what kind of IS is needed, its features, and usage when delivered. The reality, however, might be different—the IS development project might be a part of some larger business development project, the future conditions and context of the usage might not be clear, and there might not be an agreement about the features needed. In such cases, considerable effort needs to be devoted to the elicitation and analysis of the business requirements and the various business development alternatives. This is something for which the agile approaches are not well suited.

To support the modeling process of agile development teams on a macro level, Ambler (2002) proposed Agile Modeling (AM). It provides a set of best practices to support "lightweight" modeling and suggests active stakeholder involvement, which to a large extent is similar to participatory EM. Hence, Stirna and Kirikova (2008) have analyzed the potential of using EM in agile development projects. While many artifacts used for IS design in agile projects can be replaced by similar artifacts used in EM, the main contribution of EM to AM is in terms of the way of working with business issues such as goals, processes, concepts, and requirements.

Ambler (2007) introduced Agile Model-Driven Development (AMDD) as a framework for iterative and incremental modeling to be used in agile projects. AMDD presents the overall way of working without specifying which IS design artifacts should be modeled. Table 10.2 takes the EM process as a basis and shows how it contributes to AMDD. An additional contribution to Iteration 0 is achieved by the preparatory phase of the EM process including activities such as identifying the project objectives and preinterviewing the stakeholders. In this context, we then

Table 10.2 Combining AMDD with the EKD modeling process

AMDD stage	EM support
Iteration 0: envisioning	
Initial requirements modeling (identify high-level scope and an initial requirements stack)	A participatory EM session with all key stakeholders to establish the business goals of the IS, to explore the business requirements, and to set the overall strategy of the project. The intangible benefit is the consensus about these issues
Initial architecture modeling	A participatory EM session to identify architecture components of the IS on a crude level and to align them with business requirements
Iteration 1–n	
Iteration Modeling: Thinking Through What You'll Do This Iteration	Participatory modeling to elaborate detailed issues concerning the iteration, for example, elaboration of the business process that needs to be supported, designing a specific information structure
Model storming (work through specific issues, just-in-time (JIT) modeling, stakeholders actively participate)	Short participatory sessions in the development team to resolve specific modeling issues that they have, involving stakeholder representatives that are available on site. Involving other stakeholders would have to be planned in advance. Short participatory but developer-driven sessions because, in this case, it might be too resource consuming to involve a dedicated modeling facilitator; hence, the members of the development team should be able to model alone
Executable specification via test-driven development	EM supports this task by providing explicit linking to business goals, rules, and requirements, which can serve as measurable constraints

Adapted from Stirna and Kirikova (2008)

foresee that enterprise models may be among the results of Iteration 0 and in the subsequent iterations more IS-oriented models such as UML models might be created.

In addition, the following principles of EM are in alignment with the agile way of working:

– *Iterative elaboration of multiple perspectives*, such as process, information, and rules. Developing an enterprise model that answers various questions and stakeholder perspectives ensures that the agile team has a repository of explicit knowledge about the business environment of the system as well as about the software design. The agile team should not, however, aim at developing a complete enterprise model first and only then begin developing software because that would be against the principle of iterative and incremental development. The tangible benefit of this is a repository/model of business knowledge about the system and its intended usage. The intangible benefit is a better commitment to the use and acceptance of the new IS.
– *Involvement of different stakeholder types*. Agile projects should involve various stakeholder types, such as end users and occasional users as well as the stakeholders that have an indirect relation to the system, such as high-level managers who will benefit from the system in terms of improved work efficiency. The agile team is to be involved in the EM process to become familiar with the models and with the stakeholders. The modeling facilitator should be a part of the agile team. The tangible benefit is the discovery and integration of various views and opinions about the requirements, thus increasing the completeness of knowledge about the IS to be built. This makes the iterative and incremental development more efficient, because less redesign and rework is needed. The intangible benefit is the promotion of the system and its increased acceptance by the stakeholders.
– *Links of IS models with enterprise models*. The philosophy of agile projects is that the IS development should begin as soon as the team has enough knowledge to begin the development. Hence, the enterprise model does not need to be complete from the beginning; it can gradually be extended, and other IS development artifacts should be linked to the enterprise model to ensure traceability of decisions. Even if the agile mind-set is not favorable to documentation of the system, the tangible benefit of such a linking is the possibility to identify how different features of the IS contribute to business goals, process, and requirements. The intangible result is a reduced need for redesign and rework.
– *Simple tool support*. Agile teams prefer using simple and effective tools, which is in alignment with the principle of EM to use simple tools such as the plastic wall and simple drawing tools for documentation. The main motivation for using simple tools is that every stakeholder is able to contribute to the model at any time.

10.4.2   Goal-Oriented Requirements Engineering

GORE is based on using goal modeling approaches for capturing business require-ments, often for the purpose of exploring various systems development and config-uration alternatives. GORE is commonly based on approaches such as i* (Yu 1997), Tropos (Castro et al. 2002), and KAOS (Dardenne et al. 1993), but it can also use other goal modeling languages. GORE is typically performed before the elaboration of detailed IS requirements. Donzelli (2004) proposes a process for GORE consisting of the following phases: the start-up phase, the goal modeling phase consisting of soft goal modeling and hard goal modeling, as well as the organization modeling phase for further model refinement. In principle, this is similar to the general EM project process described in Chap. 5, and hence, participatory GORE sessions should follow the same principles of modeling and facilitation as for EM in general.

Pohl (2010) suggests practical criteria for choosing i* or KAOS for goal model-ing in conjunction with requirements elicitation. Other modeling languages such as 4EM can also be applied. Concerning the modeling concepts used, we have observed that stakeholders without prior experience have difficulties deciding on, for instance, whether a goal is a soft goal or a hard goal; hence, such more subtle aspects of goal modeling should be taken care of by the modeling facilitator. In the process of GORE, it is also possible to switch to other types of modeling, such as use case modeling, as suggested by Cooper et al. (2006). In this case, the facilitator would need to ensure that the stakeholders understand the rationale for the shift from the vision (goals) to more specific means of realizing the vision by specifying IS functional requirements with use cases.

10.4.3   IS Analysis and Design with UML

Modeling is a common practice in information system development. It is used for IS analysis—the process of eliciting and documenting what are the real-world require-ments for the IS to be built—and design—the process of specifying the IS that should be built to satisfy the requirements. There are various approaches to IS development such as plan driven, for instance, the Unified Process (Kroll and Kruchten 2003), and agile (cf, for instance, Schwaber and Beedle 2002). This section will discuss the issues to consider when carrying out participatory modeling with UML (OMG 2015).

UML consists of a number of diagrams:

- *Structural diagrams:* class diagram, component diagram, composite structure diagram, deployment diagram, object diagram, package diagram, profile diagram
- *Behavioral diagrams:* activity diagram, communication diagram, interaction overview diagram, state machine diagram, sequence diagram, timing diagram, use case diagram

In principle, all of them could be used in participatory modeling sessions, but the usefulness of such actions would be questionable. In our opinion, the following diagram types and the aspects of the system analysis or design they address would particularly benefit from a participatory way of working, whether involving stakeholders or just among developers.

Use Case Diagrams The main focus of use case specification is to capture and document functional requirements. Use case modeling consists of two parts—use case diagramming and documenting textual descriptions of use cases. Hence, each use case should be described. The descriptions can either be in a simple story format or according to a template consisting of several fields, such as use case name, actor, preconditions, main success scenario, extensions, and post-conditions; such elaborated use case description formats are often called fully dressed. In practice, discussing use case diagrams in a participatory setting gives the project team a broad understanding of which functionality the system should support. Writing fully dressed use case descriptions in a participatory setting is deemed too time-consuming in most cases. Therefore, in a participatory setting, the use cases in the diagram should be specified in the simple format including the main extensions. The modeling facilitator should explain to the participants that after the session, the use case would most likely need to be elaborated in detail. It might even be possible to assign different participants to specify the initial versions of the different use cases in the diagram.

Class Diagrams The main purpose of class diagrams is to specify the information needs of the IS to be built. In a participatory setting, class modeling typically focuses on the business needs and how they are to be handled by the IS. There are a number of recommended approaches for the identification of candidate classes, such as identification of noun phrases, category list, analysis of the use case descriptions, and class-responsibility-collaboration (CRC) cards (Beck and Cunningham 2012). For more details on the practical aspects of class design, see, for instance, Larman (2004). In a participatory session, the modeling facilitator can start by posing a number of driving questions similar to the ones used for concepts modeling in EM (Sandkuhl et al. 2014), as follows:

– Which are the main concepts/classes of this application? How are they related?
– Why is this concept/class needed?
– What do we need to know about the concept in the application? What are its properties? When and where do we need this (with reference to the activity diagram or use case diagram)?
– How many instances of this concept/class are there?
– How does an instance of this class come into existence? What makes an instance of this class come into existence?
– What makes an instance cease to exist? How does an instance cease to exist?

Moreover, the purpose of class modeling might evolve from a more general discussion about the main information objects to more specific identification of information objects. Table 10.3 shows an example of how class modeling can evolve

Table 10.3 Example of how concepts and classes can evolve

Initial model: A concept Dish with attributes Ingredient and Calories. Such a model might emerge from an initial discussion among stakeholders or from the initial analysis of the use case descriptions

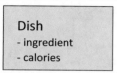

Refinement cycle 1: Attributes of the initial concept Dish are discussed in FoodIngredient that is introduced as a class

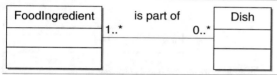

Refinement cycle 2: Class Dish is renamed to Recipe to represent the purpose of this class and to represent the Ingredients of the Dish. Appropriate attributes for both classes are introduced

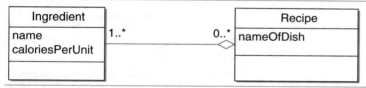

Refinement cycle 3: Aggregation of Ingredients into Recipe is discussed, and a new class RecipeContents is introduced to store the amount of units of an Ingredient that are included in a particular Recipe

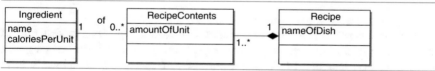

from concepts modeling depending on the purpose of modeling. In principle, the incremental refinement of the model toward making it more suitable for IS development might stop at any point as soon as the developers decide that a satisfactory level of detail enabling software development is reached. Considering this example, it might also be that the initial model and, for instance, the two first cycles are done together with the domain experts and more details added later by IS developers.

In a project that would focus on developing an information system, the resulting model in Table 10.3 can be further refined by creating a sequence diagram for calculating the total number of calories in a Recipe (Fig. 10.1) and then further developing the class diagram by setting attribute types and operations (Fig. 10.2). These kinds of tasks can be done after the participatory session, in a more analyst-driven way.

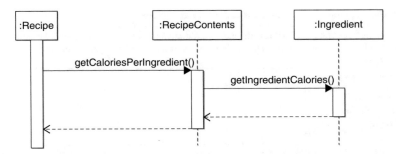

Fig. 10.1 Example of a sequence diagram for calculating the total number of calories in a Recipe

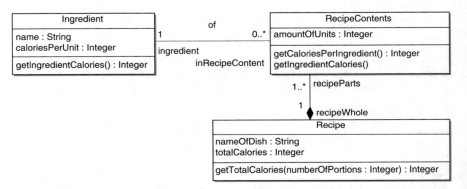

Fig. 10.2 Example of a design class diagram showing operations for calculating the total number of calories in a Recipe

Component Diagrams This type of diagram is used to specify the structure of information systems in terms of their components. They can be of varying size and complexity, and one of the main purposes of specifying components is to support component-based development and analyze the possibilities for the reuse of existing components. In a participatory setting, component diagrams can also be used to discuss the responsibilities and main communication pathways between components. In our experience, a productive discussion on this issue can be achieved by applying the principles of high cohesion (each component should be as single purpose as possible) and low coupling (the dependencies among components should be kept to a minimum).

Activity Diagrams These diagrams are similar to Business Process Models in terms of the application purpose and notation. Hence, they can be used in a participatory setting according to the same principles as in EM (Chap. 5). In an IS development project, activity diagrams can be used, for instance, to focus on the workflow from a business perspective or to specify use cases more explicitly than textual use case descriptions.

What we have discussed in this section are the diagram types that benefit most from being used in a participatory setting. There are other diagram types that might be useful in specific project settings as well. The discussion in this section followed the assumption that the participatory modeling session is prepared similarly to the recommendations in Chap. 5. This also assumes that there is a modeling facilitator and a group of stakeholders. Considering the nature of IS development projects, this makes participatory modeling sessions more suitable for the early phases, focusing on requirements and analysis. Another way of using these modeling techniques in a participatory way is that a group of developers just use class diagrams or sequence diagrams to support their discussion about a specific design or implementation issue. In such cases, this is usually done without the presence of a facilitator, and the resulting models are merely notes of the decisions made. In such cases, more UML diagram types become useful, for example, sequence or communication diagrams for deciding on object responsibilities, state charts, and interaction overview diagrams. This kind of agile and "on-demand" modeling within an IS development project is outside the scope of this book. More about modeling in agile development projects is available in Ambler (2002).

10.4.4   Capability Driven Development to Support Run-Time Variability

Capability Driven Development (CDD) is an approach to design context-dependent business solutions and to manage them during run-time (Grabis et al. 2016). In essence, it is a development approach that supports both IS design as well as deployment and run-time adjustments. It consists of a number of method components for:

- *Enterprise Modeling.* The component guides the creation of enterprise models that are used as input for capability design. The 4EM approach is incorporated for the purpose of this component.
- *Capability design process.* It gives an overview of how to design capabilities by using process models, goal models, and other types of models.
- *Context modeling.* It describes the method components needed for analyzing the capability context and the business process variations needed to deal with variations in the context.
- *Reuse of capability design.* This component contains guidelines for the elicitation and documentation of patterns for capability design.
- *Run-time delivery adjustment.* It is used in the development of capability run-time adjustments including implementation of capability delivery adaptation algorithms.

CDD also contains a number of method extensions for capability design in various business areas and for addressing more specific organizational problems. All method components are described in terms of purpose, modeling language, and notation used, as well as the way of working according to the principle of method component provided in Goldkuhl et al. (1998).

The way of working with all method components is specified in terms of steps to be taken, for example, which artifacts (models or sub-model) should be developed, on the basis of what information, and who should do what in the process. The decision-making about when the method components should be used in a participatory setting and when the work should be done in a more analytical way is not, however, specified. The method component Enterprise Modeling with 4EM should be performed in a participatory manner. In our opinion also, method components for capability design and context modeling would be able to reap the benefits from the participatory approach. For example, the capability design could start with capability elicitation on a strategic level in a group of stakeholders. Initial analysis of the capabilities and existing process variations in a group of experts could have positive effects on context modeling.

We see the application of the participatory way of working to CDD as an area for future development. Particular attention should be devoted to incorporating the run-time data about the context situation and IS performance in the participatory process.

10.5   Summary

This chapter discussed the use of the participatory approach to modeling along with other modeling approaches. We addressed a set of typical requirements for a modeling approach to be considered if the approach is to be used in a participatory setting. We also discussed the main principles of the ways of working with business modeling methods, such as Business Model Canvas; Enterprise Architecture frameworks; as well as Balanced Scorecard development. Participatory modeling is also suitable for various activities in IS development. In this regard, we discussed aspects of facilitation using agile approaches, UML, Goal-Oriented Requirements Engineering, and Capability Driven Development.

There are many more methods than can be addressed in a chapter such as this. Many of them have the potential of utilizing the participatory approach to modeling. We hope that this chapter might trigger practitioners using those approaches to extend their ways of working.

References

Ambler, S.: Agile Modeling: Effective Practices for Extreme Programming and the Unified Process, 1st edn. Wiley, New York (2002)

Ambler, S.: Agile Model Driven Development (AMDD): The Key to Scaling Agile Software Development. http://www.agilemodeling.com/essays/amdd.htm (2007)

Beck, K.: Extreme Programming Explained: Embrace Change. Addison-Wesley, Boston, MA (2004)

Beck, K., Cunningham, W.: A Laboratory for Teaching Object Oriented Thinking. ACM SIGPLAN Notices, NY, USA. Abg, **24**(10), 1–6 (2012). https://doi.org/10.1145/74878. 74879, ISBN 0-89791-333-7

Bubenko, J.A., Jr, Persson, A., Stirna, J.: User Guide of the Knowledge Management Approach Using Enterprise Knowledge Patterns. Deliverable D3, IST Programme project HyperKnowledge – Hypermedia and Pattern Based Knowledge Management for Smart Organisations. Project no. IST-2000-28401. Department of Computer and Systems Sciences, Royal Institute of Technology, Stockholm, Sweden (2001)

Castro, J., Kolp, M., Mylopoulos, J.: Towards requirements-driven information systems engineering: the Tropos project. Inf. Syst. **27**(6), 365–389 (2002)

Cooper K, Abraham SP, Unnithan RS, Chung L, Courtney S: Integrating visual goal models into the rational unified process. J. Vis. Lang. Comput., Volume 17, Issue 6, pp 551-583 (2006). doi: https://doi.org/10.1016/j.jvlc.2006.10.005, ISSN: 1045-926X

Dardenne, A., van Lamsweerde, A., Fickas, S.: Goal-directed requirements acquisition. Sci. Comput. Program. **20**(1–2), 3–50 (1993)

Department of Defense: DoDAF Architecture Framework Version 2.02. http://dodcio.defense.gov/ Portals/0/Documents/DODAF/DoDAF_v2-02_web.pdf (2009)

Donzelli, P.: A goal-driven and agent-based requirements engineering framework. Requir. Eng. **9** (1), 16–39 (2004)

Goldkuhl, G., Lind, M., Seigerroth, U.: Method integration: the need for a learning perspective. IEEE Proc. Softw. **145**(4), 113–118 (1998)

Grabis, J., Henkel, M., Kampars, J., Koç, H., Sandkuhl, K., Stamer, D., Stirna, J., Valverde, F., Zdravkovic, J.: Exploitation Package – The Final Version of Capability Driven Development Methodology, CaaS – Capability as a Service for Digital Enterprises. FP7 project no. 611351, Rostock University, Germany. http://caas-project.eu/ (2016)

Hüttermann, M.: DevOps for Developers. Apress, Heidelberg (2012). ISBN 978-1-4302-4570-4

Johannesson, P., Boman, M., Bubenko, J., Wangler, B.: Conceptual Modelling. In: Hoare, C.A.R. (Series ed.) Prentice Hall International Series in Computer Science, 280 pp. Prentice Hall (1997)

Kaplan, R.S., Norton, D.P.: The Balanced Scorecard: Translating Strategy into Action. Harvard Business School Press, Boston, MA (1996)

Kroll, P., Kruchten, P.: The Rational Unified Process Made Easy: A Practitioner's Guide to the RUP (2003). ISBN 0-321-16609-4

Larman, C.: Applying UML and Patterns: An Introduction to Object-Oriented Analysis and Design and Iterative Development, 3rd edn. Prentice Hall PTR, Upper Saddle River, NJ (2004)

Martinsons, M., Davison, R., Tse, D.: The balanced scorecard: a foundation for the strategic management of information systems. Decis. Support Syst. **25**(3), 71–88 (1999)

Niehaves, B., Stirna, J.: Participative enterprise modelling for balanced scorecard implementation. In: Proceedings of ECIS 2006. http://aisel.aisnet.org/ecis2006/80 (2006)

OMG: OMG Unified Modeling Language, version 2.5. OMG Document Number formal/2015-03-01. http://www.omg.org/spec/UML/2.5 (2015)

Osterwalder, A., Pigneur, Y.: Business Model Generation: A Handbook for Visionaries, Game Changers, and Challenger. Wiley, New York (2010). ISBN: 978-0-470-87641-1

Pohl, K.: Requirements Engineering – Fundamentals, Principles, and Techniques. Springer, Heidelberg (2010)

Sandkuhl, K., Stirna, J., Persson, A., Wißotzki, M.: Enterprise Modeling – Tackling Business Challenges with the 4EM Method. The Enterprise Engineering Series. Springer, Heidelberg (2014)

Schwaber, K., Beedle, M.: Agile Software Development with SCRUM. Prentice Hall, Upper Saddle River, NJ (2002)

Stirna, J., Kirikova, M.: Integrating Agile Modeling with participative Enterprise Modeling. In: Halpin, T.A., Proper, H.A., Krogstie, J. (eds.) Proceedings of the 13th International Workshop on Exploring Modeling Methods for Systems Analysis and Design (EMMSAD'08) held in conjunction with the CAiSE'08 Conference, Montpellier, France, 16–17 June 2008, pp. 171–184. http://ftp.informatik.rwth-aachen.de/Publications/CEUR-WS/Vol-337/paper14.pdf (2008)

The Open Group: TOGAF Version 9.1, an Open Group Standard. The Open Group online. http://pubs.opengroup.org/architecture/togaf9-doc/arch/index.html

UK Ministry of Defence: Proposed NAF v4 Meta-Model (MODEM). NATO Architecture Framework v4.0 Documentation. http://nafdocs.org/modem (2013)

Yu, E.: Towards modeling and reasoning support for early-phase requirements engineering. In: Proceedings of the 3rd International Symposium on Requirements Engineering (RE'97), Washington (1997)

Chapter 11
How to Become a Professional Enterprise Modeling Practitioner

Chapter 6 described the roles and needed competence of the main stakeholders in an EM project, of which the EM practitioner is one. In this chapter, we discuss how to become a professional EM practitioner. This chapter provides recommendations on how to build a suitable competence profile for working professionally with EM, in particular participatory EM.

The following core abilities of an EM practitioner were defined in Chap. 6:

- Ability to model, which means that a person is able to construct an enterprise model that is syntactically correct according to the used EM language and that the model in a reasonable way reflects the domain and problem in question
- Ability to facilitate modeling sessions, which means that a person is able to lead a group of domain experts in creating/refining an enterprise model and doing it in such a way that the group's knowledge and abilities work together to create a high-quality model
- Ability to manage EM projects toward fulfilling their goals and making the best of the project resources

The core abilities build on each other so that the most advanced stage of expertise is the ability to manage modeling projects. It was concluded that the progression from being able to create an enterprise model to being able to manage a modeling project was the result of having collected substantial experience over time.

Building expertise in EM often means that modelers, gradually and with experience, become aware of the important aspects of EM. With growing expertise, they are able to tackle more and more complex issues.

Which are then the aspects that modelers gradually become aware of? The novice modelers are mainly concerned with constructing models using a modeling language. With growing experience, issues about managing the process of modeling, ensuring the quality of models, and gaining the desired effects of modeling come into focus. We will now discuss these stages, starting at the bottom of Fig. 11.1.

© Springer International Publishing AG, part of Springer Nature 2018   183
J. Stirna, A. Persson, *Enterprise Modeling*,
https://doi.org/10.1007/978-3-319-94857-7_11

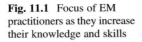

Fig. 11.1 Focus of EM practitioners as they increase their knowledge and skills

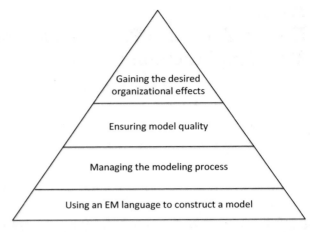

Gaining the desired organizational effects

Ensuring model quality

Managing the modeling process

Using an EM language to construct a model

11.1 Using an EM Language to Construct a Model

The novice modeler naturally focuses on how to *construct a model* that is syntactically correct according to a chosen EM language. Questions about how to transfer information about the organization to an enterprise model are in focus. Modeling is a matter of discovering facts about an organization and using the constructs of the EM language to construct a model that correctly reflects those facts. As a complete novice, one would most likely try to create a model of some kind that reflects the current state of an organization. Often the easiest model to start with is a process model, and then it could be wise to combine that with a concepts model to describe the information that flows in such a model. After that, the other model types will follow. The novice modeler often finds it a bit challenging to understand how model types are related to each other, and working actively with inter-model links will help in that process.

University courses about EM are mostly about constructing models. Courses in EM usually build on courses in IS analysis and design and requirements engineering; they can be aligned with courses in similar topics such as Enterprise Architecture and Business Process Management. Our recommendation is to study such courses thoroughly, because in practice EM practitioners usually master more than one modeling method. Broad and deep knowledge about the current modeling methods allows to choose suitable modeling methods based on factors such as the organization's internal standards and guidelines, project portfolio of methods and tools to be used, the modeling problem at hand, purposes of models, etc. Most EM practitioners have a portfolio of modeling methods and tools from which they assemble a method and tool set for a specific modeling project.

Modern courses in modeling usually include group work in order to prepare the students for the majority of real-life projects that require models to be created collaboratively. Hence, a part of being able to construct a model is also the ability to collaborate with colleagues in modeling.

11.2 Managing the Modeling Process

With some more experience comes the insight that in order for the model to be useful in some sense, a *process* needs to be organized to discover the relevant facts to include in the model. Often this means involving stakeholders of the modeling result. Learning about different elicitation approaches and when they can be used is, hence, the next step. In Chap. 2, the most common elicitation approaches are described: interviews, observations, document analysis, work diary, and participatory modeling sessions. The elicitation approach that is the most difficult to manage is the facilitated modeling sessions, where the EM practitioner plays the role of a facilitator (see Sects. 6.2 and 7.1 and Chap. 8 about contingencies in modeling sessions).

The question is then, how can EM practitioners become skilled in using various elicitation approaches? In university courses, the focus is often on learning modeling languages, and too little effort is put into teaching about the process of modeling. As discussed in this book, the participatory modeling session is a complex process that requires knowledge and skills and, therefore, is the elicitation technique that is the hardest to master. Becoming a modeling facilitator takes time and extensive practice. The following quote from an interview with an experienced EM practitioner involved in a project for training modeling facilitators illustrates the problem:

> We interviewed 73 or 74 potential facilitators. Out of these we chose 15 who we thought were at least reasonably good. Towards the end we had seven left. This is the real situation. We lost some on the first level. They didn't really have the ability to model. Some we lost on the second step. They didn't have the ability to facilitate modeling sessions. (Interviewee in Persson 2001)

Deep knowledge about facilitation of participatory modeling sessions is seldom included in university courses. Hence, a common mistake that novices make is that they believe that just because they have learned to use a modeling language, they will be able to carry out a participatory modeling process. Their mistakes will most likely lead to poor project results and require costly rework.

However, it may be challenging for instructors to provide practical experience in facilitation to students in an educational setting since it requires quite a bit of experience from facilitating participatory modeling. The lab part should primarily consist of performing group modeling with an EM language for a given purpose on a sample case. The students should be asked to observe each other and to take turns in facilitation. The work should be allowed to take considerable time (e.g., periodically over several weeks) so that all participants in the group have the opportunity to act as facilitators. Instructors should observe the group work and provide constructive comments.

One aspect of the training should also be to practice the management of behaviors of modeling participants in relation to stereotypes discussed in Chap. 7. This could be achieved by using role-play, where certain behaviors are assigned to participants in the group. For example, one participant should suddenly change his or her opinion on a matter completely and strongly advocate this in the session or one participant wants to push for a certain and somewhat awkward solution. The other students should observe, take notes, and then discuss with the assigned facilitator about what happened. Reflecting on what happened is an essential part of the learning process, so this should be given some time, not only for a course but also throughout a facilitator's career.

However good a course may be at letting the students practice their skills in facilitation, the real learning takes place in true practice. Our suggestion for people that want to become modeling facilitators is to start with courses and books on topics that this book has addressed as well as to team up with one or more experienced facilitators.

Facilitators who are just starting their learning path toward becoming expert facilitators should never facilitate alone, since the errors made during modeling will negatively influence the outcome of the process where modeling is used. To become really good at facilitation, one needs to collaborate with more experienced colleagues. In essence, the experienced facilitator should take a mentor's role for the junior facilitator. They both can work in tandem facilitating modeling sessions. This way the junior facilitator gets first-hand experience in tasks that the facilitator normally carries out. They should also reflect on the work they have accomplished as facilitators from a learning perspective, for example, in terms of what was done, what was achieved, what was not, what worked, what did not, and what to do next and why.

Even with access to mentors, it can be difficult to organize such learning by doing, with feedback loops in a systematic and practical way, particularly if a group of people need to be trained at the same time. A complicating factor here is that the person being trained needs to be subjected to a variety of situations, in order to be prepared for future assignments. Also, since the situation in real projects is often sensitive, there is no room for critical mistakes. This means that the number of skilled facilitators unfortunately increases very slowly.

Facilitated meetings are not only used in EM. It is also used in other organizational settings where a group of people meets to solve a problem. There are books on the subject, which can contribute to learning about facilitation in EM (c.f. Hunter 2009). Similarly, courses on performing and managing other kinds of people-based activities, such as brainstorming and coaching, can also enhance one's skill set for facilitating modeling sessions.

11.3   Ensuring Model Quality

With more experience, modelers often start to become concerned with different quality aspects of the model resulting from the modeling process. There is a considerable body of knowledge about EM quality (e.g., Heravizadeh et al. 2008; Krogstie et al. 2006; Krogstie 2012; Larsson and Segerberg 2004; Moreno-Montes de Oca et al. 2015; Sandkuhl et al. 2014; Stirna and Persson 2009). Being aware of the quality criteria enables the modeler to plan the process of modeling. However,

Table 11.1 Summary of model quality requirements depending on purposes of EM

Purpose of EM	Model quality requirements
Develop the business	
Develop visions and strategy	Understandability, correctness, simplicity, flexibility
Design/redesign the business	Completeness, correctness, flexibility, integration, understandability, usability
Develop an information system	Completeness, correctness, flexibility, integration, usability
Ensure the quality of business operations	
Ensure acceptance for business decisions	Completeness, correctness, integration, simplicity, understandability, usability
Maintain and share knowledge about the business	Correctness, integration, understandability, usability
Use EM as a problem-solving tool	
Use EM to analyze and solve a specific business problem	Correctness, flexibility, understandability

the experienced EM practitioner knows that the different purposes of modeling will decide which criteria are important (Bubenko et al. 2010).

Chapter 3 discussed which quality criteria are relevant to which EM purpose (Table 11.1). Some practical advice for quality assurance in EM, which relates to the criteria of Larsson and Segerberg (2004), can be found in Chap. 12 of Sandkuhl et al. (2014).

However, the main approach to learning how to assess the quality of models comes from participating in a number of modeling projects and evaluating the usefulness of created models with respect to the goals of those projects. One important aspect of learning about the quality of one's own models is to subject them to the scrutiny of colleagues and to be open to constructive critique from them.

11.4 Gaining the Desired Organizational Effects

At the highest level of maturity, the EM practitioner is concerned with achieving positive effects with using EM, which entails making an impact on an organization's development. People with this level of maturity are able to manage modeling projects. Learning about the purposes of EM (Chap. 3) and what is required to achieve those purposes is essential at this stage. The contents of this book can help in this process.

At this stage, all levels of competence come into play. A person at this stage of maturity needs to be able to define the goals and negotiate the resources of a modeling project as well as to guide the project toward its goals. In order to do that, the purpose and related quality criteria need to be known. Based on that, the plans for the modeling process needs to be drawn up, which requires knowledge about which elicitation approaches are suitable in different situations and how elicitation can be supported by professional EM practitioners, for instance, facilitators. The project will also need to choose the EM language to be used in the project, which requires knowledge about how different languages could fit the purpose of the EM project, its context, and relationships to other projects. It goes without saying that this is not a job for the novice modeler. Being aware of the different focus areas in Chap. 3 is the basis for developing one's abilities over time.

11.5 Summary

In this chapter, we have briefly discussed some basic strategies for building the knowledge and abilities necessary to become a professional EM practitioner. We discussed that these are built-in stages reflecting the maturity that comes with increasing experience. The stages were:

1. Using an EM language to construct a model
2. Managing the modeling process
3. Ensuring model quality
4. Gaining the desired organizational effects

It was concluded that becoming a professional EM practitioner needs experience and substantial practice.

References

Bubenko Jr., J.A., Persson, A., Stirna, J.: An intentional perspective on enterprise modeling. In: Intentional Perspectives on Information Systems Engineering. Springer, Heidelberg (2010)

Heravizadeh, M., Mendling, J., Rosemann, M.: Dimensions of business processes quality (QoBP). In: International Conference on Business Process Management, pp. 80–91. Springer, Heidelberg (2008)

Hunter, D.: The Art of Facilitation - The Essentials for Leading Great Meetings and Creating Group Synergy. Wiley, Hoboken (2009)

Krogstie, J.: Model-Based Development and Evolution of Information Systems: A Quality Approach. Springer, Heidelberg (2012)

Krogstie, J., Sindre, G., Jørgensen, H.: Process models representing knowledge for action: a revised quality framework. Eur. J. Inform. Syst. 15(1), 91–102 (2006)

Larsson, L., Segerberg, R.: An approach for quality assurance in enterprise modelling. MSc thesis, Department of Computer and Systems Sciences, Stockholm University, no 04–22 (2004)

Moreno-Montes de Oca, I., Snoeck, M., Reijers, H.A., Rodríguez-Morffi, A.: A systematic literature review of studies on business process modeling quality. Inf. Softw. Technol. 58, 187–205 (2015). https://doi.org/10.1016/j.infsof.2014.07.011

Persson, A.: Enterprise modelling in practice: situational factors and their influence on adopting a participative approach. Ph.D. Thesis, Department of Computer and Systems Sciences, Stockholm University (2001)

Sandkuhl, K., Stirna, J., Persson, A., Wißotzki, M.: Enterprise Modeling: Tackling Business Challenges with the 4EM Method. Springer, Heidelberg (2014)

Stirna, J., Persson, A.: Anti-patterns as a means of focusing on critical quality aspects in enterprise modeling. In: Enterprise, Business-Process and Information Systems Modeling, pp. 407–418. Springer, Berlin (2009)

Chapter 12
Outlook on the Practice and Research of Participatory EM

This chapter discusses the issues that are pertinent to the use of participatory Enterprise Modeling (EM) in practice, such as adoption of it in organizations, including building the organizational structure for modeling, and integration of EM with other approaches sharing similar principles of work for which participatory EM can help. The chapter ends with a discussion on emerging issues of participatory EM.

12.1 Adoption and Institutionalization of Participatory EM

In this book, we have mostly assumed that Enterprise Modeling (EM) is used in a project setting and that EM method competence is either available within the organization or brought in by external consultants. While the latter is an efficient approach in many cases, the former should be preferred for an organization to be able to work more independently and without the need to procure external help. In Sandkuhl et al. (2014), a process for EM adoption in organizations consisting of the following phases has been presented:

– Deciding that an EM method should be adopted as part of the organization's set of institutionalized methods
– Selecting a suitable method

  • Selecting a suitable modeling language depending on the purpose of modeling and the organization's existing portfolio of methods and tools already used.
  • Defining a modeling process. In most cases, the approaches to modeling will be a blend of participatory and analyst driven depending on the specifics of the different modeling projects. What needs to be done at the stage is to agree on a common process for carrying out EM projects. It should be similar to the one presented in Chap. 5.

© Springer International Publishing AG, part of Springer Nature 2018
J. Stirna, A. Persson, *Enterprise Modeling*,
https://doi.org/10.1007/978-3-319-94857-7_12

- Selecting EM tool support. More about this has been discussed in Chap. 9 and in Sect. 5.3 of Sandkuhl et al. (2014), while a more in-depth analysis can be found in Stirna (2001).

– Implementing the method within the organization

- Acquiring the chosen modeling method
- Adapting the method according to the specific needs of the organization
- Acquiring internal modeling competence
- Carrying out pilot projects
- Evaluating and adjusting the modeling method and tool
- Carrying out organization-wide implementation activities

The above process requires developing and maintaining in-house competence, which is a fairly challenging task. In essence, the organization should be prepared to establish a team of EM practitioners as well as work out a plan on how to involve the rest of the employees. In Sandkuhl et al. (2014), this dedicated unit is referred to as a *modeling department*. The following roles should be considered for inclusion in a modeling department:

– *Facilitator*—as discussed in Chaps. 5 and 6, the modeling facilitator leads and advises the modeling participants during modeling sessions.
– *Method expert*—knowledgeable about the modeling method (or several methods) used in their organization and responsible for the development and maintenance of the modeling method used and, if necessary, integration with other methods and approaches used.
– *Tool expert*—responsible for supporting other tool users in the organization about advanced functionality of the tool as well as responsible for tool maintenance and other aspects of operation, such as integration with other tools.
– *Model maintenance expert*—responsible for keeping enterprise models up to date.
– *Model presentation expert*—responsible for improving the presentation quality of models, publishing the models on the intranet, etc.

Building a modeling department is motivated by the intention of using EM long term in the organization. If the intention also is to model without external consultants and/or to keep models "alive," then the organization has to develop its own in-house EM competence.

The success of developing in-house EM competence in an organization depends heavily on people's enthusiasm and commitment supported by competence and skills. Naturally, this needs to be supported by adequately allocated resources, but in our experience, the commitment and competence are the most critical factors in successful introduction and adoption of EM in an organization. In principle, a number of EM "champions" are needed. There are people who see real business needs and how EM can address them. They can be regarded as internal "champions" for EM. There should also be people who understand the area of modeling methods and tools well, know best practices of EM use in organizations, as well as are able to

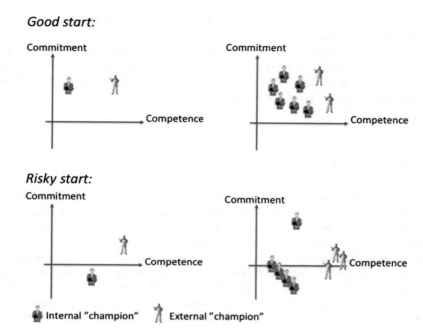

Fig. 12.1 Commitment and competence situations of method adoption

support the organization in the process of method selection and institutionalization. These people are often coming from outside and, hence, called external "champions." Usually, several people in both categories are preferred.

Figure 12.1 illustrates typical situations in terms of commitment and competence of internal and external champions. In our opinion, the most important factor for a good start of an EM adoption process is high commitment of internal champions. They might not immediately be very competent in EM methods and tools. Basic understanding of the principles of modeling and the main ways of working is sufficient because a more experienced external champion can provide the more advanced knowledge. The process is even faster and more successful if there is a group of committed and competent champions, internal as well as external.

If, however, the internal champions are not strongly committed or most of them are not more than casually interested, then, even if the competence level is higher, the EM adoption process is at risk of stalling. The lack of internal commitment cannot be compensated by the competence and engagement of external champions.

Once the initial core team of EM champions has formed and the process of EM adoption has started, there is a need to involve the rest of the people in the organization. This will ensure their awareness of the participatory way of working. Their involvement will also ground the EM activities in the "normal" work processes of the company. In Grabis et al. (2016) and Sandkuhl and Stirna (2018), two stereotypical philosophies have been elaborated for a Capability Driven

Development method used in organizations. They are denoted "All Do Some" (ADS) and "Some Do All" (SDA).

Between these opposites, there are hybrid variants combining elements of ADS and SDA, for instance, when in larger organizations, some business units practice ADS and others SDA in their internal work. In the following, we will disregard the hybrids and focus on the core SDA and ADS.

12.1.1   Some Do All

According to Sandkuhl and Stirna (2018), "Some Do All" (SDA) represents the philosophy that all EM competence should be concentrated in a single organizational unit that provides method support, tool support, and other services within the organization; in essence, this means that the modeling department is the central part of the SDA philosophy. Its benefits are efficient ways of standardizing methods and tools used, easy management of competence profiles and resources, as well as centralized planning and competence development. The drawback of concentrating all competence in one unit is the risk of encountering problems with EM acceptance in the rest of the organization because others may perceive this unit as "outsiders" in relation to their own organization.

In practice, SDA means that the organizational roles for a modeling department have to be filled. Not every role necessarily requires a separate person, but the competences required for the roles have to be made available. Concerning the allocation of roles for the modeling department, Table 12.1 shows which roles in an SDA setting can be performed in a decentralized way and which roles should be established in a new organizational unit. In the case of assigning to existing organizational roles, the EM support tasks are to be included within the area of responsibility for the corresponding role.

Table 12.1 Model department roles according to SDA philosophy

Role in modeling department	Assign to existing roles (example)	Modeling department, how many needed
Facilitator		Yes, probably several
Method expert		Yes, at least one. Several in larger organizations or if many methods used
Tool expert		Yes, at least one. Several in larger organizations or if many methods used
Model maintenance expert		Yes, several
Model presentation expert	Can be assigned to people responsible for internal documentation	Yes, several

Table 12.2 Model department roles according to the ADS philosophy

Role in modeling department	Assign to existing roles (example)	Establish centrally or outsource
Facilitator		Yes, probably several
Method expert	Quality manager	
Tool expert	IT department, responsible for similar types of tools	
Model maintenance expert	Each unit has a responsible person, process owners	
Model presentation expert	Responsible for internal documentations, process owners and quality managers	

12.1.2 All Do Some

According to Sandkuhl and Stirna (2018), "All Do Some" (ADS) represents the principle that whenever there is the need for EM somewhere in the organization, the local employees will be offered training and support to enable them to do it in a self-supported way. The support tasks required for this training and enablement are either provided by external consultants or organized in a central unit within the organization of the smallest possible size. It can be considered as a "grassroots" approach if many people in an organization engage in EM. This usually increases the acceptance of EM and supports a wider establishment of organizational practices.

Table 12.2 shows which roles in an ADS setting can be performed in a decentralized way and which roles should be established centrally. In principle, even the facilitator tasks can be assigned to existing roles, if they have the necessary competence and experience. However, since becoming a facilitator takes considerable time and effort (see Chap. 11 about facilitator training and Chap. 6 about the needed competences), this might not be a feasible action in most cases.

In this case, assigning to existing organizational roles means that the corresponding roles receive appropriate training and mentoring and that the EM support tasks become their areas of responsibility.

12.2 Future Research Directions

In the past 20 years, the participatory way of working has been gaining a lot of recognition, and nowadays, many people in organizations have had at least some experience with approaches that are based on group work. While this is, of course, positive, to some it has also created a false impression that all group work approaches are the same and, in some cases, that they can be performed in a relatively haphazard manner without affecting the outcome. In this book, we have tried to advocate the opposite. There are a number of relevant techniques and approaches to organizational and information system (IS) development that can benefit greatly from participatory modeling if adequately prepared and properly carried out. In most cases, the participatory approach would improve the results of those approaches in terms of increased stakeholder understanding of the domain, consensus, and commitment to decisions. At the same time, facilitation and organization of participatory modeling sessions are often seen as somewhat peripheral topics of the area of information system development. In our opinion, if applied properly, it can lead to great benefits in terms of clear requirements, better understanding of the business, as well as stronger commitment to decisions and organizational change.

The research fields of computer science and information systems produce a large number of valuable results in terms of methods and tools for making IS requirements elicitation, analysis, and design more efficient. Many of these contributions would benefit from considering the participatory way of working, but currently these aspects are unexplored, and we know too little about facilitation in business and IS development projects. This section points to some research issues that warrant more in-depth analysis.

Investigation of the Effects of Facilitation   So far, the positive effects of facilitation have been observed in practice, which has motivated this book. In our opinion, more in-depth studies concerning the impact of facilitation should also be undertaken.

Facilitator Styles   The current base of knowledge about facilitation of modeling sessions is mostly based on practical experiences. It is insufficiently explored from a research point of view. For example, what the different types of facilitation are and how they can be used depending on the situations in the project and in the organization are far from clear. This book has been based on experience from using the Scandinavian strand of participatory EM in practice. Consequently, we have advocated certain ways of working, recommended certain actions for problem-solving, and advised against doing some things that might, for some reason, appear attractive. To broaden the view on facilitation, we recommend reading an investigation by Rosemann et al. (2011) on different facilitation styles, such as:

- Communication style—talks vs. listens
- Power style—assertive vs. empathic
- Adaption style—static vs. flexible
- Disagreement style—embraces conflict vs. avoids conflict
- Control style—centralized vs. decentralized
- Model behavior—does model vs. lets model
- Facilitation behavior—does facilitation vs. lets facilitate
- Involvement style—involves vs. ignores
- Work style—structured vs. unstructured
- Domain knowledge style—domain agnostic vs. domain expert

Some of these styles seem to contradict what we have proposed in this book. They also seem impractical, at least for the purpose of achieving stakeholder commitment. However, from the point of view of research, these aspects are insufficiently investigated.

Group Dynamics in Modeling Group dynamics is a system of behaviors and psychological processes occurring within a social group or between groups. Group dynamics was proposed by Lewin (1947). It has roots in social psychology, and over the years, it has been studied considerably, including the aspects of group dynamics in software development projects. What is much less researched in group dynamics is modeling sessions and how the facilitator should act in various situations. This book proposes numerous dos and don'ts based on practice, but more detailed investigations from the point of view of research are needed.

Facilitation in the Age of Social Media Social networks have the potential of directly reaching and involving large groups of stakeholders, including groups that traditionally have been more difficult to involve. Current investigations in the area of requirements engineering (cf., for instance, Seyff et al. 2015) and software development (cf., for instance, Singer et al. 2014; Bajic and Lyons 2011) show promise. In the future, we envision the need to extend the EM process and the facilitation approaches, such as the ones described in this book, with activities that allow involving modelers via social media.

Facilitation in the Age of Data If, in the past, we were assuming that the main source of requirements is stakeholders, the current trends of system analysis and development go beyond that toward the inclusion of large data sets, such as run-time data, customer behavior data, market data, social media data, etc. Much of this is raw data and needs skillful and purposeful analysis to elicit information that can be used for requirements elicitation or design. Because this work is purposeful in nature, it is not very efficient to be done at the early stages of a modeling project because one needs to know what to look for in the data. Hence, the participatory modeling might need to be done in cycles of participatory stakeholder-driven and analyst data-driven sessions. It is also likely that in such cases the plastic wall will need to be combined with more advanced tools for model creation and fusion from various sources.

Modeling Tools Tools for activities such as requirements engineering, modeling, and design have been an area of considerable interest since the late 1980s and will continue to be so. While there are interesting research prototypes emerging almost all the time, tools that can be used industrially are still few, and they do not offer significant advancements for participatory modeling in addition to the common multiuser editing of models. At the same time, hardware categories such as smart boards and projectors evolve and offer more advanced features. Since the primary targets of these software and hardware advancements are activities such as presentations and simple brainstorming sessions, researchers in the field of EM should continuously monitor development in the tool area and assess their potential for improving the EM process.

12.3   Recommendations for Additional Reading

This book has presented a practice-based view on participatory EM. The purpose of the book has been to discuss the aspects of facilitation and EM project management without going into details of specific approaches and methods. It is based on the experience and research of its authors and their colleagues. There is however a great deal more to read and learn—the fields of EM, business process modeling, and IS analysis and design have numerous interesting and useful sources to recommend. From the point of view of advancing one's knowledge in EM and for those interested in specific modeling approaches or more detailed areas of application of EM, we would suggest the following sources:

– A book on the 4EM method by Sandkuhl et al. (2014)
– Another EM approach, MERODE, by Snoeck (2014)
– A book that collects experiences and recommendations of practitioners from Scandinavia edited by Nilsson et al. (1999)
– A book about Active Knowledge Modeling for continuous use of models in enterprises by Lillehagen and Krogstie (2008)
– A book on domain-specific modeling and using the OMiLAB environment edited by Karagiannis et al. (2016)
– A book on facilitation of workshops by Hunter (2009)
– A book on the quality aspects of business processes by Krogstie (2016)
– Books on enterprise architecture development and management by Greefhorst and Proper (2011) and Lankhorst (2013)

References

Bajic, D., Lyons, K.: Leveraging social media to gather user feedback for software development. In: Proceedings of the 2nd International Workshop on Web 2.0 for Software Engineering, Web2SE '11, 1–6, ACM, New York, NY (2011)

Grabis, J., Henkel, M., Kampars, J., Koç, H., Sandkuhl, K., Stamer, D., Stirna, J., Valverde, F., Zdravkovic, J.: Exploitation package - the final version of Capability Driven Development methodology, CaaS – capability as a service for digital enterprises. FP7 Project no 611351, Rostock University, Rostock. http://caas-project.eu/ (2016)

Greefhorst, D., Proper, E.: Architecture Principles - The Cornerstones of Enterprise Architecture. The Enterprise Engineering Series, vol. 4, pp. 1–151. Springer, Heidelberg (2011)

Hunter, D.: The Art of Facilitation - The Essentials for Leading Great Meetings and Creating Group Synergy. Jossey Bass Wiley, Hoboken (2009)

Karagiannis, D., Mayr, H.C., Mylopoulos, J.: Domain-Specific Conceptual Modeling, Concepts, Methods and Tools. Springer, Cham (2016)

Krogstie, J.: Quality in Business Process Modeling. Springer, Cham (2016)

Lankhorst, M.: Enterprise Architecture at Work - Modelling, Communication and Analysis. The Enterprise Engineering Series, 3rd edn. Springer, Berlin (2013)

Lewin, K.: Frontiers in group dynamics: concept, method and reality in social science; social equilibria and social change. Hum. Relat. 1(1), 5–41 (1947). https://doi.org/10.1177/001872674700100103

Lillehagen, F.M., Krogstie, J.: Active Knowledge Modeling of Enterprises. Springer, Berlin (2008)

Nilsson, A.G., Tolis, C., Nellborn, C. (eds.): Perspectives on Business Modeling Understanding and Changing Organisations. Springer, Berlin (1999)

Rosemann, M., Hjalmarsson, A., Lind, M., Recker, J.: Four facets of a process modeling facilitator. In: ICIS 2011 Proceedings, 3. http://aisel.aisnet.org/icis2011/proceedings/projmanagement/3 (2011)

Sandkuhl, K., Stirna, J.: Organizational adoption of capability management. In: Capability Management in Digital Enterprises. Springer, Heidelberg (2018)

Sandkuhl, K., Stirna, J., Persson, A., Wißotzki, M.: Enterprise modeling—tackling business challenges with the 4EM method. In: Dietz, J.L.G., Proper, H.A., Tribolet, J. (eds.) The Enterprise Engineering Series, pp. 1–299. Springer, Heidelberg (2014). ISBN 978-3-662-43724-7

Seyff, N., Todoran, I., Caluser, K., Singer, L., Glinz, M.: Using popular social network sites to support requirements elicitation, prioritization and negotiation. J. Internet Serv. Appl. 6(1), 7 (2015). https://doi.org/10.1186/s13174-015-0021-9

Singer, L., Figueira Filho, F., Storey, M.-A.: Software engineering at the speed of light: how developers stay current using twitter. In: Proceedings of the 36th International Conference on Software Engineering, ICSE 2014, pp. 211–221. ACM, New York, NY (2014)

Snoeck, M.: Enterprise Information Systems Engineering - The MERODE Approach. The Enterprise Engineering Series. Springer, Heidelberg (2014)

Stirna, J.: The influence of intentional and situational factors on enterprise modelling tool acquisition in organisations. PhD Thesis, Department of Computer and Systems Sciences, Royal Institute of Technology, Stockholm, Sweden, ISSN 1101-8526 (2001)

Index

© Springer International Publishing AG, part of Springer Nature 2018
J. Stirna, A. Persson, *Enterprise Modeling*,
https://doi.org/10.1007/978-3-319-94857-7

Printed in the United States
By Bookmasters